Financial Dynamics and Business Cycles

Financial Dynamics and Business Cycles

New Perspectives

Edited by

Willi Semmler

M. E. Sharpe, Inc.
Armonk, New York   London, England

Available in the United Kingdom and Europe from M. E. Sharpe,
Publishers, 3 Henrietta Street, London WC2E 8LU.

Library of Congress Cataloging-in-Publication Data

Financial dynamics and business cycles : new perspectives / edited by
    Willi Semmler.

        p. cm.
    Bibliography: p.
    ISBN 0-87332-531-1
    1. Business cycles—Mathematical models. 2. Economic stabiliza-
tion—Mathematical models. 3. Debts, External—Mathematical models.
I. Semmler, Willi.

HB3722.F56 1989   88-30857
338.5'42'0724—dc 19   CIP

Printed in the United States of America

MV 10 9 8 7 6 5 4 3 2 1

Contents

II

Stabilization Policy in Nonlinear Dynamical Models with Money and Finance

III

Empirical Evidence on Debt and Financial Instability

Foreword

Hyman P. Minsky

As the 55th anniversary of the bank holiday of March 1933 approached, financial instability was a main topic in the financial press. Daily reports appeared of international debt crises, of the covert bankruptcy of deposit insurance, and of the near bankruptcy of one great financial institution after another.

The great stock market crash of October 19 and 20, 1987, demonstrated that extreme instability can happen. It is generally asserted that the consequences of October 19th and 20th would have been disastrous if the Federal Reserve and Treasury interventions had not set things right. As a result of these interventions, subsequent asset prices and financing terms were different from what unconstrained markets would have generated. However, the various and assorted statements in the financial press, even by exalted economists, are not clear on what caused the free fall of the 19th and 20th, and on how the interventions that took place led to more normal behavior of the economy and various financial markets.

In 1933, financial markets in the United States and throughout the capitalist world collapsed. The bank holiday of March 1933 remains an extreme example of a policy intervention that dominates market processes. But in the nice, polite, but largely apologetic economics of the time, breakdowns such as occurred during the period from October 1929 to March 1933 were not supposed to happen. This position of the orthodox theory of the early 1930s is quite surprising, as financial breakdowns had occurred with regularity ever since modern capitalism emerged, with its expensive, long-lasting capital assets, markets in which activity and positions in capital are financed, and entrepreneurial banks riding high on a crest of new technology.

In the light of historical experience, the past 55 years are the anomaly. During this time span, no financial or economic collapse has taken place which comes close to the magnitude of either the great collapse of 1929–1933 or even that of 1907. However, the orthodox economic theory of today, like the apologetic economics of the 1920s, does not offer a lucid account of why the economy is now so much more stable than in the past. Why are income, employment, and price level repercussions of the so-evident financial instability now contained?

In the early 1930s a race was on among the eminent economists of the day to explain the great collapse as a normal result of interactions among the monetary, production, and portfolio management spheres of the economy. The announced aim of Keynes's research program was to develop a theory of a monetary production economy that was rich enough to encompass a smoothly expanding economy, a constrained cyclical economy, and an economy that from time to time collapses into depressions or explodes into accelerating inflation. In the verbal exposition of *The General Theory,* endogenously determined changes in liquidity preference could lead to rapid movements in the relative prices of different types of assets and of assets and output. In turn, these changes can lead to rapid and large movements in output and employment.

In this exposition, it was quite clear that the properties of a capitalist economy with banks and bankers of various sorts and debts denominated in money were being examined. If the structure of indebtedness was sufficiently binding in such an economy, then normal market reactions to excess supply could increase, not decrease, the excess supply. Specifically, in a financially complex economy, wage flexibility in response to unemployment could make things worse.

The General Theory carried the day as an explanation of why a capitalist economy can work as well as the American economy did in the 1920s and as miserably as it did in 1929–1933. In winning the day, *The General Theory* beat out serious efforts by von Hayek, Myrdal, and Schumpeter, who also attempted to integrate money with the financing of production.

The popular semi-mathematical statements of *The General Theory*, most particularly the successful IS/LM version of Hicks, transformed what was essentially a complex nonlinear system of the verbal exposition, which showed that the economy had various modes of possible behavior, into a nice, polite interdependent equilibrium system. In the hands of Patinkin, the Hicks version of Keynes's theory was transformed into a system that sought and sustained equilibrium: Keynes's theory was stood on its head. The dynamics of the macroeconomics that emerged out of the Hicks-Patinkin tradition of interpreting Keynes was retrograde when compared to the various operational equilibria (market, short-period, and long-period) of the Marshallian tradition in which Keynes worked. The reason for this retrogression is that the mathematical exposition of *The General Theory* in terms of a multi-market equilibrium was cut to the mathematical competence of the economists of the day, which, to put it kindly, was limited.

Poor and largely irrelevant economics does no harm when the economy behaves so as to generate a largely smooth trajectory. In the first decades after World War II, the financial structure was so robust that, in truth, money and financial relations mattered very little. Quite by accident, the fiscal structure of the United States during this period was such that modest, largely built-in deficits and surpluses were sufficient to stabilize the economy. In the era of financial tranquility, the basic message of Keynes—that the proper subject of economics is a monetary production economy and that once in a while the normal functioning of such an economy leads to deep and serious depressions—was lost.

In the 1980s, financial turbulence reappeared. The Federal Reserve no longer could assume that playing around with the money supply was sufficient to stabilize the economy. The lender of last resort function became the dominant determinant of the time and extent of Federal Reserve intervention. In the turbulent world of the 1980s, the lack of relevance of the formal models, such as rational expectations that had achieved prominence in the 1970s, became evident. Fanciful schemes to develop business cycle models on the basis of either no or poorly conceived monetary relations emerged in the 1980s. The irrelevance of these models became evident as financial turbulence and intervention to constrain the effects of this turbulence became common.

Even as financial instability emerged as a dominant observation, the combination of the ability to simulate complex dynamical behavior and greater mathematical sophistication enabled economists, who were not wearing the blinders of neoclassical orthodoxy, to develop dynamic models that were capable of generating the complex paths through time that the verbal exposition of *The General Theory* encompassed. Mathematical formulations have finally caught up with the theoretical results based upon a combination of close verbal reasoning of the repercussions of profit maximization in a monetary production economy and a close understanding of how capitalist economies behave.

The papers collected in this volume come from various backgrounds and research paradigms. A common theme runs through these papers that makes the collection both interesting and important: The authors take seriously the obvious evidence that capitalist economies progress through time by lurching. Whether a particular study starts from household utility maximization or from the processes by which productive structures are reproduced and expanded, the authors are united in accepting the evidence that financial instability is a significant characteristic of modern capitalism.

If a theory holds that a capitalist economy is best thought of as a complex interdependent system whose trajectory depends on initial conditions and an internal dynamics that is capable of endogenously generating periods of incoherence, then the question ''Why is incoherence so rare?'' moves onto the research agenda. The obvious answer is that the impact of the institutional structure and the system of interventions that result from this structure dominates the economy's endogenous dynamics. This dominance can be interpreted as the intermittent imposition of new ''initial conditions.'' Coherence is observed not because markets yield order, but because institutions and policy interventions dominate markets. In the view that follows from this argument, though not all chapters in the volume will agree on it, markets are social devices to adjust details of the economy once the structures of intervention and regulation are in place that can abort the full development of chaos.

The main message of the combination of close observation of the economy and the ability to handle complex nonlinear mathematical systems that is evident in these studies is that capitalism is too complex for laissez-faire to be an acceptable policy rule. The subtext is that because "apt government" is necessary for capitalist economies to realize their potential, economic theory will be of use as it provides insights that enable us to design "apt government."

Introduction[1]

Willi Semmler

The General Theme

The chapters in this volume were contributions to a conference on "Economic Dynamics and Financial Instability," held at the Economics Department of the New School for Social Research in April 1986. This conference focused on the role of money, finance, and debt in micro and macro dynamical models as well as on an evaluation of stabilization policy in the context of a dynamical theory of a monetary market economy. Another aim of the conference was to give an account of the state of empirical research relating to the evidence of debt and financial instability, especially in the U.S. economy. This general perspective attempted to connect the analysis of real economic activities (production, investment, and consumption) with financing activities in market economies. This view is shared, by and large, by the contributors in this volume.

The writings of Hyman Minsky, in particular, have stimulated the revival of the type of research which also considers the financial side of the economy. As can be seen from the chapters, major topics of the entire conference were initiated by Hyman Minsky's work on the financial fragility of market economies. Other writers, recently, also have pointed out that extensive external financing of economic units (firms, but also households and financial institutions) and the feedbacks from asset and financial markets to economic activities make market economies very fragile. As Tobin puts it in his Nobel Prize Lecture:

> In short, the financial and capital markets are at best highly imperfect coordinators of savings and investment, an inadequacy which I suspect cannot be remedied by rational expectation. The failure of coordination is a fundamental source of macroeconomic instability. . . . (Tobin 1982, p. 179)

Starting with Fisher (1933) and then based on the frameworks of Keynes and Kalecki, an elaborate theory of the role of money and finance in the macroeconomic process has been put forward. By referring to both Keynes and Kalecki, Minsky has elaborated a theory of financial instability in which the role of the degree of indebtedness and cash payment commitments of firms, as well as the revaluation of capital assets due to financial perturbations, are considered central (Minsky 1975, 1982, 1986). Minsky specifically stresses that the increase of firms' debt and their extensive borrowing lead to a dangerous liability structure of firms, and consequently to a fragile performance of macroaggregates.

Although Minsky refers to dynamic motions of the economy and to business cycle models in his writings on financial instability, he has not formalized his ideas in the context of dynamical models (except in Minsky 1957). A major effort, therefore, is undertaken in these chapters to formalize the role of debt financing for macro theory in the context of a dynamic theory of firms, the market, and macroaggregates. This task, however, cannot be done without some technical tools borrowed from dynamical system analysis. Many chapters in this volume apply advances in linear and nonlinear dynamical theory (particularly nonlinear dynamics of high dimensions), limit cycle models for two dimensions, and complex and chaotic dynamics for one-dimensional nonlinear difference equations, in order to model the relation of the real and financial side of the economy. The studies are divided into three sections.

In the first section, contributions appear which deal specifically with basic linear and nonlinear models of the interaction between the real and financial sides of market economies. Almost all pursue basic themes, in one way or another, of macroeconomic fragility by modeling economic motions in a way inspired, for example, by Kalecki (1971), Kaldor (1940), or Goodwin (1948, 1951, 1986) and by examining the interaction of the real economy and financial markets initiated by Minsky. Contributions for this part of the book are provided by Taylor and O'Connell, Woodford, Franke and Semmler, Shaikh, and Duménil and Lévy. All are methodologically similar. Though most of the chapters utilize basic economic models as their background (for example, IS/LM versions of macrodynamic models), they focus particularly on nonlinear dynamics when considering the interaction of financial and asset markets with the product (or labor) market. Based on a new innovative and relevant methodology, important economic results are presented in this section of the book.

The second part of the book continues these themes and deals with stabilization policy (fiscal and monetary policy) in the context of dynamic views of real and financial motions in the economy. Most papers here are of macroeconomic orientation, such as the chapter by Day which evaluates the effects of stabilization policy in a model of complex and rich economic dynamics (in the context of an economic chaos model). Asada also focuses on a macroeconomic approach by including, in a seminal way, the financial and asset markets in a Goodwin-type cycle model and discusses economic policy effects on this basis. Fazzari and Caskey, starting with a critique of the standard IS/LM presentation of the macroeconomy where usually debt and debt contracts are not accounted for, develop a critique of neoclassical policy postulates. The chapter by Albin, commencing with a microstudy of firms' behavior in a dynamic neighborhood, elaborates a complex microdynamical model evaluating economic policy (particularly monetary policy) on this basis. Both chapters by Day and Albin demonstrate how the underlying motions of a complex nonlinear economy can change due to fiscal or monetary policy actions.

The third part of the book is concerned with empirical evidence on debt and financial instability, in particular with cyclical patterns of debt and macroactivities. Niggle, starting also with Minsky's theoretical contributions, develops some empirical measures of corporate (cyclical) indebtedness from the Flow of Funds Accounts and relates this to the fluctuations of macroaggregates. Wolfson discusses empirically-oriented approaches to analyze the interrelation of debt and macroeconomic fragility and elaborates on causes of financial crisis in certain periods of the U.S. economy. Finally, the contribution by Jimenez and Nell focuses on the main determinants of debt in a developing country. A case study of a small country with an open economy is analyzed in order to include a view on this topic from a Third World perspective.

As stated above, most contributions draw more on nonconventional traditions than on standard textbook presentations of macrodynamics. In order to make the reader more familiar with these perhaps lesser-known traditions, and for the purpose of providing some background on the applications of dynamic analysis to economics, the following sections present some of the relevant concepts. An introduction to the theory of linear and nonlinear economic dynamics and macrocycle models is given. This is followed by a discussion of some recent topics on economic dynamics and financial instability. A selected bibliography on the relevant technical and economic themes of the book are then provided for the reader.

Linear and Nonlinear Dynamical Models of Economic Fluctuations

This first part attempts to give a brief justification of why models of nonlinear dynamics are utilized by the authors and why they seem to be empirically more relevant. There is a long tradition in economic theory that utilizes only linear dynamical models in macroeconomics (mostly in two dimensions, for example, IS/LM versions of macromodels). Moreover, a common tradition in modern macroeconomic writings, textbooks, and even econometric work in macrodynamics is that economic macrosystems are basically considered stable at their stationary (or steady-state) equilibrium values, and perturbations originating in unexpected random shocks are thought to be transitory and lead to a return to equilibrium after sufficient periods of time. In traditional theories, including the rational expectation view of business cycles (Sargent 1979; Lucas 1981), it generally has been accepted that stable dynamical models (i.e., stable around their equilibrium solutions) are adequate representations of economic dynamics. Numerous studies have attempted to demonstrate that cyclical co-movement of data on production, income, and employment results solely from randomly distributed shocks on monetary aggregates, productivity of firms, or consumption behavior of households. The first type of shocks is representative for monetary cycle theories (Lucas 1981), and the two latter types are relevant in real business cycle theories (cf. Kydland and Prescott, 1982; Long and Plosser, 1983). This tradition of macroanalysis started with Ragnar Frisch in the 1930s and still prevails in a large part of economic theory, for example in new classical economics (Sargent 1979; Lucas 1981; Barro 1984) and in econometric approaches to the business cycle (more extensive references to these approaches are given by Woodford in this volume).

Major new innovations in the theory of economic dynamics and cycles were already initiated in the 1940s by the application of nonlinear dynamics to the problems of fluctuating growth and erratic accumulation. The theory of nonlinear economic dynamics originally was put forward in the work of Goodwin (1948, 1951), Kaldor (1940), and Kalecki (1971) and was also present in Hicks' (1950) contribution to the theory of trade cycles. This theoretical tradition of endogenously generated economic cycles has been revived recently, mainly beause of recent mathematical advances in the theory of nonlinear oscillations (Hirsch and Smale 1974; Marsden and McCracken 1976; Guckenheimer and Holmes 1983; Gandolfo 1986) and chaotic dynamics (Li and Yorke 1975; Ruelle and Takens 1971; Smale 1967; Lasota and Mackey 1985).

The essential new view in the tradition of nonlinear modeling of economic dynamics is that the equilibrium dynamics of the economy (around its stationary or steady-state values) are inherently unstable arising from a Hopf-bifurcation for certain parameters of the model. Economically, such instability properties in the vicinity of the stationary or steady-state values of the model are well known from Keynesian economics or the growth model of Harrod-Domar type, where an unstable accelerator generates positive feedback effects in the neighborhood of the equilibrium. This is essential for the dynamics of the models of Foley (1986)[2] and Day included in this volume. On the other hand, the departure of the economy from its equilibrium value may—due to nonlinearities in the response of economic agents to economic data—generate globally stable economic systems. Such globally attracting forces may, for example, arise from the financial or liquidity side of the economy (cf. Foley [1986] and Day included here). Since the equilibrium position of the economy is normally conceived as unstable, the economy is forced to generate stable cycles around the equilibrium (e.g., limit cycles). Interesting variations of these types of analysis are represented by the chapter by Duménil and Lévy, where a transition can occur between different regimes of complex dynamics (cf. the contribution by Albin). Thus, recent applications of nonlinear (and chaotic) dynamics to economic modeling seem to yield more interesting and realistic results than the old linear dynamic models. Although in nonlinear models the dynamics are more complicated than in linear models, they allow for stable, closed cycles or bounded (erratic) fluctuations, as in the type of models presented by Day, Albin, and Woodford. The trajectories of the dynamics of the latter type frequently are only describable by probabilistic concepts (cf. Lasota and Mackey 1985).

The theoretical framework of nonlinear dynamics in economics as originally initiated by the works of Goodwin, Kaldor, Kalecki, and Hicks has led to the elaboration of different types of nonlinear cycle models: (1) nonlinear accelerator-multiplier models (Goodwin, Hicks, Minsky), (2) nonlinear wage-share employment dynamics (Goodwin), (3) nonlinear income-investment dynamics (Kaldor), (4) nonlinear profit-investment models (Kalecki), and (5) nonlinear overlapping generations models (Benhabib and Day 1982; Grandmont 1985). In addition, as mentioned, nonlinear economic dynamics are not necessarily restricted to cyclical behavior but can also generate bounded, erratic fluctuations as in the deterministic chaotic models included in this volume.

The theoretical tradition referred to above has proven to be very fruitful for macroeconomic theorizing, and recently, several further extensions of such versions of economic dynamics have been elaborated and published in economic journals. As recent work has also shown, numerous seminal extensions and applications of nonlinear theories of business cycles (or chaotic dynamics) have been developed by a new generation of theoretically-oriented researchers. On the basis of the aforementioned tradition of nonlinear dynamics, several further areas of research became important. Among them are: (1) the microdynamics of nonlinear cycle theories, (2) growth, technical change, and employment problems in the context of nonlinear short-run and long-run models, (3) economic dynamics for open economies, (4) stabilization policy in nonlinear cycle models, (5) the difference of time-continuous and time-discrete nonlinear models (chaotic dynamics), and (6) econometric tests of nonlinearities (or deterministic chaotic properties) in time series data. Many of these extensions have been worked out in recent literature. In this book, however, the authors focus mainly on the (possible nonlinear) dynamical interaction of the financial and the real side of the economy.

Dynamical Models of Macrofluctuations
with Money and Finance

Dynamical models with money and finance of linear and nonlinear types have already been developed in the context of the traditional IS/LM framework. Authors representing this approach include Schinasi (1981, 1982), Torre (1977), Stutzer (1980), Benassy (1984), and recently Taylor (1985) and Taylor and O'Connell (1985). In recent discussions, the work of Taylor and O'Connell (included in this volume) has served as a new starting point for study of the interaction of the real and financial side of the economy as verbally formulated by Minsky. Besides IS/LM versions of macromodels, such problems also have been studied in a framework of accelerator-multiplier models with money and finance (cf. Minsky 1957). For the majority of those studies, however, the investment and financing behavior of firms and the lending and borrowing under conditions of indebted units in an economy really had not been well integrated in macrodynamical models.

Recently, the economic effects of debt financing of economic units, particularly of firms, have been studied extensively in the financial and more empirically-oriented literature (cf. Brealy and Meyers 1984; Wojnilower 1982; Eckstein and Sinai 1986; Wolfson 1986). In empirical work on recent trends in corporate finance, for example, it has been stated that debt financing has become a dominant way of generating funds—slowly replacing self-financing and equity financing of firms. This, at least, holds as a secular trend, but it has also become an important way of raising funds over the business cycle (Brealy and Myers 1984; Wolfson 1986). As the contributions by both Niggle and Wolfson in this volume show, there is a strong secular as well as cyclical component in the determination of the liquidity and debt variations of corporate financial structure.

As previously mentioned in theoretical studies such as those put forward by Minsky (1975, 1982, 1986), it has been shown that high debt/asset ratios will appear as a dangerous liability structure of firms, increasing the risk of bankruptcy of economic units and possibly developing unstable macroeconomic trajectories. Following the research of Minsky and taking into account the increasing empirical relevance of debt financing of economic units, four different types of approaches can be seen which relate the conditions of financing to macroeconomic fluctuations.

The first type of model is solely concerned with exogenous credit constraints and its impact on macrofluctuations. Within this framework, it is argued that equity financing is not a viable alternative to debt financing. Thus, exogenous credit constraints, rather than interest rates, are the effective determinants of economic fluctuations (Stiglitz and Weiss 1981; Greenwald, Stiglitz, and Weiss 1984; Guttentag and Herring 1984). This idea of exogenous credit constraints (already put forward by von Hayek and Hawtrey in the 1920s) is formalized in dynamic models by Woodford (1986 and also Woodford in this volume), where credit constraints appear as a fixed upper limit of borrowing which enters as a parameter in a time-discrete macromodel generating nonlinear cycles among other types of motions.

In a second type of model, the ease and drain of finance and liquidity is more or less endogenously generated. Foley, in particular, has presented a series of papers where this approach is taken to explain self-generated liquidity-growth cycles (Foley 1986, 1987). Here, borrowing and lending are fully endogenized in an interdependent economic system. In Foley's papers, borrowing, lending, and capital outlay (the investment of firms) are essentially dependent on the profit rate and on the endogenously generated liquidity of the enterprise system as a whole.

Nonlinear macroeconomic cycles therefore, are generated in the profit rate and liquidity, where a liquidity drain appears at periods of high growth rates and an ease of liquidity occurs at low growth rates of the economy. Thus, the drain and ease of liquidity become the attracting forces of the dynamic system, whereas an unstable accelerator effect creates an unstable equilibrium. A similar relation between an unstable accelerator and a stabilizing liquidity effect is also characteristic of Day's model included in this volume. Several important features of Foley's models are that the dynamic system is considered to be a closed one, capitalist consumption is equal to zero, and there are no asset holders outside of the firms.

A third type of model allows for multiple assets being held outside of the investing firms. Specific features for economic dynamics arise here from changing asset composition, which responds to economic variables such as the rates of return of firms, their expected rates of return, and the interest rate. Models of this type are developed in Taylor (1985) and Taylor and O'Connell (1985), and also in the basic model in Taylor (1982). There, however, capitalist firms are exclusively externally financed through loans and equity issuance. The savings generated by rentier households, as suggested in Kalecki's macroeconomic writings, are channeled through the banking system to investing firms. The main new economic result in Taylor and O'Connell is that financial and asset markets can render the macrodynamics totally unstable (not to be expected in standard IS/LM models). This arises from the fact that in contractionary periods, for example, the previous debt of firms and the additional shifting of asset holders into liquidity (money) will generate a positive feedback effect during the downward movement of the economy; the further away the macroaggregates are from their normal position, the further they will depart from it. This dynamic system is also globally unstable.

A fourth type of model can be developed as a variation of the Kalecki-Taylor approach. However, this type explicitly takes into account the role of external financing and indebtedness of firms in macrofluctuations. Though the models by Taylor, and by Taylor and O'Connell develop rich macroeconomic dynamics, including financial instability as proposed by Minsky in his financial crisis theory, the role of firms' indebtedness and debt payment commitments is not studied fully. As noted before, a high degree of indebtedness and debt payment commitments of firms, however, seem to be essential causes for financial instability. The role of debt for investment and borrowing behavior of firms, as well as for lending by asset holders, is formalized and explored in the contribution by Franke and Semmler in this book. A Kalecki-Taylor type of (nonlinear) IS/LM version of a macromodel is expanded to a large dynamical system, which includes two additional dynamical equations representing the evolution of the debt/asset ratio and the state of confidence of investors. Among other scenarios, cyclical movements of rates of return, growth rates, the interest rate, the state of confidence, and the debt/asset ratio arise. In Woodford's contribution, particularly in the first part of his chapter, the debt/asset ratio is made endogenous, feeding back to a complex macrodynamics of the chaotic type. Both of the models by Franke and Semmler and by Woodford refer to Kalecki's view that higher debt leads to an increasing risk for firms—the "law of increasing risk."

In other contributions in this volume, such as the contribution by Shaikh, the implications of both debt and equity finance for macrofluctuations is explored in a framework inspired by the Marxian theory of money and credit. A framework based on nonlinear differential equations for fast and slow dynamics is developed which allows for an integrated treatment of Marxian, Kaleckian, and Keynesian ideas on external financing of firms and macrofluctuations. In Duménil and Lévy, a nonlinear dynamical macromodel with real and financial variables, derived from the microbehavior of firms, is elaborated. It not only allows for financial instability and cycles but also for stagnation as a possible scenario.

Based on the types of models presented in this book, the results for economic policy are very intriguing. Particularly, as the chapters in Part II demonstrate, stabilization policies of the monetary and fiscal variety are likely to generate transitions between different types of dynamics when a nonlinear complex type of motion of the underlying economy is allowed for. Well known and widely used economic policies can generate quite unexpected outcomes, as shown in the studies by both Day and Albin.

In sum, a number of central themes of the dynamics with money and finance and their implications for macrofluctuations and economic policy are presented, and the empirical measures and trends of debt financing are provided. It may be appropriate, however, to indicate a further research strategy that could not be pursued here fully. The following additional dimensions could be explored on these topics: (1) microeconomic studies of borrowing and investment behavior of firms and their effects in a system of interdependent dynamics; (2) empirical and theoretical studies of debt financing of firms and macrofluctuations in open economies; (3) an intercountry comparison of stylized facts concerning the evolution of the financing structure of firms, debt burden, and debt payment commitments and their impact on macrofragility; (4) major policy implications for extended versions of such models (e.g., to open economies). Subsequent research on dynamical methodology, extended models, stylized facts and trends, and policy implications will help to introduce further theoretical, empirical, and policy dimensions into the theme "Financial Dynamics and Business Cycles." The contributions to this book should be considered an important advance in this development.

Notes

1. The conference and the publication of its papers were made possible by a generous grant from Manufacturers Hanover Trust, which bears no responsibility for any views expressed in this volume. The organizers also appreciate very much the help and assistance of Marsha Lasker and Karin Ray.

2. Foley's paper was originally presented at the conference but has been published elsewhere in the meantime.

Selected Bibliography

Barro, R. J. 1984. *Macroeconomics*. New York: John Wiley.

Benassy, J. P. 1984. "A Non-Walrasian Model of the Business Cycle." *Journal of Economic Behavior and Organization* 5:77–89.

Benhabib, J., and R. H. Day. 1982. " A Characterization of Erratic Dynamics in the Overlapping Generations Model." *Journal of Economic Dynamics and Control* 48:459–72.

Bosworth, B. 1971. "Patterns of Corporate External Financing." *Brookings Papers on Economic Activity* 2:253–85.

Brealey, R., and S. Myers. 1984. *Principles of Corporate Finance*. New York: McGraw-Hill.

Chang, W. W., and D. J. Smyth. 1971. "The Existence and Persistence of Cycles in a Non-linear Model: Kaldor's 1940 Model Reexamined." *Review of Economic Studies* 38:37–46.

Clower, R. W. 1967. "A Reconstruction of Microfoundations of Monetary Theory." *Western Economic Journal* 6:1–9.

Dana, R. A., and P. Malgrange. 1984. "The Dynamics of a Discrete Version of a Growth Cycle Model." *Analyzing the Structure of Econometric Models*. J. Ancot, ed., The Hague: Nijhoff Publishing Company.

Day, R. H., and W. Shafer. 1985. "Keynesian Chaos." *Journal of Macroeconomics* 7(3): 277–95.

Eckstein, O., and A. Sinai. 1986. "The Mechanisms of the Business Cycle in the Postwar Era." *The American Business Cycle: Continuity and Change*. Robert J. Gordon, ed., NBER, Chicago: University of Chicago Press, pp. 39–105.

Fisher, I. 1933. "The Debt Deflation Theory of Great Depressions." *Econometrica* I:337–57.

Foley, D. 1986. "Stabilization Policy in a Nonlinear Business Cycle Model." *Competition, Instability, and Nonlinear Cycles, Lecture Notes in Economics and Mathematical Systems*. W. Semmler, ed., New York and Heidelberg: Springer-Verlag, pp. 200–211.

Foley, D. 1987. Liquidity-Profit Rate Cycles in a Capitalist Economy. *Journal of Economic Behavior and Organization* 8(3): 363–377.

Gandolfo, G. 1986. *Mathematical Methods and Models in Economic Analysis*. Amsterdam: North-Holland.

Goodwin, R. M. 1948. "Secular and Cyclical Aspects of the Multiplier and Accelerator." *Employment, Income and Public Policy*. Essays in honor of A. H. Hansen. New York: W. W. Norton.

Goodwin, R. M. 1951. "The Nonlinear Acceleration and the Persistence of Business Cycles." *Econometrica* 19(1): 1–17.

Goodwin, R. M., and L. F. Punzo. 1986. *The Dynamics of a Capitalist Economy*. Boulder: Westview Press.

Goodwin, R. M. 1986. "Swinging Along the Autostrada." *Competition, Instability, and Nonlinear Cycles*, W. Semmler, ed., Heidelberg and New York: Springer-Verlag, pp. 125–31.

Greenwald, B., J. E. Stiglitz, and A. Weiss. 1984. "Informational Imperfections in the Capital Good Market and Macroeconomic Fluctuations." *American Economic Review* (May):194–200.

Guckenheimer, J., and P. Holmes. 1983. *Nonlinear Oscillations, Dynamical Systems and Bifurcations of Vector Fields*. Berlin and New York: Springer-Verlag.

Guttentag, J., and R. Herring. 1984. "Credit Rationing and Financial Disorder." *The Journal of Finance* (December):1359–82.

Grandmont J. M. 1985. "On Endogenous Competitive Business Cycles." *Econometrica* 5(September):995–1045.

Hicks, J. R. 1950. *A Contribution to the Theory of Trade Cycle.* Oxford: Oxford University Press.

Hirsch, M. W., and S. Smale. 1974. *Differential Equations, Dynamical Systems and Linear Algebra.* New York: Academic Press.

Joseph, D. D. 1983. "Stability and Bifurcation Theory." *Comportement Chaotique des Systemes Deterministes,* G. Iooss, ed., Amsterdam: North-Holland, pp. 351–79.

Kaldor, M. 1940. "A Model of the Trade Cycle." *Economic Journal* 50(March):78–92.

Kalecki, M. 1971. *Selected Essays on the Dynamics of the Capitalist Economy.* Cambridge: Cambridge University Press.

Klein, L. R., and R. S. Preston. 1969. "Stochastic Nonlinear Models." *Econometrica* 37:95–106.

Kohn, M. 1981. "Loanable Funds Theory of Unemployment and Monetary Disequilibrium." *American Economic Review* (December):859–875.

Kydland F., and E. F. Prescott. 1982. "Time to Build and Aggregate Fluctuations." *Econometrica* 50(November): 1345–70.

Lasota, A., and M. Mackey. 1985. *Probabilistic Properties of Deterministic Systems.* Cambridge: Cambridge University Press.

Lakin, W. D., and D. A. Sachez. 1970. *Topics in Ordinary Differential Equations.* New York: Dover.

Li, T. Y., and J. Yorke. 1975. "Period Three Implies Chaos." *American Mathematical Monthly* 82:985–92.

Long, J. B., and C. I. Plosser. 1983. "Real Business Cycles." *Journal of Political Economy* 91(February):39–69.

Lorenz, E. 1963. "Deterministic, Nonperiodic Flow." *Journal of the Atmospheric Science* 20:130–41.

Lucas, R. E. 1981. "Understanding Business Cycles." *Studies in Business Cycle Theory,* R. E. Lucas, ed., Cambridge: MIT Press.

Marglin, S. A. 1984. *Growth, Distribution and Prices.* Cambridge: Harvard University Press.

Marsden, J. E., and M. McCracken. 1976. *The Hopf-Bifurcation and its Applications.* New York: Springer-Verlag.

Minsky, H. P. 1957. "Monetary Systems and Accelerator Models." *The American Economic Review* 47(6):859–82.

Minsky, H. P. 1975. *John Maynard Keynes.* New York: Columbia University Press.

Minsky, H. P. 1982. *Can "It" Happen Again? Essays on Instability and Finance.* Armonk, New York: M. E. Sharpe, Inc.

Minsky, H. 1986. *Stabilizing an Unstable Economy.* New Haven: Yale University Press.

Nell, E. 1986. *On Monetary Circulation and the Rate of Exploitation.* Thames Papers in Political Economy. London: Thames Polytechnic.

Rose, H. 1969. "Real and Monetary Factors in the Business Cycle." *Journal of Money, Credit, and Banking* (May):138–52.

Ruelle, D., and F. Takens. 1971. "On the Nature of Turbulence, Communications." *Mathematical Physics* XX:176–92.

Sargent, T. 1979. *Macroeconomic Theory.* New York: Academic Press.

Schinasi, G. J. 1981. "A Nonlinear Dynamic Model of Short Run Fluctuations." *Review of Economic Studies* 48:649–56.

Schinasi, G. J. 1982. "Fluctuations in a Dynamic, Intermediate-Run IS-LM Model: Applications of the Poincare-Bendixson Theorem." *Journal of Economic Theory* 28:369–75.

Semmler, W. 1986a. "On Nonlinear Theories of Economic Cycles and the Persistence of Business Cycles." *Mathematical Social Sciences* 12(1):47–76.

Semmler, W. 1986b, ed. *Competition, Instability, and Nonlinear Cycles, Lecture Notes in*

Economics and Mathematical Systems. Heidelberg and New York: Springer-Verlag.

Semmler, W. 1987. "A Macroeconomic Limit Cycle with Financial Perturbations." *Journal of Economic Behavior and Organization* 8(3):469–95.

Semmler, W., and M. Sieveking. 1988. Nonlinear Growth-Liquidity Dynamics with Bankruptcy Risk. New School for Social Research, University of Frankfurt. Mimeo.

Smale, S. 1967. "Differentiable Dynamical Systems." *Bulletin of the American Mathematical Society* 73:747–817.

Stiglitz, J., and A. Weiss. 1981. "Credit Rationing in Markets with Imperfect Information." *American Economic Review* (June):393–410.

Stutzer, M. J. 1980. "Chaotic Dynamics and Bifurcation in a Macro Model." *Journal of Economic Dynamics and Control* 2:353–76.

Taylor, L. 1982. *Structuralist Macroeconomics.* New York: Basic Books.

Taylor, L. 1985. "A Stagnationist Model of Economic Growth." *Cambridge Journal of Economics* 9:383–403.

Taylor, L., and S. A. O'Connell, 1985. "A Minsky Crisis." *Quarterly Journal of Economics* 100(Supplement):871–886.

Tobin, J. 1965. "Money and Economic Growth." *Econometrica* 33(October):671–84.

Tobin, J. 1969. "A General Equilibrium Approach to Monetary Theory." *Journal of Money, Credit and Banking* 1:15–29.

Tobin, J. 1982. "Money and Finance in the Macroeconomic Process." *Journal of Money, Credit and Banking* XIV(2):171–203.

Torre, V. 1977. "Existence of Limit Cycles and Control in Complete Keynesian System by Theory of Bifurcations." *Econometrica* 45(September):1456–66.

Wojnilower, A. M. 1982. "The Central Role of Credit Crunches in Recent Financial History." *Brookings Papers on Economic Activity* 2:289–327.

Wolfson, M. 1986. *Financial Crises.* Armonk, New York: M. E. Sharpe, Inc.

Woodford, M. 1986. Self-Fulfilling Expectations, Finance Constraints and Aggregate

Wolfson, M. 1986. *Financial Crisis.* Armonk, New York: M. E. Sharpe, Inc.

Woodford, M. 1986. Self-Fulfilling Expectations, Finance Constraints and Aggregate Fluctuations. Columbia University, New York. Mimeo.

I

Basic Models on Nonlinear Dynamics and Financial Instability

A Minsky Crisis

Lance Taylor and Stephen O'Connell

Hyman Minsky's ideas about financial crises are influential. For example, he provides much of the theoretical foundation for Charles Kindleberger's (1978) well-known book *Manias, Panics, and Crashes*. But for all his citations in the specialist literature, Minsky's work has never been elaborated formally, and he is scarcely noticed in the textbooks.

One reason for the neglect is that Minsky's theories are both microeconomically detailed and institutional. In recent essays collected in Minsky (1982), he works with at least four types of financial actors: households plus firms variously engaged in "hedged," "speculative," and "Ponzi" finance. Shifts of firms among classes as the economy evolves in historical time underlie much of its cyclical behavior. This detail is rich and illuminating, but beyond the reach of mere algebra.

What can perhaps be formalized are purely macroeconomic aspects of Minsky's theories. Two general assumptions characterize the crises he discusses. The first is that total nominal wealth in the system is macroeconomically determined, dependent on confidence and the state of the cycle. More of his flavor is captured if we further postulate that asset choices by firms and households are not coordinated. Firms build up physical capital, obtaining finance from equity or loans from intermediaries. They can also build up their own net worth. Households use intermediaries or equity to direct their savings toward firms. However, there is no effective arbitrage between valuations of physical capital held by firms and financial capital held by households. The market valuation of shares can deviate substantially from the book value of capital, with the difference being absorbed by net worth. With total wealth fluctuating over time, separate portfolio decisions by firms and households can interact to create crises.

Comments by Hyman Minsky, an anonymous referee, and Dan Raff are gratefully acknowledged.

The second major assumption is that there is high substitutability among assets in household portfolios under certain circumstances—there can be a flight to money when conditions are ripe. How often this possibility arises is an empirical matter. The crises on record show that it cannot be ruled out of court. When panics occur, interest rates rise, investment is cut back, and profit rates fall. As a consequence, the valuation of firms' capital assets declines and so does their net worth. The stage is set for the debt-deflation process that Minsky and Irving Fisher (1933) emphasize. Part of the process is extensive financial disintermediation and "disappearance" of assets. Endogenously varying levels of wealth in the macro system permit debt deflation to occur.

The text followed in developing these two ideas is titled *John Maynard Keynes* by Minsky (1975). This book has the advantage of stating Minsky's crisis story against the backdrop of *The General Theory* and the distributional accounting of Michal Kalecki (1971). We largely follow the latter's formulations, beginning with a very simple model and then indicating extensions at the end of the paper.

On the production side of the economy, there is markup pricing at a constant rate τ over the wage bill (representing prime cost). The nominal wage is w, and the labor-output ratio is b. The price level P is given by

$$(1) \qquad P = (1 + \tau)wb.$$

Minsky follows Keynes and parallels later model-builders such as Foley and Sidrauski (1971) in assuming that there are separate capital- and consumer-goods-producing sectors. That complication is dropped here for simplicity, so the price of *new* investment goods is P.

Is it legitimate to impute this price to physical capital goods in place? If so, a rate of profit r can be defined as

$$(2) \qquad r = \frac{PX - wbX}{PK} = \frac{\tau wbX}{(1 + \tau)wbK} = \frac{\tau}{1 + \tau} \frac{X}{K},$$

where X is the level of output, and K is the capital stock. Other pricing rules for physical assets would of course produce different expressions for the rate of profit—in particular, Minsky's analysis is based on prices for individual buildings and machines. Indeed, he would go further and assert that the PK term in the denominator of (2) is impossible to define after the Cambridge controversies. For that reason, all his formulas are stated as levels, while the ones here are based on division by PK. The trick simplifies differential equations for growth, at the cost of begging serious questions about the valuation of capital stock.

Minsky's investment theory is built around expected returns generated by physical capital in the process of production. In a stylized way, we can imagine firms using a rule of thumb for investment that depends on anticipated profits and a discount factor. The capitalized value of expected earnings per unit of investment is an appropriate shadow price (called P_k by Minsky) for the investment decision. It can be written as

$$(3) \qquad\qquad P_k = (r + \varrho)P/i,$$

where i is the current interest rate and ϱ reflects the difference between the anticipated return to holding capital and the current profit rate r. The variable ϱ carries a heavy burden in the story that follows. It represents expected high or low profits, which in turn depend on the overall state of confidence. In Minsky's view, financial and product market conditions, internal finance, and existing liability structures all influence P_k and, in the present treatment, ϱ.

Minsky makes investment demand depend on the price differential $P_k - P_i$, where P_i is the supply price of new investment goods (also subject to real and financial perturbations). For present purposes P_i is replaced by P, and the price differential is

$$(4) \qquad\qquad P_k - P = (r + \varrho - i)P/i$$

Algebra becomes simpler if we use the variant specification (in nominal terms):

$$(5) \qquad \text{Investment demand} = PI = [g_0 + h(r + \varrho - i)]PK,$$

where g_0 is a constant reflecting autonomous capital stock growth, and the coefficient h measures firms' investment response to the expected difference between profit and interest costs. The theory of equation (5) is quite orthodox.[1]

Income streams generated by production are the wage bill wbX and markup income τwbX (or rPK). Following Kalecki, we assume that all wages are consumed. Profits are all distributed to rentiers, who have a saving rate s^2. The aggregate saving flow is given by

$$(6) \qquad\qquad \text{Saving supply} = srPK = s\tau wbX.$$

Excess demand for goods is just the difference between (5) and (6). After dividing through by PK, the following condition for equilibrium in the commodity market is obtained:

$$(7) \qquad\qquad g_0 + h(r + \varrho - i) - sr = 0.$$

If the profit rate r or the output level X increases when there is excess demand, commodity market adjustment is stable if the condition $s - h > 0$ is satisfied—investment must respond less to profit rate increases than saving.[3] Solving (7) for r and plugging the result into the investment demand function gives a reduced form for the capital stock growth rate g $(= I/K)$ as

(8)
$$g = \frac{s[g_0 + h(\varrho - i)]}{s - h}.$$

A fall in the interest rate or an increase in anticipated profits leads to a higher growth rate. Since

(9)
$$g = sr$$

from the saving function, the profit rate and capacity utilization go up as well.

The next step is to look at the asset side of the economy along the usual portfolio balance lines. There is an outside primary asset F, or fiscal debt. It can take the form of money (M) or short-term bonds (B), held by the rentiers (workers' financial market participation is ignored, consistent with the assumption that they do not save). The capitalized value of the plant and equipment held by firms is $P_k K = (r + \varrho)PK/i$. Firms have emitted an outstanding stock of equity E; its market price is P_e, determined below. The difference between the value of capital stock and equity is firms' net worth N.[4] Their balance sheet (along with that of the rentiers) appears in Table 1. In differential form, the firms' balance sheet identity is

---

Table 1

Simplified Balance Sheets for Firms and Rentiers

Firms		Rentiers	
$\dfrac{r + \varrho}{i}$	$P_e E$	$P_e E$	
		M	W
	N	B	

---

(10)
$$P_k I + \dot{P}_k K = P_e \dot{E} + \dot{P}_e E + \dot{N},$$

where a dot above a variable denotes a time derivative. The liability counterparts of new investment or capital gains on the existing stock are new equity issues, higher equity prices, or increased net worth. We do not go into how firms decide about issuing new stock; hence the adjusting variables are the price of equity and net worth.

Total wealth of the rentiers is

$$(11) \qquad W = P_eE + M + B = P_eE + F.$$

A price for bonds does not enter in (11), since they are short term. The change in rentiers' wealth over time is

$$(12) \qquad \dot{W} = \dot{P}_eE + P_e\dot{E} + \dot{M} + \dot{B} = \dot{P}_eE + srPK.$$

Their wealth increases from capital gains and financial saving.

At each point in time, rentiers allocate their wealth across assets according to the following equations for market balance:

$$(13) \qquad \mu(i,r + \varrho)W - M = 0,$$

$$(14) \qquad \frac{\xi(i,r + \varrho)}{P_e} W - E = 0,$$

and

$$(15) \qquad - \beta(i,r + \varrho)W + B = 0,$$

where $\mu + \xi + \beta = 1$. Only two of these three equations are independent. As usual, we work with (13) and (14) for the money and equity markets with i and P_e as the equilibrating variables, respectively. The excess supply function (15) for bonds will be equal to zero when the other excess demand relationships satisfy the same condition.

The arguments in the asset demand functions are the bond interest rate i and the anticipated profit rate on physical capital $r + \varrho$. Incorporating transactions demand would require the use of X/K (or r, again) as an additional argument, but this possibility is ignored for simplicity. The notion behind using $r + \varrho$ to measure returns to equity is that wealthholders try to look through Wall Street to "fundamentals" on the production side, instead of basing share purchase decisions on the Dow Jones average P_e. A more elaborate theory of asset demand would use the expression $(r + \varrho)P/P_e + \hat{\Pi}_e$ as the return to equity, where $\hat{\Pi}_e$ is the expected growth rate of P_e. If, following the rational expectations school, the actual and expected rates of inflation of equity prices were made equal (except for a white noise error term), then (14) with $(r + \varrho)P/P_e + \hat{\Pi}_e$ as the return to equity could generate a stock price bubble. Inverting (14) would make $\hat{\Pi}_e$ a positive function of P_e, and the standard rational expectations saddlepoint solution could emerge.[5]

We ignore this possibility because bubbles do not seem central to Minsky's crisis theory, though he mentions them from time to time.[6] His argument would be that under most (but not all) circumstances, shareholders simply do not agree about expected inflation of the equity price. On average (though not for some) the arbitrage opportunity is ignored; the possibility of capitalizing economy-wide gains or losses on share prices is not exploited.[7] Folklore contends that Joseph Kennedy got out of the stock market before the crash of 1929. Most other participants did not, and their error generated a crisis of confidence of the type to be discussed below.

With bubbles excluded, the key variable in (13) and (14) is the anticipated corporate return $r + \varrho$. Note from Table 1 that higher returns bid up firms' valuation of their capital stock. The same is true of financial wealth, since from (11) and (14),

$$(16) \qquad W = \frac{F}{1 - \xi(i, r + \varrho)}.$$

An increase in r and ϱ will drive up ξ, and thus share prices and financial wealth will rise. In effect, rentiers' net worth is determined macroeconomically from their valuation of anticipated profits, feeding into market balances for asset supplies and demands. The share price can be solved for as

$$(17) \qquad P_e = [\xi/(1 - \xi)](F/E);$$

in turn, P_e determines the change in firms' net worth given their investment and issuance of new equity in (10).

From (16) it is easy to rewrite the money market excess demand function as

$$(18) \qquad \mu(i, r + \varrho) = \alpha[1 - \xi(i, r + \varrho)],$$

where $\alpha = M/F$ is the share of fiscal debt issued as money.

Using subscripts i and r to stand for partial derivatives with respect to the interest rate i and the expected profit rate $r + \varrho$, we may write the differential form of (18) as

$$(19) \qquad \eta_i di + \eta_r dr = -\eta_r d\varrho + (1 - \xi)d\alpha,$$

where

$$\eta_i = \mu_i + \alpha\xi_i$$

and

$$\eta_r = \mu_r + \alpha\xi_r$$

A higher bond interest rate cuts back on demand for money, so that μ_i is negative. Since demand for equity also falls, ξ_i is negative, making $\eta_i < 0$. The partial derivative μ_r is negative, but an increase in r or ϱ raises the demand for nominal equity. From the standard assumption that assets are gross substitutes, $\xi_r > |\mu_r|$. However, if money and equity are close substitutes in asset demand, the magnitudes of the two partial derivatives will be close to each other. Further, if α is a small enough fraction, then $\eta_r < 0$. For reasons to be made clear shortly, we shall assume high substitutability between money and equity, so that the portmanteau derivative η_r is indeed negative.[8]

Note immediately from (19) that an open market operation to increase the money supply would raise α and reduce the interest rate for a given rate of profit. From (3) and (17) there would be higher asset prices P_k and P_e; Minsky (1975) devotes long passages to justify this result. An increase in the expected extra profit rate ϱ will reduce i when there is a high degree of asset substitutability.[9]

Equations (7) for the commodity market and (18) for money form a system analogous to the usual IS/LM construct. However, it should be recognized that underlying (18) is the assumption that both the money and equity markets clear. In equilibrium, the price of equity P_e and nominal wealth W are determined along with the profit and interest rates. As shown in Figure 1, we assume that the financial market equilibrium schedule has a negative slope in (r,i) space, due to strong substitution between money and liabilities of firms. The "story" is that if realized or prospective profits increase, then rentiers wish to shift their portfolios away from money and bonds and toward claims to real assets. With a sufficiently strong shift away from money, the equilibration process requires a rise in the equity price and hence, in wealth. Interest rates fall to make households content to hold the existing stock of bonds at the increased level of wealth.

For short-run stability in our analog to the IS/LM system, the slope of the financial market curve must be shallower, i.e., less negative, than the slope of the commodity market schedule, as shown in Figure 1. An increase in ϱ will pull rentiers sharply enough toward equity to bid down the interest rate, as shown by the dashed line. In the commodity market, a higher ϱ stimulates investment demand, thus increasing output and the rate of profit. Overall, the outcome is a lower interest rate, a higher profit rate and a higher P_k—there is a positive linkage between expected profits and the actual profit rate and rate of capital stock growth. On the other hand, if prospects seem grim, a fall in anticipated profits will lead rentiers to flee toward money, drive up interest rates, and strangle growth. Tighter monetary policy (a lower α) would have a similar effect, shifting the financial market locus upward. The outcome would be a higher interest rate and a lower rate of profit.

Figure 1. **Responses of the Interest Rate and Profit Rate to an Increase in the Expected Incremental Profit Rate ϱ.**

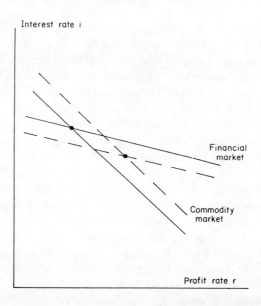

These mechanisms can generate a crisis. To see the details, the way in which anticipated profits and monetary policy evolve over time needs to be specified. The most plausible theory about the expected profit differential ϱ is that it should depend on the general state of the economy: ϱ might increase, for example, when the actual profit rate is high or the interest rate is low. Both hypotheses in fact give the same dynamics, but the interest rate link is used here, since it involves easier algebra. To do so, suppose that the "normal" dynamic story about ϱ is given by the equation,

$$(20) \qquad\qquad \dot{\varrho} = - \beta(i - \bar{\imath}),$$

When the rate of interest exceeds its "normal" long-run level $\bar{\imath}$, expected profits begin to fall.

To complete the dynamics, government policy behavior must be specified. In standard Keynesian fashion, both monetary and fiscal policy have substantial influence over the path of capital stock growth in our model. Minsky (1982) offers lengthy discussion of the interaction of monetary and fiscal interventions in a complex financial system. In the current model, the money-debt ratio α can be written as

$$\alpha = \frac{M}{F} = \frac{M}{PK}\frac{PK}{F} = \frac{M}{PK}\left[\frac{1}{f}\right],$$

where f is the ratio of outstanding fiscal debt to the capital stock. Leaving fiscal complications aside, we fix government expenditures as a proportion of the capital stock and taxes as a proportion of expenditures. On these assumptions, f is fixed, and government spending disappears as an autonomous component of the capital stock growth rate g. The money-debt ratio then evolves according to the rule,

$$(21) \qquad\qquad \hat{\alpha} = \hat{M} - g,$$

so that for a fixed money growth rate $\hat{M}$, $\hat{\alpha}$ falls as g increases.

The nonactivist monetary policy of pre-Keynesian days when financial panics occurred with some frequency could be characterized as a choice of a fixed rate of money supply growth. This sort of policy has a flavor of "leaning against the wind," since money growth does not respond to changes in g. However, it is a far cry from the activist policy pursued in many countries after World War II. The shift of October 1979 in Federal Reserve operating policies toward more precise targeting of money supply growth rates might perhaps be characterized as a move from more complicated interventions toward a rule like (21). Minsky might attribute the retreat from this policy in mid-1982 to growing realization on the part of the monetary authorities that crises still can occur.

The system (20) and (21) has a steady-state equilibrium at $i = \bar{\iota}$ and $g = \hat{M}$. With partial derivatives from (20) in the first row, its Jacobian matrix takes the form:

$$(22) \qquad \begin{bmatrix} -\beta i_\varrho & -\beta i_\alpha \\ -(g_i i_\varrho + g_\varrho) & -g_i i_\alpha \end{bmatrix},$$

where the subscripts on i stand for derivatives through the IS/LM system, (7) and (18), and the growth rate derivatives come from (8).

Equations (20) and (21) are potentially unstable. From Figure 1, an increase in ϱ lowers the interest rate and thus raises the derivative $\dot{\varrho}$ in (20). This positive feedback does not necessarily dominate the system, since the Jacobian determinant $-\beta i_\alpha g_\varrho$ is easily seen to be positive (signaling possible stability).

The phase diagram appears in Figure 2, with arrows showing directions of adjustment in the different quadrants. To explore the possibilities, assume that the economy is initially in a complete steady-state equilibrium at point A. A momentary lapse of confidence would cause ϱ to jump down from A to a point like B. Equally, a one-shot market operation to reduce the money supply would cause i to rise. For a newly set (lower) value of α, (20) shows that ϱ would start to fall from A, setting off a dynamic process like the one beginning to B.

If the authorities hold to a constant money supply growth $\hat{M}$ when the economy is away from steady-state, then a below-equilibrium value of ϱ is associated with

Figure 2. **Adjustment Dynamics When a Fall in the Expected Incremental Profit Rate ϱ from an Initial Equilibrium at A Leads Finally to a Return to Steady-State.**

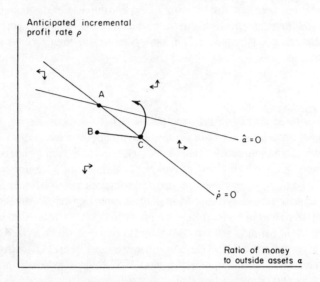

slow capital stock growth and a rising money-debt ratio α from (21). This increase would reduce the interest rate and raise $\dot{\varrho}$. If this effect were strong enough, the economy would follow a path like the one leading through C and return to equilibrium. A minor crisis occurs in the sense that the profit rate and output fall, leading to a lower interest rate, higher investment demand, and ultimate recovery.

But what happens if the (α, ϱ) trajectory does not turn the corner at C? At the micro level, the system enters a debt-deflation contraction such as described by Irving Fisher (1933). Minsky (1982, 42) describes past examples as follows:

> Whenever profits decreased hedge units became speculative and speculative units became Ponzi. Such induced transformations of the financial structure lead to falls in the price of capital assets and therefore to a decline in investment. A recursive process is readily triggered in which a financial market failure leads to a fall in investment which leads to a fall in profits which leads to financial failures, further declines in investment, profits, additional failure, etc.

In terms of Figure 2, output and investment can fall forever, or at least until the model changes. This is a true Minsky crisis, and it occurs when the derivative i_ϱ is strongly negative and the slope of the $\dot{\varrho} = 0$ locus in Figure 2 is shallow. Going back through the algebra reveals that this condition applies when there is high asset substitution. A reduction in ϱ leads the interest rate to rise and the profit rate to fall, driving rentiers into money and bidding up the interest rate further. Expected profits fall still more, and the process never ends. An unstable Minsky crisis looks like movement into a liquidity trap except that the interest rate is steadily rising. From (3) and (17), the descent into the trap is accompanied by plummeting capitalized quasi rents and equity prices—general disintermediation. Financial claims and counterclaims collapse as the microeconomic manifestation of the crisis.

To follow the financial collapse in detail is beyond our scope here. However, three observations are worth making. First, Minsky stresses the importance of intermediaries in accelerating both boom and crisis by creation and destruction of "layered" financial structures. Table 2 gives an expanded balance sheet that may illustrate what he has in mind. Firms now issue debts D_f along with equity as liabilities. These are held by intermediaries as assets, along with quantities B_i and M_i of outside bonds and (high-powered) money. They also have net worth Q and liabilities (deposits) to the rentiers in amount D_i. As far as the public is concerned, these deposits are equivalent to money. Money supply is a variable endogenous to the entire macro system, as argued by Keynesians such as Kaldor (1982).

Table 2

Amplified Balance Sheets for Firms, Financial Intermediaries, and Rentiers

Firms		
$\dfrac{r + \varrho}{i}\ PK$		P_eE
		D_f
		N
Intermediaries		
D_f		D_i
B_i		Q
M_i		
Rentiers		
$(M - M_i) + D_i$		
$(B - B_i)$		W
P_eE		

In the initial phases of an expansion, profit rates rise, and interest rates fall. The partial derivatives of firms' net worth N with respect to these variables are

$$(23) \qquad N_r = \frac{1}{r} \left[\frac{rPK}{i} - \frac{(r\xi_r/\xi)}{1 - \xi} P_e E \right]$$

and

$$(24) \qquad N_i = \frac{1}{i} \left[-\frac{(r + \varrho)PK}{i} - \frac{(i\xi_i/\xi)}{1 - \xi} P_e E \right]$$

Signs are ambiguous here, since P_k and P_e on opposite sides of the firms' balance sheet both fall with i and rise with r. However, one would expect N_r to be positive when the share of rentiers' financial wealth held in equity ξ and the share demand elasticity $r\xi_r/\xi$ are relatively small. If r and P are related positively through a rising markup or aggregate supply curve, $N_r > 0$ is still more likely. Similar arguments suggest that $N_i < 0$. If these conditions hold, then at the beginning of a boom firms' net worth will begin to rise. They will tend to borrow against this increase, creating assets that intermediaries can then expand across the economy. The process will reverse in the downswing, and the intermediaries' overall importance will shrink. At the top of the expansion, the ratio of firms' debt to their net worth rises, and they shift gradually (in Minsky's terminology) from "hedge" to "speculative" and even "Ponzi" positions. The stage is set at the micro level for financial collapse; ultimately some wave of failure sets it off. Assets and liabilities of the intermediaries contract, as the value of capitalized expected profits declines. The process carries with it bankruptcies and financial hardship, especially for the "Ponzi" firms that had been happily emitting new liabilities to cover ongoing interest costs.

Second, in his recent writings, Minsky (1982) stresses the importance of government deficits and Federal Reserve interventions in cutting off the possibility of open-ended crises as discussed above. In Kalecki accounting incorporating the government, we have

Profits = Investment + Government deficit − Current account deficit.

In crisis, investment falls, but the government deficit goes up. It can act as a source of demand to prevent endless debt deflations. In a like manner, Federal Reserve intervention to increase the growth rate of the money supply could preclude crisis. Both fiscal and monetary stabilizers could be described formally by extending our model to include government and central bank transactions explicitly.

Third, bankruptcies of firms are an intrinsic aspect of the downswing. Reductions in investment demand as firms attempt to sell off capital assets to meet inelastic cash requirements can make the "commodity market" curve in Figure 1 flat or upward sloping at low rates of profit. In this situation, monetary contraction can lead to unstable dynamics, even in the absence of high substitutability between money and capital. For details see O'Connell (1983).

In closing observe that for empirical testing, the key mechanism in the crisis theory here is the negative relationship of expected profits and the rate of interest discussed in connection with Figure 1. This linkage in turn requires a substantial degree of substitutability between equity and other assets in the aggregate portfolio. Were there less substitutability, the financial market equilibrium locus in Figure 1 would slope upward (as LM curves usually do) and an increase in ϱ would drive up i. The $\varrho = 0$ locus in Figure 2 would be answered by an immediate upward movement in that variable.

High substitutability plays a central role in other portfolio-based crisis models.[10] It represents a certain absence of inertia in the financial system, as opposed to a case where more sluggish responses to changes in returns underlie general stability. Over time, asset substitutability may rise if the central bank regularly has intervened as a lender of last resort to avert potential crises. Taking the past as a guide to the future, participants in financial markets may become accustomed to exposed positions. Their portfolio switches may become more frequent and substitution more acute when the economy is at the peak of the cycle, or dire portents are in the air. If, under these circumstances, the central bank shifts to a less interventionist policy line, the stage may be set for disaster. With sensitive asset markets, financial crisis must always be considered as a live macroeconomic possibility.

Notes

1. Using P_k as a shadow price for investment decisions, of course, resembles Tobin's (1969) use of "q." However, we depart from Tobin by *not* carrying the q-calculation over to the equity market. Separation of the investment decision from the price of equity is a corollary of the independence of households' and firms' financial actions that was mentioned at the outset.

2. In principle, the saving rate could depend on wealth or some notion of permanent income. As will become clear below, such a behavioral assumption would lead to a positive dependence of s on ϱ. The resulting aggregate demand effects would reinforce our story and are omitted for simplicity.

3. See Taylor (1983) for discussion of stability and other properties of the present model. O'Connell (1983) analyzes a model in which the commodity market stability condition is violated at low levels of capacity utilization, giving rise to unstable dynamic processes with a Fisher-Minsky flavor.

4. Large outstanding levels of corporate net worth appear to be characteristic of modern capitalism. See Atkinson (1975, 129–31) for estimates for the United Kingdom and a discussion of the difficulties this phenomenon creates for analysis of wealthholding in general.

5. In formal terms, let $\phi(i,)$ be the inverse function of $\xi(i,)$ with respect to its second argument. Then from (14) with $(r + \varrho)P/P_e + \hat{\Pi}_e$ as the return to equity we have

$$\hat{\Pi}_e = \phi\left[i, \frac{P_eE}{F + P_eE}\right] - \frac{(R + \varrho)R}{P_e} \quad ,$$

so that $\hat{\Pi}_e$ depends positively on P_e. For more on how such a relationship can generate saddlepoint instability, see Burmeister (1980).

6. See also Kindleberger (1978). The textbook example of a rational expectations bubble is the tulip mania in Holland more than 300 years ago. For an early exposition of the theory, see Samuelson (1957).

7. Analogously, investment demand never responds with enough alacrity to potential profit to drive $r + \varrho$ and i into equality. Minsky (1975) cites borrowers' and leaders' risk in the investment context and nowhere suggests the tulip mania triggers macroeconomic capitalist crises.

8. If we included transactions demands in the model, they would make η_r less negative or positive. We assume substitution effects dominate.

9. Minsky (1975) prefers to treat the negative effect of ϱ on i in terms of shifts in liquidity preference. On page 123 we learn that "during a boom the speculative demand for money decreases." Further, on page 76 if higher income from a boom "is interpreted as increasing the surety of income from capital-asset ownership, then the liquidity preference function will shift, so that for a given quantity of money, the higher the income, the higher the interest rate, and the higher the price of capital assets." In other words, for given money *and* income, higher exected profits (which drive up the price of capital assets) would have to be associated with a *lower* interest rate (because, again, speculative demand declines). The implied sign change in the derivative η_r from positive to negative as r rises could be modeled in the present framework. Its main effect would be to increase stability on the downswing and make an endless Minsky crisis of the type discussed herein impossible.

10. For example, see Dornbusch and Frenkel (1982).

References

Atkinson, A. B. 1975. *The Economics of Inequality*. Oxford: Clarendon Press.
Burmeister, Edwin. 1980. *Capital Theory and Dynamics*. Cambridge: Cambridge University Press.
Dornbusch, Rudiger, and Jacob A. Frenkel. 1982. The Gold Standard and the Bank of England in the Crisis of 1847. Paper presented at conference Retrospective on the Classical Standard 1821–1931. Hilton Head, N.C.
Fisher, Irving. 1933. "The Debt-Deflation Theory of Great Depressions." *Econometrica* I:337–57.
Foley, Duncan K., and Miguel Sidrauski. 1971. *Monetary and Fiscal Policy in a Growing Economy*. New York: Macmillan.
Kaldor, Nicholas. 1982. *The Scourge of Monetarism*. Oxford: Oxford University Press.
Kalecki, Michal. 1971. *Selected Essays on the Dynamics of the Capitalist Economy, 1930–1979*. Cambridge: Cambridge University Press.
Kindleberger, Charles P. 1978. *Manias, Panics and Crashes: A History of Financial Crises*. New York: Basic Books.

Minsky, Hyman P. 1975. *John Maynard Keynes*. New York: Columbia University Press.
————. 1982. *Can "It" Happen Again? Essays on Instability and Finance*. Armonk, New York: M.E. Sharpe, Inc.
O'Connell, Stephen A. 1983. Financial Crises in Underdeveloped Capital Markets: A Model for Chile. Department of Economics, Massachusetts Institute of Technology. Mimeo.
Samuelson, Paul A. 1957. "Intertemporal Price Equilibrium: A Prologue to a Theory of Speculation." *Weltwirtschaftliches Archiv*. LXXIX:181–219.
Taylor, Lance. 1983. *Structuralist Macroeconomics*. New York: Basic Books.
Tobin, James. 1969. "A General Equilibrium Approach to Monetary Theory," *Journal of Money, Credit and Banking* I:15–29.

Finance, Instability, and Cycles

Michael Woodford

Neoclassical optimal growth models are found to have a stable stationary equilibrium for a wide range of parameter values, including those usually judged to be empirically realistic. While examples are known in which the stationary competitive equilibrium is unstable and equilibrium cycles exist (Benhabib and Nishimura 1979, 1985), or even in which equilibrium dynamics are chaotic (Boldrin and Montrucchio 1986; Deneckere and Pelikan 1986), these depend both upon relatively extreme assumptions about the relative capital intensities of different sectors and upon a sufficiently high rate of time discount. (For sufficient conditions for the absence of cycles or chaos in optimal growth models, see Scheinkman [1976] and Dechert [1984].) It follows from the stability of the stationary equilibrium in the absence of exogenous shocks that business cycles (i.e., repetitive rather than merely transitory deviations from the stationary equilibrium) must be explained as resulting from the response of the economy to continual exogenous shocks. Repetitive aggregate fluctuations are identified with the stationary Markovian equilibria of a stochastic growth model, as in the work of Kydland and Prescott (1980, 1982), where the exogenous shocks are stochastic shifts in the production technology.

Critics of this sort of approach to business cycle theory have typically attacked the fundamental methodological postulates of equilibrium modeling—it is denied that markets should be modeled as clearing at all times, or that agents should be assumed to possess perfect foresight (or "rational expectations" in the case of a stochastic equilibrium). Neoclassical economists who object to the new classical macroeconomics typically hold that these postulates are appropriate for models of long-run equilibrium, but that business cycles are short-run phenomena which cannot be modeled in that way; more radical critics deny that these postulates are appropriate in analyses of economic dynamics at all.

I wish to suggest instead that the logic of conventional new classical accounts of the business cycle is less inexorable than such terms of debate seem to presume.

Even if one grants the postulates of spot markets for all goods that always clear and perfect foresight regarding all future spot prices, the standard results on the stability of stationary competitive equilibrium need not result if one modifies another crucial assumption of the new classical models that has received somewhat less attention—the existence of perfect financial markets.

Consider here an infinite horizon competitive equilibrium model that is orthodox in all respects, except for the introduction of certain financial constraints. These constraints seem to be reasonably descriptive of financial arrangements in complex modern private enterprise economies, and they are closely related to specifications that have often figured in non-neoclassical business cycle theories. In this model, the stationary competitive equiliibrium may be unstable, and the perfect foresight equilibrium dynamics may converge instead to equilibrium cycles or to a chaotic attractor. This possibility depends neither upon multiple production sectors nor upon a high rate of time discount, as in the examples of equilibrium cycles discussed above.

Even when the stationary competitive equilibrium is not unstable, perfect foresight equilibrium frequently is indeterminate for the model, i.e., for given initial conditions, a continuum of nearby equilibria exists. This indeterminacy— which never occurs in optimal growth models with perfect financial markets[1]— can also be regarded as a type of intrinsic instability of the competitive process. Since different dynamic paths for the economy are equally consistent with fulfillment of expectations, arbitrary events can cause agents' expectations to jump from one such path to another. Change in expectations is then self-fulfilling. In such circumstances, stationary stochastic fluctuations are possible in which autonomous shifts in "animal spirits" constantly occur and cause fluctuations in the rate of production and accumulation, but in which the economy is nonetheless always in a "rational expectations equilibrium."[2]

An Economy with Concentrated Ownership of Capital and No External Finance

The economy to be considered here is a stationary infinite horizon economy with a one-sector production technology, infinite lived agents, endogenous labor supply, and competitive spot markets for all goods (i.e., for labor and for the single produced good). It is thus like the sort of economy investigated by Kydland and Prescott (1980), except that the existence of stochastic shocks to the production technology are not assumed, but imperfections in the financial markets are assumed.

The kind of financial market imperfections of primary interest are restrictions upon the ability of economic units (households or firms) to finance expenditures other than out of their own current or past income. That is, there is no assumption of the existence of a single, economy-wide competitive market for claims to future income (including claims to income contingent upon various possible future events, as in the Arrow-Debreu framework) to which all agents have equal access. This will allow the marginal tradeoffs between present and future goods to be different for different economic units at a given point in time. Cyclical variation in the discrepancy between the marginal tradeoffs of different units in the economy is crucial to the cycle models to be developed below. In the present section, for simplicity, the extreme case of an absolute inability of any economic unit to obtain external finance at all is considered. This means that no financial assets are exchanged at all, so that each unit must spend an amount equal to its income in every period.

In order for borrowing constraints to have any effect upon economic dynamics, of course, it is necessary to assume that agents are not all identical. At certain times some agents would in fact wish to borrow on terms at which other agents would be willing to lend. Accordingly, instead of assuming a single representative infinite lived agent who both supplies labor and owns the capital stock, as in standard neoclassical growth models, assume that two distinct types of infinite lived agents exist, one for each of these two roles. Workers are assumed not to accumulate capital goods, and furthermore, the two groups are assumed not to be able to borrow from or lend to one another.

While there are other ways in which one might introduce a differentiation among agents that would allow borrowing constraints to bind, this particular differentiation seems particularly relevant to the organization of production in modern capitalist economies. Such a differentiation of roles figures prominently in many non-neoclassical business cycle theories. (Kalecki's is perhaps the most obvious example, but many less formal discussions also treat separately the decisions of capitalists and workers, or producers and consumers.) The constraint upon financial intermediation assumed here is given less attention in traditional accounts but is implicit in the treatment of the decisions of the two classes of agents by authors such as Kalecki. If workers lend to capitalists through a complete and fully competitive set of financial markets, they can effectively accumulate capital themselves, so that the distinction between the two roles is negated. (It is shown in the next section that some limited lending by workers to capitalists does not much alter the dynamics predicted by the model. As the limit upon such lending is progressively relaxed, however, one approaches an economy which is equivalent to one with a single representative agent.) Furthermore, the absence of borrowing or lending between the two groups implies that each group's expenditures in a given period are constrained by the income of that group. Some such financial constraint is thus implicit in all models which assume that workers consume exactly their wages each period, and that capitalists accumulate out of their profits. (Again, Kalecki is explicit about this, but many other studies in economic dynamics have also assumed a link of this sort between income distribution and the division of total expenditures into consumption and investment.)

Various explanations are possible of the assumption that workers do not accumulate capital and that no lending occurs between the two groups. One might assume that financial institutions treat all agents alike, but they lend only to borrowers with certain kinds of collateral. Capital goods are obviously much more transferable than is labor power, for which reason the latter sort of "wealth" makes poor collateral. If borrowing against future labor income is impossible, it need only be shown that in equilibrium workers prefer to borrow rather than save (at the rate of return earned by capitalists) in order to explain both why workers own no capital (and hence cannot borrow), and why capitalists do not borrow from workers. This, in turn, requires only the assumption that workers discount the future more than capitalists.

Under yet another interpretation, concentrated ownership of means of production results from the fact that only certain agents possess the knowledge required to recognize profitable production opportunities and organize production appropriately. Wage earners would like to lend to these entrepreneurs (at the rate of return that entrepreneurs receive upon their own capital), but they are unable to effectively monitor the uses to which the funds are put or the amount of profits actually earned. Hence they do not lend, and entrepreneurs' accumulation of capital is constrained by their profits. One needs only to show then that in equilibrium, wage earners do not wish to borrow from entrepreneurs; this occurs if wage earners discount the future less than do entrepreneurs.

This interpretation is particularly reminiscent of Kalecki's theory, in which the macroeconomic consequence of income distribution that is most emphasized is the effect of profits upon the quantity of entrepreneurial capital and hence upon the amount of investment undertaken. The similarity is even greater when it is shown, in the following section, that even if wage earners do lend to entrepreneurs, it can be assumed that there is a limit to permissible asset-liability ratios (owing to the "principle of increasing risk") in order to obtain similar results. However, the simpler case of an economy in which no lending occurs is treated first.

To be specific, consider an economy in which there are two types of infinite lived agents. Workers seek to maximize

$$\sum_{t=1}^{\infty} \gamma^{t-1}[u(c_t) - v(n_t)]$$

where c_t is consumption in period t and n_t is labor supply. Here γ is a discount factor between zero and one, u and v are twice differentiable functions satisfying:

(i) $u' > 0$, $u'' < 0$, $v' > 0$, $v'' > 0$,
(ii) $v'(0) = 0$, $v'(n) \rightarrow \infty$ for large enough n, and
(iii) $u'(c) + cu''(c) > 0$.

Assumptions (i) are standard monotonicity and concavity assumptions. Assumptions (ii) are stronger than necessary, but together with (i) insure that the single-period problem

$$\text{Max} \atop c, n \quad u(c) - v(n) \qquad \text{s. t.} \quad c = wn$$

has an optimal solution c,n > 0, for any positive real wage w. Let the labor supply that solves this problem be denoted n = s(w). Assumption (iii) then is necessary and sufficient for s(w) to be a monotonically increasing function, i.e., it is the condition that leisure and consumption be "gross substitutes."

If workers neither lend to nor borrow from capitalists and cannot accumulate capital goods themselves (presumably because of economies of scale at low levels of production), then in fact $c_t = w_t n_t$ will be workers' budget constraint each period, and so optimizing labor supply will be $n_t = s(w_t)$, and consumption demand will be $c_t = w_t s(w_t)$. Accordingly, the supply curve s(w) summarizes all aspects of workers' behavior that are relevant for the present model.

Suppose that there exists a constant returns to scale one-sector production technology (at least, with constant returns over the range of variation that actually occurs over a business cycle). The relevant aspects of this technology can be summarized by specifying r(w), the level of quasi rents per unit of capital (assuming employment of an optimal quantity of labor inputs) as a function of the real wage. The demand for labor (per unit of capital goods held by capitalists) will then be d(w) = −r'(w). It follows that for any quantity k > 0 of capital goods in existence per worker, the market-clearing real wage will be the solution to:

$$(1) \qquad\qquad kd(w) = s(w).$$

If r is assumed to be a decreasing convex function of w (as follows from profit maximization subject to a convex production set), then d(w) is a decreasing function of w, and a unique solution w(k) to (1) exists. Also note that w(k) will be an increasing function of k.

Finally, suppose that capitalists seek to maximize:

$$\sum_{t=1}^{\infty} \beta^{t-1} \log q_t$$

where q_t is consumption in period t, and β is a discount factor between zero and one. These preferences are chosen to simplify the calculations; they imply a constant savings ratio β for capitalists, regardless of their exectations regarding the future rate of profit. In the case that β is close to one, i.e., capitalists do not discount the future very much, this assumption is probably not too restrictive. (In any event, it is expected that the capitalists' savings ratio should never fall too far below one.)

Without loss of generality, in the case of a one-sector technology, complete depreciation of capital in each period's production is also assumed. Then each period's capital stock can be identified with capitalist saving in the previous period to obtain:

(2) $$k_{t+1} = \beta r[w(k_t)]k_t.$$

This gives each period's capital stock as a function of the previous period's capital stock. Analysis of the possible equilibrium paths of capital accumulation then reduces to the analysis of the properties of a one-dimensional map.

If $r(0) > \beta^{-1}$ is assumed, as is necessary in order for the capital stock not to go to zero asymptotically, we find that there exists a unique steady-state capital stock $k^* > 0$, such that if the initial capital stock per worker equals k^*, (2) yields $k_t = k^*$ forever. However, this steady- state equilibrium need not be stable. If the right hand side of (2) is written $f(k_t)$, then a necessary and sufficient condition for instability is that $f'(k^*) < -1$. (It can be shown that the assumptions above preclude the case $f'(k^*) > 1$.) In terms of the fundamental relationships of the model, this condition can be expressed as follows.

Proposition 1. Let e_s, e_d denote the elasticities of supply and demand for labor respectively, evaluated at the steady-state equilibrium, and let s_n, s_k represent the income shares of labor and capital, respectively, also evaluated at the steady-state. Then the steady-state is locally unstable if and only if

(3) $$s_n/2s_k > e_s + e_d.$$

If condition (3) holds, then for almost all initial capital stocks k_1, the equilibrium capital stock fluctuates forever within a bounded interval $[0, k^+]$, without ever converging.

The case described in Proposition 1 is depicted in Figure 1. The arrows indicate the sequence of capital stocks $(k_1, k_2, k_3, k_4, k_5, k_6)$ for an initial stock k_1 only slightly less than k^*. It is clear that k_t can quickly diverge quite far from k^*, and that the path of k_t in equilibrium may be quite erratic.

It is important to note the role of the financial constraint in allowing this kind of instability to occur. In a standard one-sector optimal growth model, k_{t+1} is necessarily a *monotonically increasing* function of k_t, and this (together with the fact that f must cross the 45° line only once and from above) insures global stability of the steady-state. This is because when the same "representative agent" receives both wages and the quasi rents to capital goods, his income equals total output, necessarily an increasing function of the capital stock. Then, assuming that future consumption is a "normal good," saving will be an increasing function of the capital stock as well. In our model, on the other hand, capital accumulation depends upon capitalists' saving, which depends upon capitalists' income. Even though a larger capital stock must mean a larger total output, capitalists' incomes may be smaller, if wages rise rapidly enough as the capital

Figure 1

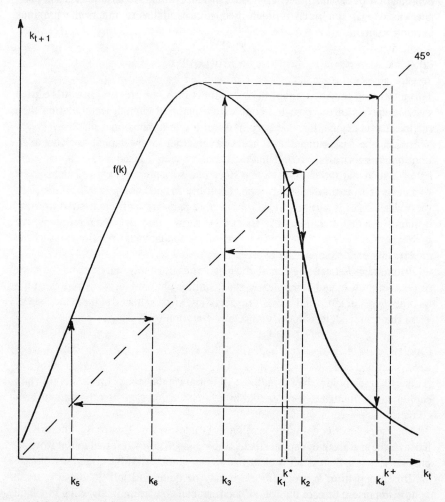

stock is increased. This explains why f may be decreasing over some values of k, and why sufficiently low elasticities of both supply of and demand for labor are necesssary for instability.

Proposition 1 does not describe the asymptotic behavior of the capital stock (and hence of production), except to say that it does not converge to a constant value; it may converge to regular periodic fluctuations, or it may be forever aperiodic. It is particularly interesting to note the possibility of *strongly chaotic* dynamics, by which we mean that:

(i) the map f has at most a countable number of periodic points and all of its periodic points are unstable; and

(ii) for almost all initial capital stocks k_1, there exists a probability measure μ

on $[0,k+]$ which is absolutely continuous with respect to Lebesgue measure (i.e., the measure μ can be described in terms of a density function g, so that $\mu(A) = \int_A g(k)dk$ for A any measurable set), and which describes the asymptotic frequency distribution for k_t (i.e., for A any measurable set with positive measure, the asymptotic frequency with which $k_t \in A$ is equal to $\mu[A]$).

In such a case, the set of initial conditions in $[0,k^+]$ that result in bounded but asymptotically aperiodic (i.e., chaotic) trajectories is of full measure. Hence the chaotic equilibrium dynamics should be "observable."[4] Furthermore, for almost all initial conditions, the equilibrium dynamics will "appear stochastic" in the sense that the long-run frequency distribution for k_t is given by an absolutely continuous measure.

Li and Yorke (1978) show that a sufficient condition for strongly chaotic dynamics is a map f that (i) maps a bounded, closed interval into itself, (ii) is piecewise C^2, and (iii) has $|f'| > \lambda > 1$ at all points where the derivative is defined. The following result gives sufficient conditions for this to occur in our model.

Proposition 2. Suppose that $s(0) > 0$ and $r'(0) > -\infty$ (i.e., $d(0) < \infty$). In addition, suppose that there exists a wage $w^+ > 0$, such that

$$\frac{e_s(w) + e_d(w)}{w} < \frac{-r'(w)}{r(w) + \beta^{-1}}$$

for all $0 < w \le w^+$, and such that the limit of the left-hand side as w approaches zero is defined and less than the limit of the right-hand side. Finally, suppose that

$$\frac{s(w^+)}{s(0)} \ge \frac{\beta r(0)r'(w^+)}{r'(0)} .$$

Then the equilibrium dynamics for the capital stock described by (2) are strongly chaotic.

This proposition is proved in section 3 of Woodford (1988). Briefly, these conditions insure that for all k less than a critical positive value, $w(k) = 0$, so that f becomes a straight line with slope $\beta r(0) > 1$. In this region, there is unemployment because of the existence of insufficient capital goods. For values of k above the critical value, the wage is positive, and it rises so fast with increases in k that f is decreasing with a slope steeper than -1, at least for k no larger than k^+.

The existence of strongly chaotic dynamics of this sort would not, of course, require that wages ever fall to zero if it were supposed that the supply of labor becomes perfectly elastic at some wage $w > 0$. Then the initial straight segment of f would have a slope $\beta r(w)$, but this would still have to be greater than one, if the capital stock is not to approach zero asymptotically. Hence under conditions similar to those described in Proposition 2, strongly chaotic dynamics are obtained.

Consequences of Limited External Finance

The above model is doubtless too extreme in assuming that all economic units must spend exactly their income. In fact, while internal finance remains the most important source of funds for firms even in an economy with such well-developed financial markets as the United States, there is some reliance upon external finance. Cyclical variations in the degree of external financing are one of the kinds of regularities to be explained. In the present section, we show that similar results can be obtained even when outsiders lend to firms, as long as there continue to be limitations upon the degree to which firms can seek external finance.

In the present section, the production technology remains as before, except that firm-specific productivity shocks that cancel out in the aggregate are introduced. To be precise, suppose that when an entrepreneur chooses to accumulate capital goods in the quantity k_{t+1}, the number of *effective* capital goods with which he is able to produce in period $t+1$ will be αk_{t+1}, where α is a random variable whose value is not known at the time of the accumulation decision. The profit function $r(w)$ now describes the (deterministic) production possibilities per unit of *effective* capital. If a continuum of identical entrepreneurs with independent drawings of α is assumed and (without loss of generality) one assumes that $E(\alpha) = 1$, then the aggregate production possibilities are deterministic and identical to those assumed in the first section. (Agents who are able to organize production will be referred to in this section as entrepreneurs to clarify the fact that they are not the only agents who earn non-wage income.)

A competitive market for riskless debt to which all agents have equal access is introduced. Because the firm-specific productivity shocks are private information, debt contracts contingent upon these shocks are not enforceable. Hence (since there are no aggregate shocks), the only kind of debt that will be issued is straight debt, the promise to pay a fixed amount at a future date. It is assumed that the penalties for default are such that debtors will repay whenever they have the funds required for repayment.

Let entrepreneurial equity e_t refer to the net worth of an entrepreneur in period t, after sale of the output produced in period t, payment of wages, and repayment of any debt issued to finance that production. The entrepreneur chooses a level of consumption q_t, and a level of capital stock to accumulate k_{t+1}; this will imply issuing debt in the quantity $k_{t+1} + q_t - e_t$. When α_{t+1} is realized, his effective capital holdings will be $\alpha_{t+1}k_{t+1}$, and he will earn quasi rents of $\alpha_{t+1}k_{t+1}r(w_{t+1})$. If the real interest rate on one-period debt issued in period t is i_{t+1}, entrepreneurial equity in period $t+1$ will then be

$$e_{t+1} = \alpha_{t+1}k_{t+1}r(w_t+1) - i_{t+1}(k_{t+1} + q_t - e_t).$$

It can be shown that optimizing behavior for an entrepreneur with equity e_t, facing an interest rate of i_{t+1}, having perfect foresight regarding the quasi rents to capital $r_{t+1} = r(w_{t+1})$, and knowing the distribution G from which α_{t+1} is drawn, is to choose

(4)
$$q_t = (1-\beta)e_t$$
$$k_{t+1} = \theta(r_{t+1}/i_{t+1})(e_t - q_t)$$

where $\theta(z)$ denotes the solution to

(5)
$$E[\frac{\alpha z - 1}{(\alpha z - 1)\theta + 1}] = 0$$

Equation (5) has a unique solution $\theta(z) \geq 0$ for all $1 \leq z < \underline{\alpha}^{-1}$, where $\underline{\alpha}$ is the lower bound of the support of G (possibly zero). This solution function is easily shown to be monotonically increasing in z; $\theta(1) = 0$, while $\theta(z) \to \infty$ as $z \to \underline{\alpha}^{-1}$. Finally, θ is greater or less than one according to whether z is greater or less than $E(\alpha^{-1})$.

The function $\theta(z)$ indicates how the degree of leverage that entrepreneurs are willing to undertake depends upon the ratio $z = r_{t+1}/i_{t+1}$, i.e., upon the amount by which the expected rate of profit exceeds the rate of interest at which they can borrow. The ratio θ is finite even when $r_{t+1} > i_{t+1}$, because of the risk of a low realization of α_{t+1}, against which the entrepreneur is unable to insure because the realization is private information. The argument is essentially Kalecki's (1939) "principle of increasing risk."[5] Dependence of the sort indicated in (4) of investment upon the amount by which r exceeds i is familiar both from Kalecki's models of aggregate dynamics and those of authors such as Foley (1986) and Franke and Semmler (1986). For these purposes, the most important thing to notice about (4) is that the level of available internal funds continues to be a major determinant of capital accumulation, even when there exists a competitive market for one-period debt, and even when θ (a measure of the degree to which external finance is used) is well above one. Because of this, the same sort of "profit squeeze" mechanism described previously makes possible endogenous cycles and chaos.

We will suppose that workers have the same preferences as before, but that they may hold the debt of entrepreneurs (when $\theta > 1$) or borrow from entrepreneurs to finance greater current consumption (when $\theta < 1$). Because we now allow $c_t \neq w_t n_t$, labor supply will not, in general, depend only upon the current real wage. However, in the special case that $u(c) = c$, $n_t = s(w_t)$ can be written, even though consumption demand will no longer equal $w_t s(w_t)$. In this case, workers' demand for riskless bonds is perfectly elastic at the interest rate $q_{t+1} = \gamma^{-1}$. The investment equation (4) then becomes

(6) $$k_{t+1} = \beta\theta\{\gamma r[w(k_{t+1})]\}e_t$$

Because the functions θ and w are monotonically increasing, and the function r is monotonically decreasing, equation (6) has a unique solution $k_{t+1} = h(e_t)$, that is monotonically increasing in e_t. This function indicates the way in which the availability of internal funds continues to determine the level of capital outlays, even when a competitive market for riskless debt exists.

It follows that the level of quasi rents per unit of effective capital in period $t+1$ is given by $r(e_t) = r\{w[h(e_t)]\}$, so that aggregate entrepreneurial equity per worker, after repayment of debt, equals

(7) $$e_{t+1} = r(e_t)h(e_t) - \beta\gamma^{-1}\{\theta[\gamma r(e_t)] - 1\}e_t \equiv f(e_t).$$

Because each entrepreneur's decision (4) is linear in his equity, one need only keep track of all the macroeconomic variables of interest. Hence, the analysis of asymptotic dynamics reduces again to the analysis of a one-dimensional map.

The map f defined in (7) can exhibit behavior like that depicted in Figure 1. The main difference is that here it can be shown that $f(e) > \gamma^{-1}\beta e$ for all $e > 0$. This is because, after consuming $(1-\beta)e_t$, an entrepreneur could obtain a *certain* level of equity $e_{t+1} = \gamma^{-1}\beta e_t$ by simply lending the remainder. If instead he chooses to invest in risky production, it must be because the distribution of possible values for e_{t+1} so obtained has a mean that is greater than this. Hence it follows that f cannot be bounded above, for all $e > 0$. Nonetheless, attention can be restricted to a bounded interval, as before.

Assume that $\beta > \gamma$, since it is obvious that otherwise e_t increases forever, until eventually entrepreneurs no longer have any need of external finance. Then it can be shown that

$$\lim_{e \to \infty} f(e)/e = \gamma^{-1}\beta.$$

It follows that there exists a bounded interval $E = [0, \hat{e}]$, such that f maps E into itself, and such that e_t eventually enters and remains forever within this interval. Hence, we can again restrict our attention to the asymptotic dynamics within a bounded interval.

If we assume again that the labor supply function s(w) is both very elastic at a sufficiently low real wage (possibly zero) and very inelastic at a sufficiently high wage, then the map f defined by (7) has the following general shape:
 • for low levels of e_t, f is increasing with a slope > 1 (wages rise little as labor demand expands, so quasi rents remain high)
 • for higher levels of e_t, f is decreasing, possibly with a slope even < -1 (rapidly rising wages in response to increased labor demand mean that aggregate

quasi rents fall as the capital stock rises)
  • for the highest levels of e_t, f is again increasing, with a slope approaching $\beta\gamma^{-1}$, which is < 1 (expected quasi rents are so low that higher e_t no longer means much of an increase in investment, the excess internal funds simply being lent out at the interest rate γ^{-1}).

The invariant interval E may or may not include values of e in all three of the above regions. It is evident that the steady-state must lie within the second region, and that its stability depends upon whether or not $f' < -1$ at the steady-state. The conditions under which this occurs are as follows:

Proposition 3. The steady-state equilibrium of an economy with limited exter-nal finance of the kind described above is *unstable* if and only if

$$(8) \qquad \frac{2s_k}{s_n}(e_s + e_d) + e_\theta(1 + \beta^{-1}\gamma) < 1 + \beta^{-1}\gamma(\theta - 1)$$

where e_θ is defined as

$$e_\theta \equiv \frac{z\theta'(z)}{\theta(z)}$$

and $z = r/i$, and where all quantities are measured at the steady-state. When (8) holds, e_t remains asymptotically within the bounded interval E, but never converges to any constant value.

Proposition 3 gives sufficient conditions for self-sustaining endogenous fluc-tuations to occur, although it does not indicate whether they are asymptotically periodic or chaotic. Either is possible. In particular, it is possible in this case, as in the previous section, to describe ranges of parameter values in which the dynamics are strongly chaotic. This is possible, in this case as before, even when the discount factors β and γ are chosen arbitrarily close to 1. Here, however, we consider only the existence of self-sustaining fluctuations more generally.

It is useful to note that (8) reduces to (3) in the case that $\theta(z) = 1$ for all z. The results here, then, are continuous with those of the previous section. It is also clear from this that self-sustaining fluctuations will be possible at least in the case of θ sufficiently insensitive to z. In addition, note that (8) certainly does not hold in the case that $\theta(z)$ is very elastic (i.e., e_θ is very large). This indicates that, if risk does not increase much with leverage so that a small change in z will induce a large change in desired leverage, instability is impossible. Thus, the case of perfect financial markets are approached in the appropriate limit as well. Finally, it is interesting to note that for a given value of e_θ, a higher value of θ at the steady-state makes instability more likely. The mere existence of external finance does not mean that instability of the sort displayed in the previous section cannot occur. Quite to the contrary—unless the desired degree of leverage is very sensitive to the ratio z, a higher degree of leverage is associated with *greater* instability. This latter conclusion is reminiscent of the conclusions of Franke and Semmler (1986).

Consequences of Monetary Exchange

In this section, an even wider range of dynamical phenomena is demonstrated to be consistent with perfect foresight equilibrium if an additional financial constraint representing the transactions role of money is introduced. In particular, it will be shown here that it is possible to obtain quasi-periodic motion on an invariant curve, and that it is possible for equilibrium to be radically indeterminate.

Assume that money must be used in certain transactions. The introduction of a cash-in-advance constraint, as advocated by Clower (1967), means that certain incomes cannot be spent until the period after that in which they are earned. The period is a time lag associated with the payments mechanism and is presumably rather short. In particular, assume that wages are paid in money and that workers must pay for the goods they consume. Therefore, the consumption expenditures of workers each period are constrained by the money they hold at the beginning of the period, representing the *previous* period's wages. Capitalists, on the other hand, are assumed not to hold money as they can spend their profits in the period in which they are earned; this might result either because producers allow each other trade credit, settling accounts only at the end of each period, or because banks extend within-period credit to agents with capital goods to pledge as collateral. The cash-in-advance constraint for workers allows us to develop a theory of the movement of money prices over the business cycle. The fact that capitalists are not cash constrained means that price level movements are caused by shifts in the desired level of investment as a fraction of total output, as in the neo-Keynesian model of Marglin (1984). In this model, however, the rate of investment desired by capitalists is not arbitrary, but represents optimizing behavior given perfect foresight.[6]

Workers are assumed to have the same preferences as in the first section and to face a sequence of period-by-period cash constraints

$$(9) \qquad p_t c_t \leq M_t.$$

Here M_t represents the money holdings of workers at the beginning of period t, which evolve according to the relation

$$M_{t+1} = M_t - p_t c_t + w_t n_t$$

where p_t is the money price of the good in period t and w_t is the money wage. For one or another of the reasons discussed above, workers do not save either by purchasing capital goods themselves or lending to capitalists.[7] And as all of the equilibria of interest here remain close to the stationary competitive equilibrium (in which the price level is constant, so that the real return upon money holdings is zero, whereas the rate of return required in order to induce workers to save is $\gamma^{-1} - 1 > 0$), they are unwilling to save by holding money either. Hence workers spend their entire beginning-of-period money balances each period, and constraint (9) always binds. It follows that $p_t c_t = M_t$ and $M_{t+1} = w_t n_t$. Hence in each period, workers choose a labor supply n_t to maximize

$$\gamma u(c_{t+1}) - v(n_t)$$

subject to the budget constraint

$$p_{t+1} c_{t+1} = w_t n_t.$$

The assumption of an infinite lived representative worker thus again turns out not to matter. The consumption and labor supply decisions of workers are in fact identical to those that would be made by overlapping generations of two-period-lived workers, each of whom works only in the first period of life and consumes only in the second, and who holds his savings in the form of money balances. Thus this model provides a reinterpretation of the results regarding the possibility of endogenous fluctuations in overlapping generations models obtained by Grandmont, among others.[8] These models are sometimes criticized because the mechanisms illustrated can only explain fluctuations that occur on time scales of approximately the lifespan of an economic agent, so that these are not "business cycle" models at all. The reinterpretation provided here answers this criticism. If one interprets these models as models with finance constrained agents, then it is plain that the time scale on which fluctuations occur has nothing to do with demography.

Capitalists are also assumed to have the same preferences as in the first section. Again it follows that they wish to save a constant fraction β of their net worth, so that

(10) $$q_t = (1-\beta)r(w_t/p_t)k_t$$

(11) $$k_{t+1} = \beta r(w_t/p_t)k_t.$$

With the assumption that the expected return on capital always exceeds that of money, capitalists never wish to accumulate money rather than capital. Since in the stationary equilibrium, the real return on capital is $\beta^{-1} > 1$ from (11), this will be true for all equilibria close enough to the stationary equilibrium.

Assume a fixed coefficients technology in which m units of period t labor are combined with each unit of capital (period $t-1$ produced good) to produce a units of period t produced good, which may be either consumed or accumulated for use in period $t+1$. Given this technology, labor demand is always

$$n_t = mk_t.$$

Also assume $a\beta > 1$. This is necessary in order for capitalists to be willing to maintain a positive quantity of capital in a stationary equilibrium.

It is now possible to derive the complete set of conditions for a perfect foresight equilibrium. Suppose, at the beginning of period one, capitalists own a capital stock $k_1 > 0$, and workers hold the entire stock of outside money $M > 0$. Given that capitalists never hold money, workers must end up holding the same stock of outside money M at the beginning of every period. This implies that in equilibrium

(13) $$p_t c_t = w_t n_t = M$$

in all periods. Because of (10)-(11), total purchases by capitalists in period t will equal $1/\beta \ k_{t+1}$ so that the condition for goods market clearing in period t is

(14) $$\frac{M}{p_t} + \frac{1}{\beta} k_{t+1} = ak_t.$$

Finally, substitution of (12)-(14) into the first-order conditions for optimal labor supply yields

(15) $$V(mk_t) = \gamma U(ak_{t+1} - \frac{1}{\beta} k_{t+2})$$

where $V(n) = nv'(n)$ and $U(c) = cu'(c)$. This is an equilibrium condition involving the evolution of the capital stock only. Any sequence of values for k_t, t $= 2,3,\ldots$, that satisfy (15) for given k_1 constitutes a perfect foresight equilibrium. For the given k_t sequence, it is possible to construct unique sequences for the price level, the wage, etc., that satisfy all of the above equilibrium conditions. (It is necessary also that certain inequalities hold at all times, which are suppressed here in the interest of brevity. Specifically, as noted above, the rate of return on capital must exceed that on money, and workers must not wish to save money. Again, these inequalities do in fact hold for all of the capital stock trajectories near the stationary equilibrium that are studied below.) Analysis of the stability of stationary equilibrium and of the existence of endogenous equilibrium cycles simply requires an analysis of the solutions to the difference equation (15).

Given the above assumptions on preferences and technology, one easily establishes that there exists a unique steady-state capital stock k^*. The perfect foresight equilibrium dynamics in the neighborhood of the steady-state may be characterized through an examination of the linearization of (15) about the steady-state, i.e.,

(16)
$$\begin{bmatrix} k_{t+2} - k^* \\ k_{t+1} - k^* \end{bmatrix} = \begin{bmatrix} a\beta & -\beta E \\ 1 & 0 \end{bmatrix} \begin{bmatrix} k_{t+1} - k^* \\ k_t - k^* \end{bmatrix}$$

where

$$E \equiv \frac{n^* v'(n^*) + n^{*2} v''(n^*)}{k^* [u'(c^*) + c^* u''(c^*)]}$$

and n^* and c^* are the steady-state values of n_t and c_t, respectively. Note one can write

$$E = (a - \frac{1}{\beta})(\frac{1}{e} + 1)$$

where e is the elasticity of labor supply with respect to w_t/p_{t+1}, evaluated at the equilibrium steady-state. Assumption (iii) on the preferences of workers then implies that $e > 0$.

Focusing on the case in which $a\beta > 1$ and $e > 0$, it is easily shown that the eigenvalues of the matrix in (16) are of the following sort:

(1) if $(a\beta/2)^2 > \beta E$ and $\beta E > 1$, there are two real eigenvalues between zero and one.

(2) if $(a\beta/2)^2 < \beta E < 1$, there are two complex eigenvalues of modulus less than one.

(3) if $(a\beta/2)^2 < \beta E$ and $\beta E > 1$, there are two complex eigenvalues of modulus greater than one.

(4) if $(a\beta/2)^2 > \beta E > 1$, there are two real eigenvalues both greater than one.

These various regions are displayed geometrically in Figure 2.

The following result is then a simple consequence of the stable manifold theorem:

Proposition 4. In the case that the elasticity of the labor supply curve e satisfies

(17)
$$e(\frac{2 - a\beta}{a\beta - 1}) > 1$$

then for each initial condition k_1 in a certain neighborhood of k^*, there is a one-dimensional continuum of perfect foresight equilibria all converging asymptotically to the stationary equilibrium. Thus, in this case, perfect foresight equilibrium is indeterminate. On the other hand, if the inequality in (17) is reversed, there exists no perfect foresight equilibrium with k_t always within a neighborhood of k^* that converges asymptotically to the stationary equilibrium, unless $k_1 = k^*$ exactly. In this case, the stationary equilibrium is unstable. Note that either case is consistent with the general assumptions made above; in fact, as shown in Figure 2, all four cases discussed in the previous paragraph occur in non-empty regions of parameter space.

It is also interesting that for *no* parameter values does the equilibrium steady-state have the "saddle path stability" property present in optimal growth models in the case of a sufficiently low rate of time discount.[9] Hence, no matter what parameter values are chosen, *some* type of macroeconomic instability is implied. In the case that (17) does not hold, perfect foresight equilibrium cannot converge to the equilibrium steady-state for generic initial conditions. The asymptotic behavior of such perfect foresight equilibria cannot be characterized in general, but in some cases, there will exist perfect foresight equilibria converging asymptotically to periodic or quasi-periodic motion on an invariant circle. The following is an immediate consequence of the Hopf bifurcation theorem for maps:

Proposition 5. Consider a one-parameter family of economies indexed by a parameter μ, and suppose that a, β, and e are all C^1 functions of μ, with $0 < a^{-1} < \beta < 1$ and $e > 0$ for all μ. Suppose further that there exists a μ^* such that

$$\beta(\mu^*)E(\mu^*) = 1$$

$$\beta'(\mu^*)E(\mu^*) + \beta(\mu^*)E'(\mu^*) \neq 0.$$

Then there exists a continuous function $\mu(\sigma)$ and a continuous family of closed curves $\Gamma(\sigma)$, for $\sigma \in (0, \bar{\sigma})$, such that as $\sigma \to 0$, $\mu(\sigma) \to \mu^*$ and $\Gamma(\sigma)$ shrinks to the equilibrium steady-state, and such that for each $\sigma \in (0, \bar{\sigma})$, $\Gamma(\sigma)$ is an invariant circle of the perfect foresight equilibrium dynamics for the economy indexed by $\mu(\sigma)$.

When a certain regularity condition is achieved,[10] Proposition 5 implies that there exist invariant circles for the perfect foresight equilibrium dynamics, either for all μ in a left neighborhood of μ^*, or for all μ in a right neighborhood of μ^*. When the invariant circles near the steady-state exist for $\beta E < 1$, only perfect foresight paths that begin on the invariant circle remain on it, whereas when the invariant circles exist for $\beta E > 1$, all perfect foresight equilibrium paths beginning close enough to the invariant circle converge to it asymptotically. Both cases are possible.[11] In either case, there exist perfect foresight equilibria that asymptotically approach the invariant circle for all k_1 in a neighborhood of k^*.

Clearly, the situation described in Proposition 5 is possible. The line labeled

Figure 2

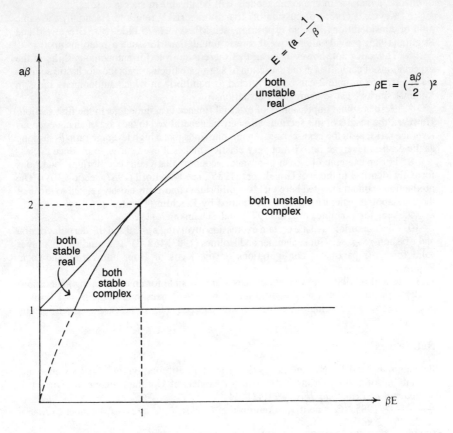

$\beta E = 1$ in Figure 2 indicates the points that satisfy the first condition, and almost all of the points must also satisfy the second condition. Note also that it is possible to satisfy these conditions with $\beta(\mu^*)$ arbitrarily close to 1. Thus in economies of the kind studied here, as above, equilibrium cycles are possible even when the agents who determine the rate of capital accumulation have an extremely low rate of time discount.

Notes

1. See Woodford (1987, section 1).
2. On the general connection between indeterminacy of perfect foresight equilibrium and the existence of stationary rational expectations equilibria in which stochastic fluctuations occur that are unrelated to any shifts in tastes or technical possibilities, see Farmer and Woodford (1984), Woodford (1984, section 4; 1986). For a general discussion of the role of imperfect financial intermediation in allowing equilibria of this kind, see Woodford (1987).

3. For details of the argument, see Woodford (1987, section 2.B).

4. Thus the criticism made by Grandmont (1985, 1026–7) of some earlier examples of chaotic dynamics in economic models will be invalid in such a case.

5. Keynes's (1936) discussion of "borrower's risk" refers to essentially the same kind of considerations. For an exposition, see Minsky (1975, 106–16). Greenwald and Stiglitz (1985) provide alternative theoretic foundations for such a relationship.

6. This does not, however, mean that there is no role for autonomous shifts in the expectations of capitalists in the causation of aggregate fluctuations; the stochastic equilibria referred to in note 2 can be interpreted as equilibria in which autonomous shifts in "animal spirits" cause aggregate fluctuations.

7. Here absolute impossibility of external finance is assumed, as in the first section. However, the results of this section can easily be generalized to the case of an endogenous leverage ratio, as in the next section. Again, one finds that a high leverage ratio θ—as long as the desired leverage ratio is not very elastic—makes it even easier to produce cycles.

8. For an example of a cash-in-advance economy that yields equilibrium conditions formally identical to those of Grandmont (1985), see Woodford (1987, section 2.A). The production economy treated here yields equilibrium conditions closely related to those of the overlapping generations economy studied by Reichlin (1986).

9. See, for example, Magill (1977) and Scheinkman (1976).

10. The condition is that a certain expression involving a,m, β and the derivitaves of u and v be non-zero. See Guckenheimer and Holmes (1983, 162–3). The condition plainly is valid for most parameter configurations on the locus of Hopf bifurcation shown in Figure 2.

11. Reichlin (1986) shows that both cases are possible for an overlapping generations model with production whose equilibrium conditions correspond to the $\beta = 1$ limit of equation (15). By continuity, both cases are also possible in the case of β sufficiently close to 1.

References

Benhabib, J., and K. Nishimura. 1979."The Hopf Bifurcation and the Existence and Stability of Closed Orbits in Multisector Models of Optimum Economic Growth." *Journal of Economic Theory* 21:421–44.
———. 1985."Competitive Equilibrium Cycles." *Journal of Economic Theory* 35:284–306.
Boldrin, M., and L. Montrucchio. 1986."On the Indeterminacy of Capital Accumulation Paths." *Journal of Economic Theory* 40:26–39.
Clower, R. W. 1967."A Reconsideration of the Microfoundations of Monetary Theory." *Western Economic Journal* 6:1–9.
Dechert, D. W. 1984."Does Optimal Growth Preclude Chaos? A Theorem On Monotonicity." *Z. Nationalokonom.* 44:57–61.
Deneckere, R., and S. Pelikan. 1986."Competitive Chaos." *Journal of Economic Theory* 40:13–25.
Farmer, R. E. A., and M. Woodford. 1984. *Self-fulfilling Prophecies and the Business Cycle.* CARESS working paper no. 84–12. University of Pennsylvania (April).
Foley, D. K. 1986. Endogenous Financial-Production Cycles in a Macroeconomic Model. Barnard College. Mimeo.
Franke, R., and W. Semmler. 1986. Debt Financing of Firms, Stability, and Cycles in a Dynamical Macroeconomic Growth Model, Disc. Paper No. 19, Fach. Wirtsch. University of Bremen, (Fall). Revised version appears in this volume.
Grandmont, J. M. 1985."On Endogenous Competitive Business Cycles." *Econometrica* 53:995–1045.

Greenwald, B., and J. E. Stiglitz. 1985. Information, Finance Constraints, and Business Fluctuations. Princeton University. Mimeo.

Guckenheimer, J. and P. Holmes. 1983. *Nonlinear Oscillations, Dynamical Systems, and Bifurcations of Vector Fields*. New York: Springer-Verlag.

Kalecki, M. 1939. *Essays in the Theory of Economic Fluctuations*. New York: Russell and Russell.

Keynes, J. M. 1936. *The General Theory of Employment, Interest and Money*. Reprint. New York: Macmillan, 1986.

Kydland, F., and E. C. Prescott. 1980. "A Competitive Theory of Fluctuations and the Feasibility and Desirability of Stabilization Policy," S. Fischer, ed., *Rational Expectations and Economic Policy.* Chicago: University of Chicago Press for NBER.

————. 1982. "Time to Build and Aggregate Fluctuations." *Econometrica* 50: 1345–70.

Li, T., and J. A. Yorke. 1978. "Ergodic Transformations from an Interval into Itself." *Transactions of the American Mathematical Society.* 235:183–92.

Magill, M. 1977. "Some New Results on the Local Stability of the Process of Capital Accumulation." *Journal of Economic Theory* 15:174–210.

Marglin, S. A. 1984. *Growth, Distribution, and Prices*. Cambridge, Mass.: Harvard University Press.

Minsky, H. P. 1975. *John Maynard Keynes*. New York: Columbia University Press.

Reichlin, P. 1986. "Equilibrium Cycles and Stabilization Policies in an Overlapping Generations Economy with Production." *Journal of Economic Theory* 40:89–102.

Scheinkman, J. A. 1976. "On Optimal Steady States of N-Sector growth models when Utility is Discounted."*Journal of Economic Theory* 12:11–30.

Woodford, M. 1984. Indeterminacy of Equilibrium in the Overlapping Generations Model. Columbia University. (May). Mimeo.

————. 1986. "Stationary Sunspot Equilibria in a Finance Constrained Economy." *Journal of Economic Theory* 40:128–37.

————. 1987. "Expectations, Finance, and Aggregate Instability," M. Kohn and S.C. Tsiang, eds. *Finance Constraints, Expectations and Macroeconomics*. Oxford University Press.

————. 1988. "Imperfect Financial Intermediation and Complex Dynamics," W. Barnett, J. Geweke, and K. Shell, eds., *Economic Complexity: Chaos, Sunspots, Bubbles, and Nonlinearities*. Cambridge University Press, forthcoming.

Debt-Financing of Firms, Stability, and Cycles in a Dynamical Macroeconomic Growth Model

Reiner Franke and Willi Semmler

The economic effects of debt-financing of firms have recently been studied in empirical as well as theoretical work. In empirical work on recent trends in corporate finance, it has been stated that debt-financing has become a dominant way of generating funds—slowly replacing self-financing and equity financing of firms. This, at least, holds as a secular trend, but it has also become an important way of raising funds in the business cycle (Brealey and Meyers 1984, 292; Wolfson 1986).

In theoretical studies, such as those put forward by Minsky (1975, 1982), it is demonstrated that high debt-asset ratios will appear as a dangerous liability structure of firms increasing the risk of bankruptcy and developing a fragile macroeconomic dynamics. At first glance, this might appear solely as a problem of financial constraints. A number of earlier articles have already dealt with the problem of liquidity and cash constraints (Clower 1967; Tsiang 1956; Kohn 1981a, 1981b). These constraints require that economic agents have the means of payment available from previous sellings before any intended demand can be made effective. As usually stated, however, firms can buy and sell without cash provided that other firms (or banks) are willing to extend credit. Thus, the problems that have subsequently been addressed are related more to credit

For helpful discussions and comments, we want to thank P. Flaschel, D. Foley, H. Minsky, E. Nell, and L. Taylor. An early version of this paper was also presented at a workshop on Dynamic Models at the University of Bielefeld, a conference of the Eastern Economic Association, and at the Econometric/Macro Workshop of the Université de Montréal. Comments of the participants are gratefully acknowledged.

constraints than to liquidity constraints.

Recent models, therefore, have focused on the impact of credit constraints on economic dynamics and macroeconomic fluctuations. Here we find two types of models. The first one is concerned with exogenous credit constraints. It is argued that equity financing is not a viable alternative to debt-financing and that exogenous credit constraints (rather than interest rates) are the effective determinants of economic fluctuations (Stiglitz and Weiss 1981; Greenwald, Stiglitz, and Weiss 1984; Guttentag and Herring 1984).

A formalization of this idea can be found in Woodford (1986a, 1986b). He designs a class of dynamic macro models in which credit constraints are built in as a fixed upper limit of borrowing. In particular, depending upon the value of this parameter, they can lead to nonlinear cycles.

By contrast, another strand of modeling seeks to fully endogenize debt-financing in an interdependent economic system. In Foley's seminal papers (1986, 1987), borrowing, lending, and capital outlays of firms are essentially governed by the endogenously determined profit rate and liquidity. With no asset holders outside the enterprise system and capitalist consumption being equal to zero, this (nonlinear) closed model generates cyclical fluctuations in these macroeconomic variables. On the other hand, there are capitalist firms which are externally financed exclusively through loans and equity issuance underlying the models of Taylor and O'Connell (1985) and Taylor (1985). The savings generated by rentier households, as suggested in Kalecki's macroeconomic writings, are channeled through the banking system to investing firms. Though these models develop a rich macroeconomic dynamics—including financial instability as studied by Minsky in his financial crisis theory—the role of firms' indebtedness and debt payment commitments is not fully worked out. A high degree of indebtedness and high debt payment commitments of firms, however, seem to be central in Minsky's theory of financial instability.

In this chapter, partly utilizing the asset-accounting framework put forward in the articles just mentioned, debt-financing of firms will be explicitly taken into account. In a fully interdependent model incorporating investing firms, savings of rentier households, commercial banks, and the government, the endogenously generated debt of firms (created through borrowing) is feeding back dynamically to the investment behavior of firms, their borrowing of funds, the asset market, the interest rate and the expected rate of return (representing the confidence of investors with regard to future development). The impact of debt-financing of firms on aggregate economic activity will be studied within this context.

First the model is introduced, which utilizes six key economic variables: the interest rate, the gross and the net rate of profit (net of interest costs), the rate of growth of the capital stock, the degree of the indebtedness of firms, and the difference between current and expected profit rates (the "state of confidence"). Two sets of markets are considered, product markets and asset markets. Both are supposed to be continuously in equilibrium, i.e., the economy evolves in a sequence of temporary equilibria. This hypothesis, however, by no means precludes it from behaving in a cyclical manner. Though various simplifications are introduced, the model will still exhibit considerable complexity.

The analysis itself is carried out in two steps. First, the temporary equilibria are investigated. Under reasonable conditions, which are made explicit, it is shown that these equilibria exist and are stable with respect to dynamical subprocesses, so to speak, which refer to the very short-run. In this way, four variables are obtained as implicit functions of the remaining two, which are the degree of indebtedness and the state of confidence.

Next, the motions of these two variables are studied in the plane and standard mathematical instruments (mainly, local stability analysis, phase diagrams, and the Poincaré-Bendixson Theorem) are utilized. On the basis of the thorough analysis of the first step, considerable information can be inferred subsequently as to the resulting movements of the other variables. Different assumptions regarding the various reaction functions make it possible to work out essentially three types of scenarios. Two of them lead to stability of the long-run equilibrium, where all of the variables mentioned cease to change and the economy is uniformly growing (in the first case stability is global, in the second at least local). The third and most interesting scenario gives rise to persistent, but nevertheless bounded, macroeconomic fluctuations of investment, economic growth, the debt-asset ratio, the expected profit rate, the interest rate and the difference of net profit rate and interest rate—all varying, partly with leads and lags, in a cyclical manner.

The proofs of the various lemmata and theorems utilized in the text are collected in an appendix.[1] Finally, it will go without saying that all functions involved are assumed to be continuously differentiable.

The Model

Here, the full model will be set up. That is, the temporary equilibrium framework is introduduced as well as the dynamical laws of change. The analysis is undertaken in the two ensuing sections.

Firms' Profits and Equities

Focusing on the flow and asset accounting of firms, the national account is followed. Let PX be the value-added aggregated over the economy, with X the flow of real output and P the corresponding price. Moreover, K denotes the physical capital stock of firms, L the stock of loans that firms have received from commercial banks, and i the current rate of interest (interest payments are assumed to be instantaneous). The gross and the net rate of profit, r^g and r, respectively, are given by

$$r^g = \frac{PX - \text{Wages}}{PK} \quad , \quad r = \frac{PX - \text{Wages} - iL}{PK}$$

Defining $\lambda := L/PK$, they are linked together by the formula

(1) $$r^g = r + i\lambda$$

We seek to capture expectations of profitability by introducing the variable ϱ. It reflects the difference between the anticipated returns to holding capital and the current profit rate. To be precise, $r + \varrho$ is the expected net rate of profits, and $r^g + \varrho$ is the expected gross profit rate (according to this interpretation, expectations with respect to changes in the interest rate or the liability structure are neglected). ϱ may be also identified with the overall "state of confidence" concerning the future development. As will be seen, it is to play an important role in the dynamic formulation of the model. The demand price P_K of capital, i.e., the capitalized value of expected earnings per unit of investment can be defined:

(2) $$P_K = \frac{r^g + \varrho}{i} P$$

Occasionally, there will be reference to

(3) $$P_K/P = \frac{r + \varrho}{i} + \lambda$$

In addition to loans, firms issue a stock of equity, E. Given K, P_K, and L, the formation of share prices P_e is determined by the equation

(4) $$P_e E = P_K K - L$$

This implies that the net worth of firms is identically zero. Moreover, as in Taylor and O'Connell (1985, 876), bubbles in the stock market are excluded since they do not seem central to Minsky's theory of financial instability.
With equation (3), we can readily derive

(5) $$P_e E/PK = \frac{r + \varrho}{i}$$

which is another equation that will prove useful further below.

Table 1

Balance Sheets in the Economy

	Assets		Liabilities
Central Banks			
High-powered money	F	D^c	Deposits of commercial banks (interest-free bank reserves)
Commercial Banks			
Bank reserves	D^c	D^o	Interest-free deposits from the public
Loans to firms	L	D^i	Interest bearing deposits from the public
Firms			
Capital stock (valued at the demand price)	$P_K K$	L	Loans from commercial banks
		$P_e E$	Equity
Public			
Deposits with commercial banks	D^o	W	Wealth
	D^i		
Equity	$P_e E$		

Asset Markets

The asset side of the economy and in particular the portfolio balance sheets are outlined in Table 1. In addition to firms, we have identified households of rentiers (the public), commercial banks, and a central bank. By hypothesis, workers do not save. Interpreting equation (4) also as a balance sheet of firms (so that their net worth is zero), the table shows the choice of economic state variables and their definitory relationships.[2] Cancelling assets against offsetting liabilities over the economy as a whole immediately leads to

(6) $$W = F + P_K K$$

Desired asset holdings of rentiers are represented by functions $d^o = d^o(r + \varrho, i)$, $e = e(r + \varrho, i)$ comparing the different (expected) rates of return. At each point of time rentiers wish to have their total wealth W split up into

$$D^o = d^o W, \quad D^i = (1 - d^o - e)W, \quad P_e E = eW.$$

It will be assumed that these plans can always be realized. Of course,

$$e_r = \partial e/\partial(r + \varrho) > 0, \; e_i = \partial e/\partial i < 0.$$

As policy variables of the monetary authorities we consider $\phi = F/PK$, the reciprocal of the velocity of base money with respect to the capital stock, and the credit multiplier $\mu > 1$ which relates bank reserves to private deposits held with the commercial banks, i.e.,

$$D^o + D^i = \mu D^c.$$

Now, taking equation (5) and substituting eW for $P_e E$ gives W/PK = $(r + \varrho)/ei$. Taking account of the equality $\mu F = \mu D^c = D^o + D^i = (1 - e)W$, we infer

(7)
$$\mu\phi = \frac{1 - e}{e} \frac{r + \varrho}{i}$$

(if e > O) or, equivalently,

(8)
$$e = \frac{r + \varrho}{r + \varrho + i\mu\phi}$$

On the other hand, we have $(F + P_K K)/PK = \phi + (r + \varrho)/i + \lambda$ from equation (3), which combined with (6) gives $\mu\phi = (1 - e)[\phi + (r + \varrho)/i + \lambda]$. Equating this to (7) and solving for e leads to

(9)
$$e = \frac{r + \varrho}{r + \varrho + i(\lambda + \phi)}$$

Comparing (8) with (9) we conclude: provided that all asset markets are in (stock) equilibrium (and $r + \varrho$ and i are distinct from zero), the firms' ratio of indebtedness λ and the policy variables μ and ϕ are connected by the equality

(10) $(\mu - 1) \phi - \lambda = 0$

It is assumed that the government does not attempt to influence λ and it allows its (positive) debt $F = D^c$ to grow at the same rate as the capital stock, so that ϕ remains constant. (Incidentally, the same is assumed in Taylor and O'Connell

[1985, 880], whereas in Taylor [1985, 393] ϕ is endogenously determined.) With respect to the supply of deposits, it imposes no restrictions on commercial banks. Consequently, because of the clearing of asset markets, μ will always adjust to fulfill (10) identically.

With these additional suppositions regarding government policy, it follows that asset markets are completely characterized by equation (9). It is analogous to the usual LM schedule. Note, however, that the function representing households' liquidity preference, d^o, has been eliminated. There shall be no further reference to it in the rest of the chapter, its role will be implicit only.

Investment and Goods Market

Planned investment of firms, I, is represented by a real function $h = h(r + \varrho - i)$ which measures the firms' responses to the expected difference between net profit and interest costs (see also Taylor and O'Connell 1985, 873). The basic argument for this device is desire to take account of risk. On the one hand, Kalecki (1937, 84–85) writes, ". . . the rate of investment decision is an increasing function of the gap between the prospective rate of profit and the rate of interest" and the difference between the "prospective rate of profit, and the rate of interest, is equal to the risk incurred."

On the other hand, it is not clear from this passage whether the gross or the net rate of profit is meant. For this purpose, the latter is chosen. Recalling that the net profit rate is $r^g - i\lambda$, it can be argued in accordance with Minsky's writings (e.g., 1975, 87) that high indebtedness and high debt payment commitments ($i\lambda$) make new investments riskier; firms may even have to turn to selling assets if the risk of default rises due to dwindling net cash flows. It is in this limited sense that the structure of financing enters into the investment decisions. For simplicity, a significance of λ beyond this point will be neglected. Nevertheless, λ will play an important part when the financing decision of firms is considered, which will be captured by another function.

Employing the function h, investment demand in nominal terms is

(11) $PI = h\,PK$

Certainly, $h' = dh/d(r + \varrho - i) > 0$.

If PG is the excess of government expenditure over taxes, and the budget deficit is solely financed by the creation of base money (cf. Tobin 1982, 178), then $PG = \dot{F}$ obtains, which, because of the hypothesis P = constant, ϕ = constant, implies

$$PG/F = \dot{F}/F = \frac{d(PK)/dt}{PK} = \dot{K}/K = I/K$$

Hence,

(12) $P\,G = \phi\,P\,I$

Besides the assumption of nonsaving workers, suppose that rentiers only save and consume from their current income, i.e., from the flow of gross profits, $r^g PK$ (they are equal to immediately distributed net profits of firms plus interest payments, which are mediated by the commercial banks). For simplicity, let the corresponding savings propensity s be fixed throughout all adjustments (o $< s \le$ 1).[3]

Finally, we postulate that all demands are satisfied. Then, from PC = total consumption = wages + (1 $-$ s)$r^g PK$, the identity PC + PI + PG = PX = Wages + $r^g PK$, and from equation (12) we deduce (1 + ϕ)PI $-$ s$r^g PK$ = 0. Thus, referring to (11) and dividing through by PK,

(13) $(1 + \phi)\,h\,(r + \varrho - i) - sr^g = 0$

In effect, (13) allows for an IS-curve for the clearing of the commodity market in the system.

Dynamics

Whereas in the previous subsection, the investment plans of firms are considered, it now has to be clarified how this is financed. That is, firms have to decide whether to issue new shares and/or raise additional loans (or pare them down). In what follows, we particularly want to concentrate on the effects of debt-financing on economic dynamics. We make debt-financing of firms dependent on their present liability structure, λ, on the one hand, and the difference between the expected gross profit rate and the rate of interest on the other.

There will be no particular problem with the dependency on λ. Since a high ratio of indebtedness increases the risk of bankruptcy, a firm finding itself in such a situation will cut down its demand for additional loans, or otherwise the banks will impose some credit constraints on it. Specifically, lenders might even reject any further application for credit (cf. Greenwald, Stiglitz, and Weiss 1984; Woodford 1986a). The way in which financing is influenced by a firm's rate of return may require more discussion. The following simple argument is offered. Facing a risky investment project, a firm compares the expected returns accruing to it with the riskless alternative of receiving interests from deposits with a bank. Since the former are profits net of interest costs, it will compare the expected *net* profit rate r + ϱ with the interest rate i. When raising credits to finance part of this new investment, of prime interest to the bank is not so much its profitability, but a sufficient margin of safety that the firm will survive. In other words, the bank is concerned that the proceeds of the firm will be sufficient to repay the principal and to cover the interests incurred. So, when granting a loan, the bank will take into account the excess of the expected *gross* profit rate, $r^g + \varrho$, over the interest rate.[4] To sum up, consider the borrowing of firms as essentially determined, directly or indirectly, by credit constraints of banks. Nevertheless, as will be seen, they might be very flexible. Formally, they are represented by a function b—where b stands for (net) borrowing—which is to govern the growth rate of debt-financing,

$$\dot{L}/L = b(r^g + \varrho - i, \lambda)$$

According to the above considerations, the signs of partial derivatives will be $b_r = \partial b/\partial(r^g + \varrho - i) \geq 0$, $b_\lambda = \partial b/\partial \lambda \leq 0$. The two arguments of the function b may well differ in their importance. There are several possibilities how they are related to each other, i.e., to what extent b will increase or decrease if one of them is changing. This gives rise to different scenarios, which will be studied in the Long-Run Dynamics section.

Taking account of P = constant, the change of λ itself is given by $\dot{\lambda}/\lambda = \dot{L}/L - \dot{K}/K$.[5] So letting g denote the rate of growth of the capital stock (cf. equation [11]), we obtain

(14) $g = h(r + \varrho - i)$

(15) $\dot{\lambda} = \lambda[b(r^g + \varrho - i, \lambda) - g]$

It remains to be considered how expectations regarding future profits evolve over time. They have been represented by the parameter ϱ which indicates the state of confidence. It should depend on the general state of the economy, in particular on the actual profitability of real investment and the burden of interest payments. We suppose that ϱ increases if the difference between the net rate of profit and the interest rate is great, and ϱ decreases if it is only small. Furthermore, the intensity of these changes may depend on the degree of indebtedness of firms. Whereas the difference of net profit rate and interest rate (r-i) indicates the liquidity position of firms (increased liquidity giving rise to an increase in ϱ), the degree of indebtedness is considered as a measure of risk of default, and the rise of λ will cause ϱ to fall. This generalizes the formalization in Taylor and O'Connell (1985, 880). In formal terms,

(16) $\dot{\varrho} = v(r - i, \lambda)$

where $v_r = \partial v/\partial(r - i) > 0$, $v_\lambda = \partial v/\partial \lambda \leq 0$.

These are all the elements of the model. The constituent variables are r^g, r, i, g, λ, and ϱ. Their motion is determined by the equations (1), (9), (13)-(16) (recall that ϕ was assumed to be fixed). (1) and (14) can be readily substituted, so that there will be four equations (E1)-(E4) for the four variables r, i, λ, and ϱ.

(E1)
$$e(r + \varrho, i) - \frac{r + \varrho}{r + \varrho + i(\lambda + \phi)} = 0$$

(E2)
$$(1 + \phi) h(r + \varrho - i) - s(r + i\lambda) = 0$$

(E3)
$$\dot{\lambda} = \lambda [b(r + i\lambda + \varrho - i, \lambda) - h(r + \varrho - i)]$$

(E4)
$$\dot{\varrho} = v(r - i, \lambda)$$

The evolution of λ and ϱ is directly governed by the differential equations (E3) and (E4). The determination of r and i is only implicit: given λ and ϱ, they adjust instantaneously (and simultaneously) such as to clear the commodity market and the asset markets, i.e., such as to satisfy equations (E1) and (E2). Market equilibria being established, a subsequent—so to speak—change of λ and ϱ will also bring about a change in the two rates of profit and interest. This, in turn, influences the changes of λ and ϱ, etc. The study will reveal further that system (E1)-(E4) is indeed a complete and consistent description of the dynamics in the economic model.

When both (E1) and (E2) are satisfied, we shall speak of a temporary equilibrium (with respect to λ, ϱ given). Accordingly, (E1)-(E4) generate a sequence of temporary equilibria (in continuous time), and r and i will cease to change if $\dot{\lambda} = 0$ and $\dot{\varrho} = 0$. If this should happen, the economy finds itself in a position of long-run equilibrium or steady growth.

Analysis of Temporary Equilibria

The aim in this section is to obtain the rate of interest i and the net profit rate r as functions of λ and ϱ, denote them by $r = R(\lambda, \varrho)$ and $i = J(\lambda, \varrho)$, such that the two market clearing equations (E1) and (E2) are identically fulfilled. We proceed in two steps. First, besides λ and ϱ, r is also considered as given. We look for an interest rate that brings about equilibrium on the asset markets, i.e., that establishes equation (E1), and designate it $i = j(\lambda, \varrho, r)$. In the second step, with respect to a given pair (λ, ϱ), a net profit rate r is sought such that putting $i = j(\lambda, \varrho, r)$, equation (E2) is satisfied. If this r is designated $R(\lambda, \varrho)$ and $r = R(\lambda, \varrho)$, $i = J(\lambda, \varrho) : = j[\lambda, \varrho, R(\lambda, \varrho)]$ is inserted in (E1) and (E2), then, by construction, both equations will be simultaneously fulfilled.

In the course of this study, several assumptions on the behavioral functions $e = e(r + \varrho, i)$ and $h = h(r + \varrho - i)$ will be put forward. Some of them are almost inevitable to ensure existence of the two functions $R(\lambda, \varrho)$ and $J(\lambda, \varrho)$. Others will help simplify the analysis and the exposition. In particular, they will permit some definite, global results concerning the signs of the partial derivatives of R and J.

Step 1. Suppose that λ, ϱ, as well as r are given, $0 \le \lambda \le 1, r + \varrho > 0$. Define

$$\epsilon = \epsilon(\lambda, \varrho, r, i) : = \frac{r + \varrho}{r + \varrho + i\,(\lambda + \phi)}$$

By allowing the degree of indebtedness to fluctuate between zero and one, assume that there is a maximum risk of bankruptcy at $\lambda = 1$ beyond which firms would not extend (or lenders would not concede to) their indebtedness. Most likely there is, as Woodford (1986a) argues, a maximum $\lambda < 1$ up to which firms (or banks) would allow the debt ratio to rise. The results would not be affected by this in any essential way.

Given the (independent) variables λ, ϱ, and r, (E1) is satisfied for those values of i at which the two functions $i \rightarrow e(r + \varrho, i)$ and $i \rightarrow \epsilon(\lambda, \varrho, r, i)$ intersect. Existence of such a point, along with the property that the interest rate falls short of the expected net rate of profit, is ensured by the first assumption. It is illustrated in Figure 1.

Assumption 1. For all values of r, ϱ with $r + \varrho > O$ the following holds:
(i) $0 < e(r + \varrho, 0) \le 1$ and there is a point i such that $e(r + \varrho, i) > \epsilon(0, \varrho, r, i)$
(ii) $i \ge r + \varrho$ implies that $e(r + \varrho, i) < \epsilon(1, \varrho, r, i)$

Assumption 1(i) expresses the idea that rentiers are sufficiently inclined to hold equities. According to (ii), however, this willingness appreciably declines if the expected rate of return from shares gets close to the interest rate (this can be explained by risk-aversion of the majority of households).

Thus we can present

Lemma 1. Let λ, ϱ, and r be given, $0 \le \lambda \le 1, r + \varrho > 0$, and suppose that Assumption 1 holds true. Then there exists a rate of interest $i > 0$ such that (E1) is satisfied and $i < r + \varrho$ for all these i.

As a matter of fact, if $e(r + \varrho, 0)$ is less than unity then there are at least two positive interest rates—i_1 and i_2—bringing about (E1) (in Figure 1 they are marked with respect to $\lambda = 1$). So the question arises which one to choose. Moreover, at future stages in the analysis it will become important whether at these points $e_i > \partial\epsilon/\partial i$ (which is the case with i_1), or whether $e_i < \partial\epsilon/\partial i$ (as with i_2). This question is decided by means of the following consideration.

Let L, PK, μ, r, and ϱ be given and fixed, and take i as an independent variable. Referring to the behavioral functions d^o and e, the supply of deposits $D^o + D^i$ by rentiers can be expressed as a function of i, $D = D(i) = D^o(i) + D^i(i)$ (in the

Figure 1

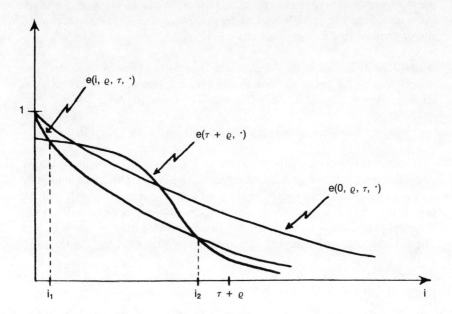

proof of Lemma 2 it will be shown that $D(i) = (r + \varrho)[1 - e(r + \varrho, i)]PK/[e(r + \varrho, i)i]$. By the same token, $D^c = D^c(i) = D(i)/\mu$. Now, suppose that at some i_o, $D(i_o) < D^c(i_o) + L = D(i_o)/\mu + L$ results. In this situation, we make use of the idea that competition among commercial banks forces some of them to raise the interest rate they offer to households in order to attract more deposits. Others will follow, so that there will be a general rise in the rate of interest until $D(i) = D(i)/\mu + L$ is reached (for a similar argument, cf. Kohn 1981b, 864). Note that stock market transactions of shares will have simultaneously taken place. Thus, a very short-run process in which the interest rate is the only adjusting variable has been sketched. It finally drives excess demands on the asset markets to zero. Of course, the process can only work if $D(i)$ is an increasing function. It is just this stability condition (in a local sense) that furnishes the next assumption. Beforehand, by relating $D(i)$ and its derivative $D'(i)$ to the points of intersection i_1 and i_2 in Figure 1, Lemma 2 ensures that it is indeed meaningful.

Lemma 2. Let L, PK, μ, r, and ϱ be given ($0 \le L/PK = \lambda \le 1$, $r + \varrho > 0$, $\mu = (\lambda + \phi)/\phi$, i.e., μ satisfies equation [10]). Then $i^* > 0$ is a rate of interest establishing (E1) if and only if $D(i^*) = D(i^*)/\mu + L$, where $D(i)$ is the function defined in the text above. Moreover, $D'(i^*) > O$ is equivalent to

$$e_i = \partial e(r + \varrho, i^*)/\partial i < \partial \epsilon(\lambda, \varrho, r, i^*)/\partial i.$$

On the basis of this lemma, the rate of interest which is most to the right out of the two (or even more) points of intersection of the curves $e(r + \varrho,.)$ and $\epsilon(\lambda, \varrho, r,.)$ is chosen. Figure 1 shows that necessarily $\epsilon_i \leq \partial\epsilon/\partial i$. In Assumption 2, simply suppose that this inequality is strict.

Assumption 2. For all values λ, ϱ, r with $0 \leq \lambda \leq 1$, $r + \varrho > 0$, and with respect to $i = j(\lambda, \varrho, r)$, defined as the greatest number i that brings about $e(r + \varrho, i) = \epsilon(\lambda, \varrho, r, i)$, the following strict inequality holds,

$$e_i = \partial e[r + \varrho, j(\lambda, \varrho, r)]/\partial i < \partial\epsilon[\lambda, \varrho, r, j(\lambda, \varrho, r)]/\partial i$$

It is evident that the just defined function $j(\lambda, \varrho, r)$ is continuous (even continuously differentiable).[6] If the additional Assumption 3 is employed, definite statements on the sign of its partial derivatives can be made. This will simplify calculations considerably in the further analysis. In essence, Assumption 3 says that locally around $i = j(\lambda, \varrho, r)$, the function e is of the form $e = e(r + \varrho - i)$. The ensuing Lemma 3 completes the first step of this section.

Assumption 3. For all $0 \leq \lambda \leq 1$, $r + \varrho > 0$, and with respect to the function $j(\lambda, \varrho, r)$ defined in Assumption 2, the following equality holds,

$$e_i = \partial e[r + \varrho, j(\lambda, \varrho, r)]/\partial i = -\partial e[r + \varrho, j(\lambda, \varrho, r)]/\partial(r + \varrho) = -e_r$$

Lemma 3. Let Assumptions 1–3 be satisfied. Then the function $j(\lambda, \varrho, r)$ defined in Assumption 2 is continuously differentiable and
  $\partial j/\partial r = \partial j/\partial \varrho = A_i/A_r > 0$,
  $\partial j/\partial \lambda = i(r + \varrho)/A_r > 0$,
where A_r: $= A_o e_r - (r + \varrho)(\lambda + \phi) > 0$,
     A_i: $= A_o e_r - i(\lambda + \phi) > 0$,
and A_o: $= [r + \varrho + i(\lambda + \phi)]^2$.

Step 2. With respect to a given pair (λ, ϱ), $0 \leq \lambda \leq 1$, we are now prepared to look for a point r_o making the function $r \to F(\lambda, \varrho, r)$ vanish, where

(17) $F(\lambda, \varrho, r): = (1 + \phi) h[r + \varrho - j(\lambda, \varrho, r)] - s [r + j(\lambda, \varrho, r)\lambda]$

Assume that even in the presence of very high differences between the expected net rate of profit $r + \varrho$ and the corresponding interest rate $i = j(\lambda, \varrho, r)$ that clears the asset market, the planned rate of growth of the capital stock is bounded from above (since, e.g., the volume of employment cannot increase at an infinite speed). It follows that $F(\lambda, \varrho, r)$ will be negative for all r sufficiently large. Hence, the IS-equation (E2) can be satisfied if a profit rate r exists that causes $F(\lambda, \varrho, r) > 0$. This positivity means that, at least for some medium values of r (or r + ϱ, respectively), firms' willingness to invest is sufficiently strong—in relation to s[r + j(λ, ϱ, r)λ] (observe that by virtue of Lemma 3 this term is falling if r is decreasing). Along with the previous assumptions, remarkably no more than these two ideas are needed to also infer uniqueness of the root r_o, as well as the sign of the derivative $\partial F/\partial r$ at this point.

Assumption 4. For all values of λ and ϱ ($0 \le \lambda \le 1$) the following holds:

(i) There is a real number $\bar{h}$ such that h(r + ϱ − i) $\le \bar{h}$ for all i > 0, r + ϱ > 0.

(ii) There exists a value r such that r + ϱ > 0 and $(1 + \phi)$ h[r + ϱ − j(λ, ϱ, r)] > s[r+j(λ, ϱ, r)λ].

Lemma 4. Let Assumptions 1–4 be satisfied. Then for every pair (λ, ϱ), $0 \le \lambda \le 1$, there exists a net rate of profit r_0 > − ϱ bringing about F(λ, ϱ, r_0) = 0. It is uniquely determined and $\partial F(\lambda, \varrho, r_0)/\partial r < 0$.

$\partial F/\partial r < 0$ could be interpreted as a condition ensuring stability in a dynamic process in which λ and ϱ remain fixed, and the profit rate r responds to excess demands, while the interest rate is continuously clearing the asset markets. A similar idea can be found in Taylor (1983, 19–20; cf. also Taylor and O'Connell 1985, 874). There, however, the rate of interest also is given and does not change during the (very short-run) process. Moreover, the negative slope of the function that corresponds to this F(λ, ϱ,.) (with i fixed) is introduced as an assumption. By contrast, in our treatment $\partial F/\partial r < 0$ is not assumed but results from a stability assumption that refers to dynamic adjustments in a different set of markets. These are the asset markets with the rate of interest as the (only) adjusting variable. Since the latter are commonly regarded as having the fastest dynamics, it may be argued that our choice of a stability assumption (i.e., Assumption 2 along with Lemma 2) is preferable.

As stated earlier, we now only need to set R(λ, ϱ) = r_0, with respect to the r_0 of Lemma 4, and then define J(λ, ϱ) = j[λ, ϱ,R(λ, ϱ)]. It is obvious that by putting r = R(λ, ϱ), i = J(λ, ϱ), both (E1) and (E2) will be satisfied for all λ and ϱ. On the basis of Lemmata 1–4 and their proofs, the partial derivatives of J and R as well as of R + ϱ − J can be determined. Since g = h(r + ϱ − i) and h' > 0, the latter provides information about *ceteris paribus* changes of the growth rate of the capital stock. The results are given in the following theorem.

Theorem 1. Suppose that Assumptions 1–4 apply. Then there exist two continuously differentiable functions R: [0,1] x R → R, J:[0,1] x R → R_{++} (R_{++} is the set of strictly positive real numbers) such that (E1) and (E2) are satisfied if we put r = R(λ, ϱ), i = J(λ, ϱ). R(λ, ϱ) + ϱ is always positive. Over the whole domain, the signs of the partial derivatives are as follows:

$\partial R/\partial \lambda < 0$, $\partial R/\partial \varrho < 0$, $\partial J/\partial \varrho > 0$, and $\partial J/\partial \lambda$ has the same sign as the expression, $-(1 + \phi)(r + \varrho)h' - s[A_i - (r + \varrho)]$ (A_i as defined in Lemma 3).

If $g(\lambda, \varrho)$ denotes the rate of growth of the capital stock in a temporary equilibrium (E1), (E2) induced by λ and ϱ, then

sgn $\partial g/\partial \lambda$ = sgn $(\partial R/\partial \lambda - \partial J/\partial \lambda) < 0$

sgn $\partial g/\partial \varrho$ = sgn $(\partial R/\partial \varrho + 1 - \partial J/\partial \varrho) < 0$

Remark 1. An apparent puzzle is the possible derivative $\partial J/\partial \lambda < 0$. The first reaction to a rising λ occurs directly on financial markets: in order to satisfy the increased demand for loans, the rentier households have to increase $D^o + D^i$, i.e., (1-e) must rise or e must fall, subsequently giving rise to a higher i (cf. Lemma 3, $\partial j/\partial \lambda > 0$). This, however, leads to an imbalance in the IS relation. Saving, $S = s(r + i\lambda)PK$, will rise with λ and i increasing, and investment, $PI = h(r + \varrho - i)PK$, will fall.

Thus, $PI < S$ is to be corrected. This could occur by a fall in r causing a simultaneous fall in PI and S. If the reaction of h to r is not too strong (i.e., h' is small) the balance of PI and S will be achieved. If, however, h' is large, then the fall in interest rate i has to be sufficiently strong, possibly below its previous value, in order to adjust PI to S. Note that since financial markets have been ignored, this line of reasoning may be incomplete. A mathematical analysis is inevitable to predict how the rate of interest in a temporary equilibrium will change if, *ceteris paribus*, the ratio of indebtedness increases.

Remark 2. Though g only stands for the growth of the capital stock, under the additional assumption of a constant mark-up rate τ, its changes are closely related to changes in the level of economic activity, i.e., to capacity utilization X/K: X/K rises (falls) if and only if g rises (falls). This can be demonstrated in two steps. First, equation (13) points out that $g = h(r + \varrho - i)$ increases if and only if the gross rate of profit, r^g, does. Secondly, movements of r^g are in step with those of X/K. To see this, use the mark-up pricing rule, $PX = (1 + \tau)$Wages, in the determination of r^g with τ the mark-up over wages. It leads to

$$r^g = \frac{PX - \text{Wages}}{PK} = \frac{\tau}{1 + \tau} \frac{X}{K}$$

Thus, given τ, changes in the profit rate r^g (respectively in the growth rate g) reflect changes in the utilization of capacity.

Before turning to a dynamic analysis, a proposition is presented concerning the impact of a change in the monetary policy parameter ϕ on economic activity. Of course, it is of a purely comparative-static nature. The result may be constrasted with Tobin (1965).

Theorem 2. Suppose that the economy is in a temporary equilibrium (E1), (E2), that the monetary authorities increase ϕ, and that without any change in λ and ϱ, a new temporary equilibrium comes about. Then under Assumptions 1–4, the new rate of growth of the capital stock will have decreased, $\partial g(\lambda, \varrho, \phi)/\partial \phi < 0$, in obvious notation.

Without further assumptions on the relative size of h' and e_r, no further statements are possible with respect to the resulting change of the equilibrium values of r and i.

Long-Run Dynamics

With the aid of Theorem 1, it is now possible to write equations (E3), (E4) as a closed dynamical system of its own. In compact form,

$$\dot{\lambda} = U\,(\lambda, \varrho)$$

(*)

$$\dot{\varrho} = V\,(\lambda, \varrho)$$

where

$$U(\lambda, \varrho): = \lambda\{b[R(\lambda, \varrho) + \varrho - (1 - \lambda)\,J(\lambda, \varrho), \lambda] - h[R(\lambda, \varrho) + \varrho - J(\lambda, \varrho)]\}$$

$$V(\lambda, \varrho): = v[R(\lambda, \varrho) - J(\lambda, \varrho), \lambda]$$

First consider borrowing by firms, i.e., the function $b = \dot{L}/L$ and impose the following assumption on it. With expectations of positive net profits presupposed, the planned rate of growth of loans (or the one conceded by banks) exceeds the growth rate of the capital stock if the degree of indebtedness λ is low, and it falls short of it if λ is already very high. Recall that the degree of indebtedness λ is also an indicator of the risk of bankruptcy. If λ is high, investors may restrict themselves concerning new borrowing, or banks may constrain credit for firms with a high λ. Conversely, credit constraints are loosened if λ is low. This explains the subsequent Assumption 5(i). Its second item looks more technical and is mainly made for convenience. It serves to rule out any bifurcation of the curve U = O.

Assumption 5(iii), on the other hand, is a requirement on the function v which governs adjustments of expectations. It can be explained as follows. Theorem 1 infers that, with respect to each fixed $\lambda = \bar{\lambda}$, the expression $r - i = R(\bar{\lambda}, \varrho) - J(\bar{\lambda}, \varrho)$ is strictly decreasing in ϱ. The same is true for $V(\bar{\lambda}, \varrho)$. Now, if ϱ is sufficiently high, the difference $r - i$ will have become so low, perhaps negative, that this optimism can no longer be justified (note that $\partial R/\partial \varrho - \partial J/\partial \varrho < -1$). Hence $\dot{\varrho} = V(\bar{\lambda}, \varrho) < 0$. In the presence of a considerably negative ϱ, the situation is reversed: $r - i$ will have increased so much that previous pessimism is no longer maintained and ϱ begins to rise, $V(\bar{\lambda}, \varrho) > 0$. It then follows that there exists a $\varrho = \bar{\varrho}$ bringing about $V(\bar{\lambda}, \bar{\varrho}) = 0$. In Assumption 5(iii) this is postulated for the extreme values $\bar{\lambda} = 0$ and $\bar{\lambda} = 1$.

Assumption 5.
   (i) For all values r, ϱ, i with $r + \varrho > i$, there is a $\bar{\lambda} > 0$ such that
$$b(r + i\bar{\lambda} + \varrho - i, \bar{\lambda}) > g = h(r + \varrho - i), \text{ whereas}$$
$$b(r + i\bar{\lambda} + \varrho - i, \bar{\lambda}) < g = h(r + \varrho - i) \text{ if } \bar{\lambda} = 1.$$
   (ii) If $U(\lambda, \varrho) = 0$, then either $\partial U(\lambda, \varrho)/\partial\lambda \neq 0$ or $\partial U(\lambda, \varrho)/\partial\varrho \neq 0$ (or both).
   (iii) There are numbers ϱ_0 and ϱ_1, such that $V(0, \varrho_0) = 0$ and $V(1, \varrho_1) = 0$.

Lemma 5. Let Assumptions 1–5 be satisfied. Then to each $\varrho \epsilon R$, there exists at least one λ, $0 < \lambda < 1$, such that $U(\lambda, \varrho) = 0$. The set

$$M_\lambda := \{(\lambda, \varrho)\epsilon[0,1] \times R : U(\lambda, \varrho) = 0\}$$

consists of one or more (isolated) smooth curves in the (λ, ϱ) plane. (Precisely, at each point $(\bar{\lambda}, \bar{\varrho})\epsilon M_\lambda$, λ can be locally represented by a continuously differentiable function of ϱ, $\lambda = \lambda(\varrho)$, with $\lambda(\bar{\varrho}) = \bar{\lambda}$ and $U[\lambda(\varrho), \varrho] = 0$ identically, or, if this is not possible, it is ϱ that can be locally represented by a continuously differentiable function of λ).

To each $\lambda\epsilon[0,1]$, there exists one and only one ϱ with $V(\lambda, \varrho) = 0$. The set

$$M_\varrho := \{(\lambda, \varrho) \epsilon [0,1] \times R : V(\lambda, \varrho) = 0\}$$

is a single connected smooth curve which is downward sloping.

From Lemma 5, we conclude that the two sets M_λ and M_ϱ have at least one point (λ_o, ϱ_o) in common. This will be a stationary point of system (*): $\dot{\lambda} = 0$ and $\dot{\varrho} = 0$. With Assumption 6 below, further study will be based on the hypothesis that $\varrho_o = 0$. Before this, briefly consider how to proceed if $\varrho_o \neq 0$. Since the analysis will reveal that (λ_o, ϱ_o) cannot be a saddle point, two cases are distinguished. First, let (λ_o, ϱ_o) be repelling. If, in addition, this rest point is unique, then the global analysis can run along essentially the same lines as Scenario 3 below, though the dynamics, and in particular the limit cycles, may be less regular. On the other hand, suppose that (λ_o, ϱ_o) is an attractor and that the process is already very close to it. This implies that r and ϱ have practically ceased to change, and that the expected net rate of profit $r + \varrho$ persistently deviates from the realized one. Hence, sooner or later the expectations have to be revised, which in the formulation of the model means that the function $v(.,.)$ has shifted. In this case, virtually a new dynamic process is set up and new motions are initiated. If the stationary point (λ_o, ϱ_o) of this modified system is again an attractor, where ϱ_o is different from zero, this procedure might be repeated, etc. Of course, a shifting of the function $v(.,.)$, or even of another function, might also occur before the process gets near a rest point. In fact, this seems to be the correct way to view what is actually happening in a dynamic economy.

Nevertheless, to reveal and discuss unambiguously the tendencies inherent in the economy as modeled above, the assumption that the formation of expectations is (already) consistent is employed.

Assumption 6. If (λ, ϱ) is a point where the two sets M_λ and M_ϱ defined in Lemma 5 intersect, then $\varrho = 0$ at that point.

Lemma 6. There is one and only one point (λ^*, ϱ^*) of process (*) such that $U(\lambda^*, \varrho^*) = 0$ and $V(\lambda^*, \varrho^*) = 0$.

All the information for an analysis of the dynamics is available but one. It concerns the reaction coefficients of the involved behavioral functions and their relative size, i.e., the derivatives or partial derivatives of $e(.,.)$, $h(.)$, and $b(.,.)$. Remarkably, they shall be needed at one point only, the long-run equilibrium (λ^*, ϱ^*). In conjunction with the previous assumptions, it will be possible, nevertheless, to arrive at global results. With respect to $r^* = R(\lambda^*, \varrho^*), i^* = J(\lambda^*, \varrho^*)$, these derivatives are

$e_r = e_r(r^* + \varrho^*, i^*)$—reactions of households in their share holdings to changes of expected net profits;

$h' = h'(r^* + \varrho^* - i^*)$—investment reactions of firms to changes of the difference between expected net profits and interests, $r + \varrho - i$;

$b_r = b_r(r^* + i^*\lambda^* + \varrho^* - i^*, \lambda^*)$—reactions of firms in debt-financing to changes of the difference between expected gross profits and interests, $r^g + \varrho - i$;

$b_\lambda = b_\lambda(r^* + i^*\lambda + \varrho^* - i^*, \lambda^*)$—reactions of firms in debt-financing in response to changes in their present degree of debt-financing.

It can now be shown that different assumptions on the relationships between these adjustment parameters lead to different motions of process (*) and possibly even to a different stability behavior. Three scenarios of economic dynamics will be distinguished. In technical terms, they correspond to the cases (1) $U_\lambda < 0$, $U_\varrho < 0$, (2) $U_\lambda < 0$, $U_\varrho > 0$, (3) $U_\lambda > 0$, $U_\varrho > 0$ (where $U_\lambda = \partial U(\lambda^*, \varrho^*)/\partial\lambda$, $U_\varrho = \partial U(\lambda^*, \varrho^*)/\partial\varrho$). The fourth possibility, $U_\lambda > 0$, $U_\varrho < 0$, shall be left aside since, as can be verified shortly, it requires a special conjuncture of the parameters. To grasp the economic meaning of these inequalitites, the explicit calculations of U_λ and U_ϱ are given. Also the partial derivatives of $V(.,.)$ will turn out to be of some interest.

Lemma 7. With respect to $\lambda = \lambda^*$, $\varrho = \varrho^* = 0$, $r = R(\lambda^*, \varrho^*,)$, $i = J(\lambda^*, \varrho^*)$, and to e_r, h', b_r, b_λ just specified, define (as in Lemma 3),

$A_i(e_r)$: $= [r + \varrho + i(\lambda + \phi)]^2 e_r - i(\lambda + \phi) > 0$

$A_r(e_r)$: $= [r + \varrho + i(\lambda + \phi)]^2 e_r - (r + \varrho)(\lambda + \phi) > 0$ and furthermore,

$$A_1: = (r + \varrho - i)(\lambda + \phi) > 0$$
$$A_2: = [(r + \varrho - i)\phi - i\lambda](1 + \phi)$$
$$A_3: = s[(1 - \phi)(r + \varrho) + i(\lambda + \phi)] > 0$$
$$A_F: = (1 + \phi)A_1h' + s[A_r(e_r) + \lambda A_i(e_r)] > 0$$

Then the partial derivatives of U and V, evaluated at $(\lambda, \varrho) = (\lambda^*, \varrho^*,)$, are,

$$U_\lambda = \lambda b_\lambda + \frac{i\lambda}{A_F} \{s[A_i(e_r) - (r + \varrho)]b_r + [A_2b_r + A_3]h'\}$$

$$U_p = \frac{s\lambda}{A_F} \{[\lambda A_i(e_r) - A_1]b_r + A_1h'\}$$

$$V_\lambda = v_\lambda - \frac{iA_3}{A_F} v_r < 0$$

$$V_\varrho = \frac{-1}{A_F} [(1 + \phi)A_1h' + s(1 + \lambda)A_i(e_r)]v_r < 0$$

There are several possibilities for the adjustment parameters e_r, h', b_r, and b_λ to fall within one of the three scenarios. Only the most striking ones will be illustrated. To begin, e_r will be called "small" (or "large") if in both U_λ and U_ϱ the coefficients associated with b_r, $[A_i(e_r) - (r + \varrho)]$ as well as $[\lambda A_i(e_r) - A_1]$, are negative (or positive, respectively—recall that $A_i(e_r) > 0$). Then the following cases are considered, where again, all statements are confined to the steady-state position.

Scenario 1: $U_\lambda < 0$, $U_\varrho < 0$. Households are rather inflexible when deciding the proportion of shares to hold. Firms, on the other hand, are reserved in their investment reactions—compared to their adjustments of debt-financing in response to changes in gross profitability over interests. Their response to the debt structure, however, is not relevant. In short, e_r is small, h' is small in relation to b_r, and the size of b_λ does not matter. More precisely, the coefficients of b_r in U_λ and U_ϱ are both negative. h' is so small that, in U_ϱ, A_1h' falls short of (-1) $[\lambda A_i(e_r) - A_1]b_r$, and similarly in U_λ.

Scenario 2: $U_\lambda < 0$, $U_\varrho > 0$. The outstanding feature of this scenario is the high responsiveness of firms to their debt structure. They (or their banks) are so cautious that the present flow of borrowing is sharply reduced if the degree of indebtedness, λ, only slightly increases. That is to say, b_λ is strongly negative. How negative it is depends on the other parameters. For example, e_r may be small and investment reactions may be strong (h' large), such as to render U_ϱ positive. Or, alternatively, households may respond very quickly in their distribution of assets, i.e., e_r is large, so that $U_\varrho > 0$ in any case. The second term in U_λ will probably be positive here, but this is supposed to be outweighed by the size of b_λ.

Scenario 3: $U_\lambda > 0$, $U_\varrho > 0$. As indicated in the signs, $U_\lambda > 0$, $U_\varrho > 0$, the increase in debt as well as the rise of expected rates of return exert a positive feedback effect on the degree of indebtedness of firms. This will result under the following conditions. A change in the debt structure has only a minor influence on firms' borrowing (b_λ is small), whereas share holding of rentiers is quite responsive to relative changes in the rates of return, i.e., e_r is large. This makes U_ϱ positive. If, on the other hand, A_2 is positive, the same is true for the term in the curved brackets in the formula for U_λ. If A_2 is negative, it is hypothesized that either b_r is so small that $A_2 b_r + A_3$ is positive. Should the latter expression be negative, reactions in investment are so reserved that $s[A_i(e_r) - (r + \varrho)]b_r$ dominates $[A_2 b_r + A_3]h'$. Finally, b_λ is so close to zero that the positivity in the formula is preserved. This third scenario is economically the most interesting one, because it generates persistent cycles. It will be discussed further below.

In the following three theorems, the stability (or instability) results that can be derived for the three scenarios are given.

Theorem 3. Suppose that Assumptions 1–6 hold and that $U_\lambda(\lambda^*, \varrho^*) < 0$, $U_\varrho(\lambda^*, \varrho^*) < 0$. The long-run equilibrium position (λ^*, ϱ^*) is globally asymptotically stable. Considered locally, (λ^*, ϱ^*) is a stable node, i.e., all trajectories approach the equilibrium directly (not in spirals). The essential characteristics of the motions of process (*) are given in Figure 2.

Remark. From Lemma 5, it is known that the curve M_ϱ is strictly falling (everywhere). M_λ is strictly falling in the vicinity of (λ^*, ϱ^*). At a greater distance, however, a positive slope may result. In this case some trajectories will display a "bouncing" behavior, as is illustrated in Figure 3. Similar things may happen in the economies treated below. It is appropriate to point out the possibility of the existence of these short-term, or intermediate, cycles on this occasion.

For an unambiguous formulation of Theorem 4 and 5, the concept of a limit set is referenced. The basic idea is already expressed by the very name of it. The precise definition is given in the mathematical appendix.

Theorem 4. Suppose that Assumptions 1–6 hold and that $U_\lambda(\lambda^*, \varrho^*) < 0$, $U_\varrho(\lambda^*, \varrho^*) > 0$. Then (λ^*, ϱ^*) is a locally asymptotically stable equilibrium of process (*). Moreover, if a trajectory starts from a point with $\lambda > 0$, then its limit set is either the steady-state (λ^*, ϱ^*) itself or a closed orbit in the (λ, ϱ) plane. The

Figure 2

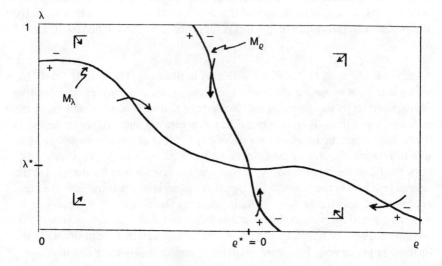

Figure 3

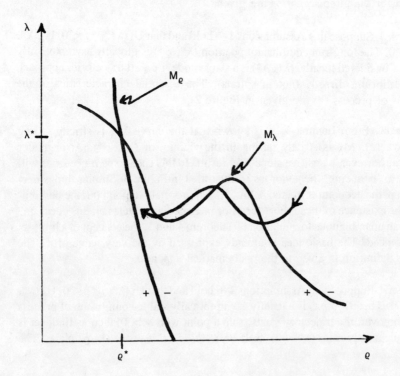

Figure 4

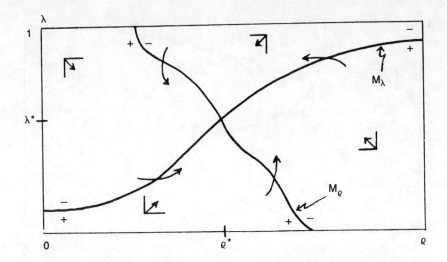

essential characteristics of the motions are given in Figure 4.

Figure 4 and the data given are not yet sufficient to indicate whether (λ^*, ϱ^*) is a stable center, i.e., whether it is (at least locally) approached in a cyclical manner. This will happen if

$$(18) \qquad (U_\lambda - V_\varrho)^2 < 4 \, U_\varrho \mid V_\lambda \mid$$

(see the proof of the theorem 4). If the inequality is reversed, then from four directions the trajectories tend directly towards (λ^*, ϱ^*) (see Coddington and Levinson 1955, 384). On the other hand, whether (λ^*, ϱ^*) also will be a global attractor depends on the position and the slopes of the curves M_λ and M_ϱ relative to each other.

Actually, the stability tendencies that are revealed by Theorems 3 and 4 should not be overestimated. By holding the price level constant, possible destabilizing deflationary (and inflationary) effects are disregarded (cf. note 5). On the other hand, the assumed formation of expectations—via the adjustment function v—is already consistent, i.e., $\varrho = 0$ if the process comes to a halt (see Assumption 6 and the Remark preceding it).

As indicated above, perhaps the most interesting case within the framework is obtained if scenario 3 prevails. The following result can be derived.

Theorem 5. Suppose that Assumptions 1–6 hold and that $U_\lambda(\lambda^*, \varrho^*) > 0$, $U_\varrho(\lambda^*, \varrho^*) > 0$. If expectations of future profit rates are very responsive to changes in $r - i$, that is, if the coefficient v_r is so large that $\mid V_\varrho \mid > U_\lambda$, then the steady-

Figure 5

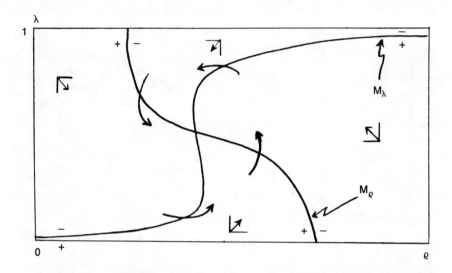

state (λ^*, ϱ^*) is locally asymptotically stable. If these adjustments are comparatively sluggish, such that $| V_\varrho | < U_\lambda$, it is locally repelling.

The limit set of each trajectory that starts at a point with $\lambda > 0$ is either (λ^*, ϱ^*) itself or a closed orbit. A phase diagram typically looks like that of Figure 5.

The theorem says, in particular, that in the unstable case each (nontrivial) trajectory will tend towards a closed orbit. Sufficient conditions for the generation of persistent cycles exist. The central ones, we repeat, are as follows. By way of Assumption 5(i) the firms' degree of indebtedness, λ, is globally bounded by zero and one, and the equilibrium point itself, (λ^*, ϱ^*), is a repeller (locally totally unstable). The latter property is implied by the inequalities $U_\lambda > 0$, $U_\varrho > 0$ and $| V_\varrho | > U_\lambda$. The conditions for U_λ, $U_\varrho > 0$ are listed in the statement concerning the third scenario. The most important ones are that near the rest point (λ^*, ϱ^*), the firms' borrowing responds only weakly to the level of firms' debt, whereas households respond strongly with their equity holdings to the net profit rate.[7]

In addition to the the motions of the constituent variables λ and ϱ of the reduced process (*), the resulting behavior of some other key variables are of interest. The way in which the respective peaks and troughs follow each other can be noted so that the different stages of a cycle can be singled out. This can be done by making reference to the functions and properties that previously have been established. In order to avoid unnecessary complication, the choice will be restricted to three additional variables: the rate of interest, $i = J(\lambda, \varrho,)$, the difference between the actual net rate of profit and the interest rate, $r - i =$

$R(\lambda\varrho) - J(\lambda\varrho)$, and the growth rate of the capital stock, $g = h(r + \varrho - i)$. Recall that, according to Remark 2 subsequent to the formulation of Theorem 1, the movements of g can be identified with the changes in the level of economic activity or capacity utilization, as well as with the realized gross rate of profit r^g. Figure 6 shows the succession and the relative position of the upper and lower turning points of all these variables (a proof can be found in the mathematical appendix. To be precise, it has been supposed that $\partial J/\partial\lambda < 0$ not only at (λ^*, ϱ^*), which readily follows from Theorem 1 and the scenario's characterization, but on the entire (λ, ϱ) plane. This assumption is by no means necessary. It has merely been employed to simplify the argument). However, it has to be stressed that this is the only information Figure 6 is able to provide. In particular, it is not meant to indicate that the time intervals $[t_k, t_{k+1}]$ have equal length. In fact, nothing is known about their relative lengths. And, the upswings and downswings need not be as regular as they have been sketched.

Recall, finally, that the dynamic development of λ is not only regulated by the growth of loans of firms, $b = \dot{L}/L$, but also by the growth rate of the capital stock (see equation [15]). In case the elasticity of b with respect to λ and r is small ($|b_\lambda|$ and b_r small), in essence, the development of λ is passively regulated by the growth of the capital stock; more precisely, it is regulated inversely by the growth rate g. This is fully confirmed by Figure 6.

The model presented here examines the impact of debt-financing of firms on aggregate macroeconomic activity. In particular, it explores the complexity of macroeconomic dynamics resulting from a high degree of debt-financing of firms and internal mechanisms by which the latter is reduced again. The analysis proceeds in two steps. First, slightly modifying a framework already employed several times in the literature, the product and asset markets are modeled and their short-run stability properties are investigated. In this context, the ratio of indebtedness of firms and the economy's "state of confidence" (the difference between present and expected profit rates) are considered to be exogenously given. The corresponding temporary equilibria of these markets are not assumed. They are demonstrated to exist and to be (locally) stable—under some reasonable conditions that are made explicit.

In a second step, the debt-asset ratio and the state of confidence are endogenized and, based on the hypothesis of continuous market clearing, it is formulated how they change over time. Merging the two steps, the interrelated motions of six economic key variables are obtained. In addition to the debt-asset ratio and the state of confidence, they are the current gross and net rates of profit, the interest rate, and the growth rate of the capital stock.

Though the resulting dynamics are quite complex, different assumptions on the diverse reaction functions make it possible to work out essentially three types of scenarios. Two of them exhibit local (if not global) stability with respect to a unique long-run equilibrium of steady growth. The other one, the most interesting case, generates persistent fluctuations in the aforementioned variables,

Figure 6

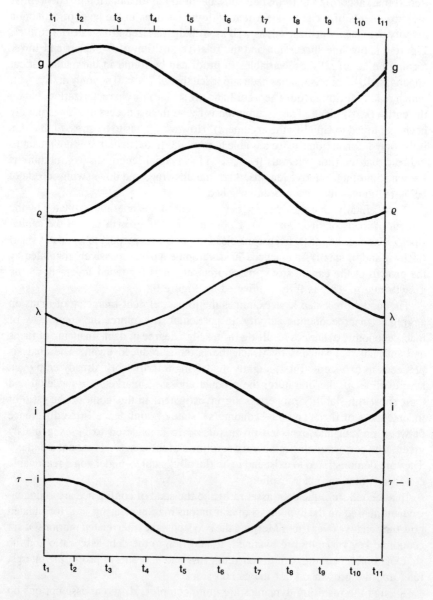

tending to a closed orbit (so that a growth cycle results). Conclusively, it should be stressed in particular that the method utilized here does not need to assume exogenously fixed upper limits of lending and borrowing. Rather, the model gives a fully endogenous treatment of all the variables involved.

Notes

1. Because of limited space the appendix with the mathematical derivations are not included in this version. The appendix is available from the authors at request.

2. There are several similarities to the economy-wide balance sheet in Taylor (1983, 93), whereas, however, in Taylor (1985, 392) the capital stock of firms is valued at P, instead of P_K.

3. Savings by private wealth holders increase the stocks of D^o, D^i, and P_eE. In what proportions is already grasped by the functions d^o and e introduced in the preceding subsection.

4. The analysis in the following sections is by no means dependent on this device. There would be only minor changes if the net profit rate entered as an argument into the borrowing function, i.e., if below $b = b(r + \varrho - i, \lambda)$, instead of $b = b(r^g + \varrho - i, \lambda)$

5. Setting P = constant leaves aside the (possibly additional) destabilizing effects of debt deflation in our dynamics, which should be considered subsequently (cf. Minsky 1975, 54, Tobin 1975).

6. To be mathematically precise, this is ensured by the Implicit Function Theorem. For further details see the proof of Lemma 3 in the appendix.

7. In more general terms, as formulated in Lemma 7, we can state that in the determination of $U_\lambda > 0$, the coefficients for the firms' investment response to $(r^* + \varrho^* - i^*)$ and the firms' borrowing response to r outweigh the response of firms' borrowing to the level of debt. On the other hand, for $U_\varrho > 0$, it is required that the linear combination of the coefficients for firms' borrowing response to r and investment response to $(r^* + \varrho^* - i^*)$ generate a positive feedback effect on ϱ These two positive feedback effects together with $|V_\varrho| > U_\lambda$ will turn the equilibrium into a repeller and generate globally persistent cycles. The conditions for those cycles to occur bear a close resemblance to the conditions of the equilibrium dynamics sketched by Kalecki in his business cycle theory (1937), but in a much simpler framework and only for a stationary economy.

References

Brealey, R., and S. Myers. 1984. *Principles of Corporate Finance*. New York: McGraw Hill.

Clower, R. W. 1967. "A Reconsideration of Microfoundations of Monetary Theory." *Western Economic Journal* 6:1–9.

Coddington, E. A., and N. Levinson. 1955. *Theory of Ordinary Differential Equations*. New York: McGraw Hill.

Foley, D. 1986. "Stabilization Policy in a Nonlinear Business Cycle Model." *Competition, Instability, and Nonlinear Cycles, Lecture Notes in Economics and Mathematical Systems*. W. Semmler, ed. New York and Heidelberg: Springer-Verlag.

Foley, D. 1987. Liquidity-Profit Rate Cycles in a Capitalist Economy. *Journal of Economic Behavior and Organization* 8(3):363–377.

Greenwwald, B., J. E. Stiglitz, and A. Weiss. 1984. "Informational Imperfections in the Capital Market and Macroeconomic Fluctuations." *American Economic Review* (May):194–200.

Guttentag, J., and R. Herring. 1984. "Credit Rationing and Financial Disorder." *Journal of Finance* (December):1359–82.

Kalecki, M. 1937. "A Theory of the Business Cycle." *The Review of Economic Studies* (February):77–97.

Kohn, M. 1981a. "In Defense of Finance Constraint." *Economic Inquiry* (June):177–195.

Kohn, M. 1981b. "A Loanable Funds Theory of Unemployment and Monetary Disequilibrium." *American Economic Review* (December):859–879.

Minsky, H. P. 1975. *John Maynard Keynes.* New York: Columbia University Press.

————. 1982. *Can "It" Happen Again? Essays on Instability and Finance.* New York: M. E. Sharpe, Inc.

Stiglitz, J .E., and A. Weiss. 1981. "Credit Rationing in Markets with Imperfect Information." *American Economic Review* (June):393–410.

Taylor, L. 1983. *Structuralist Macroeconomics.* New York: Basic Books.

————. 1985. "A Stagnationist Model of Economic Growth." *Cambridge Journal of Economics* 9:383–403.

Taylor, L., and S. A. O'Connell. 1985. "A Minsky Crisis." *Quarterly Journal of Economics* 100:871–86.

Tobin, J. 1965. "Money and Economic Growth." *Econometrica* 33(October):671–84.

Tobin, J. 1975. "A Keynesian Model of Recession and Depression." *American Economic Review* 65:195–202.

Tobin, J. 1982. "Money and Finance in the Macroeconomic Process." *Journal of Money, Credit and Banking* XIV(2):171–203.

Tsiang, S .C. 1956. "Liquidity Preference and Loanable Funds Theories, Multiplier and Velocity Analysis: A Synthesis." *American Economic Review* (September):540–64.

Woodford, M. 1986a. Finance, Instability and Cycles. Paper prepared for conference Economic Dynamics and Financial Instability, New School for Social Research, March. Revised version included in this volume.

————. 1986b. Self-Fulfilling Expectations, Finance Constraints and Aggregate Fluctuations. Columbia University, New York. Mimeo.

Wolfson, M. 1986. *Financial Crisis in the U.S. Economy.* New York: M. E. Sharpe, Inc.

Accumulation, Finance, and Effective Demand in Marx, Keynes, and Kalecki

Anwar Shaikh

This chapter develops a new approach to the theory of effective demand. The familiar relationships between aggregate demand, supply, and capacity are linked to a corresponding relationship between finance and debt. These cross-links provide a natural foundation for a macroeconomic model of internally-generated cyclical growth. The scenario which results from the model will be very similar to the classical and Marxian descriptions of normal accumulation, with supply and demand fluctuating erratically around a cyclical growth path with an endogeneous trend. Moreover, whereas current theories of effective demand generally need to resort to exogenous factors such as technical change, population growth, or bursts of innovation in order to explain economic growth (Mullineaux 1984, 87–89), this classical/Marxian approach will be able to explain growth endogeneously through the normal rate of profit.

The framework developed in this chapter is grounded in Marx's schemes of reproduction, in Chipman's (1951) illuminating treatment of Keynesian flows, and in the pioneering elaborations of the Marxian schema by Duménil (1977) and Foley (1983). The results are distinct from either of the two major traditions in modern macroecomics, since neither Say's Law (aggregate production generates a matching demand) nor Keynes's/Kalecki's Law (aggregate demand induces a matching supply) is assumed. On the contrary, as in Marx, both aggregate supply and demand are found to be themselves regulated by more basic factors (Kenway 1980; Foley 1983). Because capitalist production is fundamentally anarchic, this regulation process is always characterized by constant shocks and discrepancies. Nonetheless, the inner mechanisms of the system continue to operate. The end

The framework used in this paper was first presented at the International Conference on Competition, Instability, and Nonlinear Cycles at the New School for Social Research, New York, March, 1985.

result is a turbulent and erratic pattern in which supply and demand cycle endlessly around an endogeneously-generated growth trend (Bleaney 1976, ch. 6; Shaikh 1978, 231-2; Garegnani 1979, 183-5).

It is important to note that the present analysis is concerned solely with the relationship between effective demand and accumulation in the absence of any changes in technology or potential profitability. These themes are central to Marx's schemes of reproduction, to Keynes's theory of output, employment, and effective demand, and to Kalecki's theory of effective demand and cycles. More importantly, such considerations are a necessary prelude to the analysis of factors which may modify the path of accumulation and even transform it into a general crisis.

A Framework Linking Aggregate Demand, Supply, and Finance

This section will develop a general framework linking aggregate demand, supply, and capacity to their duals in finance and debt. The aim is to make this framework broad enough to encompass the basic approaches in Marx, Keynes, and Kalecki, while still keeping it manageable. Therefore, the price level, money wages, and the rate of interest will be held constant, since their variations are not central to the above approaches. Similarly, we assume that the aggregate consumption of workers' equals their wages, so that aggregate personal savings derive only from capitalist personal income. However, there is no assumption of any a priori balance between aggregate demand and supply in the short run (as in Keynes and Kalecki), nor between aggregate capital disbursements and internal finance (as in Marx's schemes of reproduction). Indeed, it is one of the central themes of this paper that the linked imbalances in the above two domains play a crucial role in regulating the overall reproduction process.

Aggregate Demand, Supply, and Capacity

Following Marx, the period of production is taken as the basic unit of time, and it is assumed that the difference between inputs purchased and used in each period is small enough to be treated as a relatively small random variable (which will be reintroduced in the simulations). Inputs entering production at time $t - 1$ lead to output at time t. By definition, potential profit on production (the money form of aggregate surplus value) in period t is the difference between the money value of aggregate supply Q_t in period t and the sum of materials costs M_{t-1}, labor costs W_{t-1} and depreciation DEP_{t-1} on inputs used to produce current output. The money value of aggregate supply in period t can be written as

(1) $$Q_t = M_{t-1} + W_{t-1} + DEP_{t-1} + P_t$$

Current aggregate demand D_t is composed of the current demand for materials M_t and for new plant and equipment (gross fixed investment) IG_t, for desired additions to final goods inventories $CINV_t$, and for workers'and capitalists' consumption $CONW_t$ and $CONR_t$, respectively. All of the above items require actual expenditures, except for $CINV_t$ which represents the portion of output which capitalists would like to retain in final goods inventories in order to attain some desired inventory level. When supply and demand do not balance, the actual change in final goods inventories—which equals the difference between gross output (additions) Q and gross sales (deductions) $M + I + CONW + CONR$— will differ from the desired change CINV.

(2) $$D_t = M_t + IG_t + CONW_t + CINV_t + CONR_t$$

Excess demand E_t in any period t can be defined as the difference between aggregate demand and aggregate supply. Note that when excess demand is positive, realized profits will be greater than potential profits.

(3) $$E_t = D_t - Q_t$$

Combining equations (1) - (3), recalling that workers'consumption $CONW_t$ equals their wages W_t, and grouping like terms, yields

(4) $$E_t = A_t + I_t + CINV_t + CONR_t - P_t$$

where

$A_t = (M_t - M_{t-1}) + (W_t - W_{t-1})$ = accumulation of circulating capital

$I_t = IG_t - DEP_{t-1}$ = net accumulation of fixed capital

          = net fixed investment[1]

$CINV_t$ = desired accumulation in final goods inventories

Equation (4) could be expressed in terms of the more familiar balance between total accumulation expenses ("ex ante investment"), $A + I + CINV$, and total nonconsumed surplus product ("ex ante savings"), $P - CONR$; but, this would be misleading for several reasons. First, the so-called total investment would then be a hybrid of actual accumulation in circulating capital A (investment in inventories of raw materials and goods-in-process) and desired accumulation in final goods inventories CINV, both of which tend to be ignored in conventional accounts. Second, the so-called total savings would then merely represent the excess of the surplus product over and above the personal consumption demand of the capitalist class, which in no way corresponds to any quantity of money revenue withdrawn from immediate expenditures ("saved"). Indeed, the accounting device of representing the money value of this nonconsumed surplus product as the sum of the personal savings of capitalists (which *do* represent money withdrawn from immediate expenditure [Keynes 1964, ch. 16]) and the "retained earnings" of the business sector (which *do not* not necessarily correspond to any money revenue withdrawn from expenditure [see equation 8 below]) simply conflates the relation between the supply/demand for commodities and the sources/uses of funds. This conflation obscures important connections between these two domains and are, therefore, treated separately.

Since we are abstracting from changes in technology, wages, and working conditions, aggregate capacity (normal capacity output) N_t will be proportional to the aggregate fixed capital stock Kf_t: $N_t = vKf_t$, where v = the constant capital-capacity ratio (as in Harrod). Defining capacity utilization u_t as the ratio of output to capacity (so that $u > 1$ implies above normal capacity utilization), we can write

$$(5) \qquad u_t = Q_t/N_t = v(Q_t/Kf_t)$$

The last step is to consider the effects of circulating and fixed investments on output and capacity, respectively. Given the constant fixed capital-capacity ratio v assumed above, the change in capacity is proportional to the level of fixed investment (since this is the change in the fixed capital stock).

$$(6) \qquad N_t - N_{t-1} = (1/v)I_{t-1}$$

On the other hand, given some real period of production which will be taken as the unit of time, current output Q_t and current potential profit P_t are the results of inputs M_{t-1} and W_{t-1} purchased and used in the previous period. Given a constant profit margin on costs, $m = P_t/(M_{t-1} + W_{t-1})$, the change in current potential profits is proportional to the change in past inputs. Since the latter is simply the circulating capital investment in the last period (see equation 4), it can be written

$$(7) \qquad P_t - P_{t-1} = mA_{t-1}$$

Equation (7) expresses the connection between circulating investment and the expansion of production. This relation is often neglected these days, even though it has always been an integral part of classical and Marxian schema. Modern national income accounts tend to lose sight of circulating investment because they adopt the convention of treating current expenditures for materials and labor $(M_t + W_t)$ as the production costs (intermediate inputs) of current output Q_t (BEA 1980, 6–9). This implicitly assumes a zero time of production, which is tantamount to assuming away the production process altogether.

Equations (4)–(7) define the fundamental equations of aggregate production and effective demand. It is important to note that any a priori balance between demand, supply, or capacity is never assumed.

Aggregate Finance and Debt

In treating finance, assume that firms pay dividends R to capitalists, who in turn consume a portion, CONR, and save the remainder, SAVR. Also assume, as does Kalecki (1965, 97) that firms borrow these personal savings of capitalists, SAVR, by issuing stocks or bonds to that amount. This is more or less equivalent to Marx's assumption that capitalists draw their personal consumption directly out of profits, leaving the rest available for use by the firm (Marx 1967, vol. 2, ch. 21). Any borrowing or lending above this amount is then assumed to be mediated by the banking sector. Additionally, assume that this banking sector is willing and able to fulfill the needs of its borrowers or depositers *without having to change the interest rate*. This assumption is made merely in order to duplicate the Keynesian and Kaleckian assumption that bank finance can be freely acquired (or lending be freely accepted) at some given rate of interest below the potential rate of profit. In an important and insightful paper, Asimakopulos points out that Keynes and Kalecki justify their treatment of planned investment as unconstrained by (i.e., independent of) the current flow of savings precisely through the assumption of "freely gotten finance" (Asimakopulos 1983, 222–27). By adopting the very same assumption, hopefully it will be clear that the basic differences between Marxian and conventional theories of effective demand have nothing to do with the presence or absence of credit.[2]

The need for external finance arises because the projected expenditures of firms may exceed the projected internally available sources of funds. Borrowing must, therefore, precede the actual expenditures it aims to finance (Robinson and Eatwell 1973, 218–19). In general, this borrowing will be assumed to consist of two parts: direct borrowing of current capitalist savings $SAVR_t$ through the issue of new stocks or bonds and bank borrowing B_t for any needs beyond this level.

Total Borrowing = Total Planned Uses − Total Internal Sources

Bank Borrowing + Stock/Bond Issues = Planned Uses − Sources

(8) $\qquad B_t + SAVR_t =$ Planned Uses − Sources

The output Q_t forthcoming over any period t is determined by the materials and labor set into motion in the previous period. Of this current projected output, the amount $CINV_t$ represents the desired additions to inventories of final goods, so that it is the remainder which is projected for sale. Since any financial receipts of principal and interest on past lending by firms are treated as negative finance charges on the side of uses of funds, the total projected internal sources of funds of the business sector in period t simply equals projected sales, $Q_t - \text{CINV}_t$. Over the same period, the total planned uses of funds must encompass five basic categories: circulating capital expenditures for materials M_t and wages W_t to be purchased in this period (in order to produce output for the next period), fixed capital expenditures for gross investment in plant and equipment IG_t, the payment of finance charges F_t which represent currently due principal and interest charges on past borrowing (or when negative, the current receipt of principal and interest revenues on past lending), disbursements of dividends R_t to capitalists for whom they will serve as current income, and any planned changes in money reserve levels CMR_t. It should be noted that since the money reserves of firms may be fed by past borrowing, government increases in the money supply, or even by increases in the supply of a money commodity such as gold (as in Marx), the term CMR_t represents any desired adjustments over and above these other sources of changes in money reserves. Thus equation (8) becomes

(9) $B_t + \text{SAVR}_t = M_t + W_t + \text{IG}_t + F_t + R_t + \text{CMR}_t - (Q_t - \text{CINV}_t)$

Combining equations (1) and (9) results in

$$B_t + \text{SAVR}_t = M_t + W_t + \text{IG}_t + F_t + R_t + \text{CMR}_t$$
$$- [(M_{t-1} + W_{t-1}) + \text{DEP}_{t-1} + P_t) - \text{CINV}_t]$$

$$= [(M_t - M_{t-1}) + (W_t - W_{t-1})] + (\text{IG}_t - \text{DEP}_{t-1})$$
$$+ \text{CINV}_t + F_t + \text{CMR}_t - (P_t - R_t)$$

(10') $B_t + \text{SAVR}_t = [A_t + I_t + \text{CINV}_t] + [F_t + \text{CMR}_t - (P_t - R_t)]$

The second term in brackets on the right side of equation (10') is the difference between financial uses $F_t + \text{CMR}_t$ and retained earnings $P_t - R_t$. Therefore, retained earnings correspond to financial leakages from expenditures only when all "investment" $(A_t + I_t + \text{CINV}_t)$ is deficit financed (i.e., financed entirely through borrowing, $B_t + \text{SAVR}_t$). Since this will not generally be the case, it is incorrect to treat retained earnings as a form of business savings.

Finally, noting that capitalist revenue R = consumption CONR + saving SAVR, equation (10') can be rewritten

(10) $B_t = (A_t + I_t + \text{CINV}_t + \text{CONR}_t - P_t) + F_t + \text{CMR}_t$

All of the above quantities represent planned expenditures and projected revenues, as anticipated at the beginning of period t. But if it can be assumed that short-run expenditure plans are revised between periods, not within them, and that short-run revenue estimates are relatively accurate (in a stochastic sense), then from equation (4) the first term in parenthesis on the left hand side of equation (10) is simply excess demand E_t plus a small random variable (which is reintroduced during the simulation process). Thus,

$$(11) \qquad\qquad B_t = E_t + F_t + CMR_t$$

where,

B_t =   bank borrowing by firms
E_t =   excess demand
F_t =   finances charges (principal due + interest due)
CMR_t =   desired changes in money reserves

Note that all these terms may be either positive or negative, with corresponding interpretations.

Equation (11) is the fundamental equation of finance. It says that the bank borrowing of the business sector must cover its own planned deficit finance of current expenditures (which will then show up as excess demand E_t), plus finance charges due on past borrowing, plus any funds needed to adjust money reserves to desired levels. The terms F_t and CMR_t play a particularly important role here, because they reflect the feedback of past events on current borrowing.

Equation (11) above can also be read in another way.

$$(11') \qquad\qquad E_t = (B_t - F_t) - CMR_t$$

The term in parentheses on the right side is the net bank borrowing of the business sector, since it is the difference between current new borrowing B_t and current repayments of principal and interest F_t. Equation (11) then reveals that when excess demand is zero, any desired adjustments in money reserves (in light of any direct injections of new money) must be covered by net bank borrowing. In a growing system, this implies a growing level of net borrowing, though this may well be a constant proportion of total profits or total output. More importantly, *any excess demand E must therefore be fueled by an injection of bank credit over and above the amount required for money reserve adjustments*. But any such additional borrowing implies future finance charges. Thus episodes of excess demand carry the seeds of their own negation, because the net injections of credit which fuel them also carry over into the future as accelerated leakages. This feedback will play a vital role in bounding the growth cycles of the system.

It is interesting to note that the above feedback effect was essentially ignored by both Keynes and Kalecki when they formulated their respective theories of effective demand. What is more, even after criticisms of their work led them to admit that they had implicitly relied on "credit inflation" (Kalecki) or increased "bank finance" (Keynes) as the crucial foundation of their explanation of increases in business activity (Asimakopulos 1983, 223–26), neither author ever really analyzed the impact of this "credit inflation" on the level of business debt. Instead, both ended up focusing on its impact on the level of the interest rate, thus deflecting attention away from the magnitude of business debt associated with it. This left the interest rate as the principal regulator of investment decisions, as is evident in Keynes. This same emphasis on the interest rate has been revived recently by several authors (Taylor 1985; Foley 1987) as a means of breaking out of the impasse generated by the apparent instability of growth within conventional theories of effective demand. But while the influence of interest rate movements is clearly important, it is not necessarily the central factor regulating accumulation. It will be seen that even when the interest rate is assumed to be held constant, say through some "appropriate" set of state policies, the feedback between finance, debt, and accumulation will turn out to be sufficient to stabilize accumulation. The resulting theory of effective demand is very much in the classical/Marxian tradition, with the internal profitability of the system driving accumulation and the consequent debt burden constraining it. Any such construction vitiates all claims that there is an inherent contradiction between theories of effective demand and classical and Marxian theories of growth. The next section will therefore develop a simple model embodying the above principles.

A Macro Model of Internally Generated Cyclical Growth

The model developed below focuses on profits, investment, savings and finance, because these are the critical variables in the debate surrounding the relationship between effective demand and accumulation. The adjustment of inventory and money reserve stocks will not be treated here, because they play a relatively secondary role in the basic analysis in Marx, Keynes, and Kalecki, and because space limitations preclude the necessary development.

An important aspect of the approach is the distinction between fast and slow variables. Slow variables are assumed to have decision periods longer than those of corresponding faster variables (e.g., years instead of months), so slow decisions are effectively cast in terms of moving averages of the faster variables. Although one can conceive of many different sets of variables with each set operating at its own intrinsic speed, the present analysis is confined to just two speeds. The basic fast variable will be the proportion of potential profit (surplus value) which is invested in circulating capital. In Marxian terminology, this is the rate of accumulation in circulating capital, and it regulates the relation between supply and demand. The corresponding slow variable will be the rate of accumulation in fixed capital, which regulates the relation between supply and capacity.

In what follows, the (relatively) fast adjustment process is modeled first and then the (relatively) slow one. They may be thought of as "short-run" and "long-run" adjustments, provided that two things are understood. First, the corresponding time horizons are defined within this framework and may not correspond to those implicit in other frameworks. Second, the short- and long-run balance points are not equilibrium points in the conventional sense, but rather centers of gravity around which the system cycles.

The (Relatively) Fast Adjustment Process

The relationships between aggregate excess demand, bank borrowing, and investment in circulating capital in equations (4), (7), and (11), respectively, form the core of the fast adjustment process. Noting that we are abstracting from stock adjustments, we can write

$$(12) \qquad E_t = A_t + I_t + CONR_t - P_t$$

$$(13) \qquad (P_t - P_{t-1}) = mA_{t-1}$$

$$(14) \qquad B_t = F_t + E_t$$

The next step is to define the interrelationships among the terms of the above equations. Assume that the ratio of capitalist consumption to potential profits is a constant c (on the grounds that dividends are proportional to profits and capitalist consumption is in turn proportional to dividends), and that the rate of accumulation in fixed investment k is a constant in the short-run, since it is a slow variable. Finally, the essential link between past borrowing and present debt service is captured by assuming that all borrowing or lending by firms must be paid back at a constant interest rate i within one period. Accordingly,

$$(15) \qquad CONR_t = cP_t$$

$$(16) \qquad I_t = kP_t$$

$$(17) \qquad F_t = (1 + i)B_{t-1}$$

The remaining step is to model the behavior of the rate of accumulation in circulating capital a = A/P. This ratio expresses the strength of the tendency to expand production and is generally determined by various factors ranging from the level and trends of past profits to various expected gains and costs. *There need be no specific assumption about the determinants of the level of the rate of accumulation.* Instead, simply assume that firms attempt some arbitrary rate of accumulation, which they then modify based on the results of their attempt. Specifically, assume that if any arbitrary initial attempted accumulation rate results in a level of internally available finance above potential profit (surplus value), then the accumulation rate in the next period will be higher. The opposite holds when internal finance falls below potential profit. In this way, the rate of change in the rate of accumulation becomes linked to the financial strength of the firm.

At the beginning of any period t, firms must assess their internally available finance and formulate their borrowing and expenditure plans for the period. As the internally available and borrowed funds are actually expended, the resulting demand serves to realize a particular level of aggregate profit. Thus, realized profits in period t are themselves the result of expenditures undertaken in period t (Kalecki 1965, 45–46). It follows that only the profits realized in period $t-1$ can enter into finance which is internally available at the beginning of period t.

Actual internally available finance at the beginning of period t is defined as profits realized in the previous period $t-1$ minus any debt service payments which firms are obligated to pay over the coming period t. Aggregate profits in $t-1$ are realized by aggregate purchases $(A+I+CONR)_{t-1}$, and from equation (4) these equal the sum of potential profits and excess demand $(P+E)_{t-1}$. Debt service payments over period t are given by equation (7). Thus at the beginning of period t, the internally available internal finance is

$$X_t = \text{(Realized Profits in } t\text{-1)} - \text{(Debt Service in } t)$$
$$= (P+E)_{t-1} - F_t = (P+E)_{t-1} - (1+i)B_{t-1}$$

The *accumulation reaction function* then states that the change in the rate of accumulation in circulating capital is proportional to the percentage of the excess of internally available finance over potential profit (surplus value).

(18) $$(A/P)_t - (A/P)_{t-1} = h[(E - (1 + i)B)/P]_{t-1}$$

Equations (12)-(18) describe the complete short-run model. At this point, it is useful to consolidate the above equations, express all terms as proportions of potential profit, and write them in their continuous time equivalents, so as to facilitate subsequent proofs. Combining (12), (15), and (16), letting e = excess demand as a proportion of potential profit, a = the rate of accumulation in circulating capital, recalling that c and i are constant and k is constant in the short-run because it represents the slowly changing rate of accumulation in fixed capital, and using the notation $\dot{P}$ to signify the instantaneous rate of change of P, etc., it follows that

(19) $$e = a + k + c - 1$$

(20) $$\dot{P}/P = ma$$

(21) $$\dot{a} = h[e - (1+i)b]$$

Combining equations (14) and (17) gives $B_t = (1+i)B_{t-1} + E_t$. Translating into continuous time, $\dot{B} + B = (1+i)B + \dot{E} + E$, where i now stands for the instantaneous interest rate. Dividing through by potential profit P, letting $b = B/P$, and noting that $\dot{b} = \dot{B}/P - (\dot{P}/P)b$ and $\dot{e} = \dot{E}/P - (\dot{P}/P)e$, the equation of finance can be expressed as

$$\dot{B}/P + b = (1+i)b + \dot{E}/P + e$$
$$\dot{b} + (\dot{P}/P)b + b = b + ib + \dot{e} + (\dot{P}/P)e + e$$

(22) $$\dot{b} = \dot{e} + ib + e + (\dot{P}/P)(e - b)$$

Equations (19) - (21) can be reduced still further. Since c is constant, and k is constant in the short-run, (19) implies $\dot{e} = \dot{a}$, which can then be substituted into (21). On the other hand, $\dot{P}/P = ma$ from (20) and $a = e + d$ from (19), where d $= 1 - (c+k)$, all of which can be used to rewrite (22). On this basis, the result is two nonlinear differential equations which describe the essential mathematical structure of the fast adjustment process.

(23) $$\dot{e} = h[e - (1+i)b]$$

(24) $$\dot{b} = \dot{e} + (1+i)e + (md - i)(e - b) + me(e - b)$$

where e, b represent excess demand and borrowing as fractions of potential profit, respectively, and

c = the constant propensity to consume out of profits
k = the rate of accumulation in fixed capital (constant in the short run)
d = $1 - (c + k)$
m = the constant profit margin on costs
i = the constant rate of interest

The short run adjustment process summarized above has several remarkable properties (proofs are in the Appendix). First of all, it has only one stable critical point at $e = 0$ and $b = 0$, which implies that the system automatically converges around a generally growing path on which supply and demand balance (e=0) and accumulation is self-financing (b=0). This path is none other than the *aggregate equivalent of the Marxian expanded reproduction path implied by the parameters c,k* (of which simple reproduction is a special case).[3] Second, the stability of this model is assured by the simple and plausible economic requirement that in the vicinity of expanded reproduction, the funds reinvested by firms be capable of earning an incremental rate of return which is greater than or equal to the rate of interest. In other words, active capital should be capable of earning at least as much passive capital. Third, subject to the above condition, the model is extremely robust, because it is stable for all positive values of the reaction coefficient h and is cyclically convergent for all plausible values of h.

The above properties imply that from any arbitrary initial situation, the model will converge in a cyclical fashion towards aggregate expanded reproduction. But this does not imply that the system will ever be in expanded reproduction, because

Figure 1. **Excess Demand and Debt.**

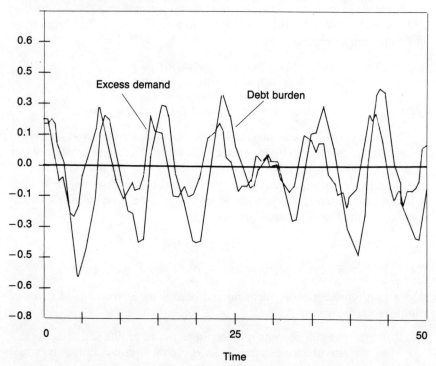

Time

once the effects of the anarchy of capitalist production are simulated by subjecting the model to recurrent random shocks, the system cycles endlessly around expanded reproduction without ever coming to rest upon it. The simulation results are shown in Figure 1 in which excess demand, e, and the debt burden, b, cycle erratically around the balance point of zero. Figure 2 shows how this translates into the fluctuation of actual profit (realized surplus value) around potential profit (produced surplus value). Taken as a whole, these figures exemplify Marx's conception of expanded reproduction as the inner tendency—the regulating average—of the erratic path of the actual system.

The short-run model has several other interesting properties. To begin with, since excess demand e is approximately zero in the short-run, equation (19) implies that

$$(25) \qquad\qquad a = 1 - (c+k) = d$$

When averaged over short-run fluctuations, the rate of accumulation in circulating capital, a, is inversely proportional to the propensity to consume, c, and to the fixed investment accumulation rate, k. This means that even though an exogeneous rise in either c or k may initially stimulate the system, the financial

Figure 2. **Produced and Realized Profit.**

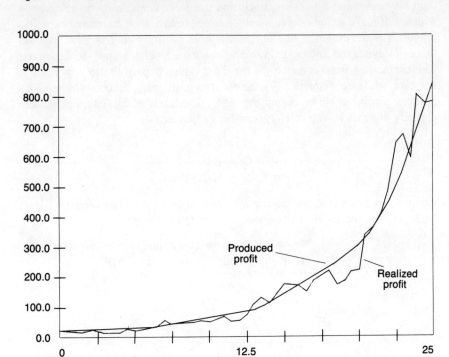

drag created by the additional debt will end up lowering a by the same amount, at least over the average short-run cycle.

The average short-run rate of return on fixed investment is also inversely proportional to c and k. Defining this as

$$r = \dot{P}/\dot{K}f = (\dot{P}/P)/(I/P)$$

where $I/P = k$, $\dot{P}/P = ma$ from equation (18) and a is given by (25), so that

$$r = md/k = \frac{m(1 - c - k)}{k} = \frac{m(1 - c)}{k} - m.$$

Once again, an exogeneous rise in c or k may initially raise the short-run rate of return on fixed investment by initially stimulating a, but will end up actually lowering it as the new short-run average level is established.

Lastly, it can be shown that the rate of capacity utilization will be roughly constant over the average short-run cycle at some level which will, in general, be different from normal capacity utilization. While this is reminiscent of the standard Keynesian and Kaleckian conclusion that there is no short-run mechanism which will make actual output equal "full employment" (i.e. normal capacity) output, it is worth noting that our results hold for a growing system, whereas those of Keynes and Kalecki hold solely for a static level of output. To derive our result, note that from equation (5) the fixed capital/capacity ratio $v = Kf/N$ is constant, while from equation (7), the constant profit margin on costs m implies a constant profit margin on output $n = P/Q$. The levels of capacity, output, and capacity utilization, respectively, can be written as

(26)
$$N = Kf/v$$
$$Q = P/n$$
$$u = Q/N = (1/r_n)\ P/Kf$$

where $r_n = n/v$ = the normal-capacity rate of profit on fixed capital.

To analyze the short run behavior of $u = Q/N$, note that

$$\dot{N} = \dot{K}f/v = I/v = (k/v)P \text{ and}$$

$$\dot{Q} = \frac{\dot{P}}{n} = \frac{(\dot{P}/P)P}{n} = \frac{maP}{n} = \frac{m(1 - c - k)P}{n} \ .$$

Thus $\dot{Q} = p\dot{N}$, where

$$p = \frac{mv[(1 - c)/k - 1]}{n}$$

is constant in the short run. Integrating both sides, $Q = pN + (Q_0 - pN_0)$, where the term in parentheses is the constant of integration evaluated at some time t_0. Rewriting,

$$u = Q/N = p + (u_0 - p)\ N_0/N$$

from which it is clear that as the system grows and N rises over time, u approaches p. A rise in c or k will, therefore, tend to lower the average short-run level of capacity utilization by lowering its asymptote p.

The (Relatively) Slow Adjustment Process

In the analysis of the short-run, the rate of accumulation in fixed capital k is taken as given on the grounds that it represents a slow variable. But since the short-run level of capacity utilization will generally differ from the normal level of capacity utilization, it is to be expected that k will slowly react to any such discrepancy. Defining a longer unit of time T (e.g., years instead of months) to accommodate this slow adjustment process, the reaction function for the rate of accumulation in fixed capital k is written as

(27)
$$\dot{k}/k = g(u - 1)$$

where u = the level of capacity utilization (normal level = 1)

g = the reaction coefficient (a positive constant)

The effects of such a reaction function depend on the counter-response of capacity utilization to k. Now, from equation (25) it is known that the fast adjustment process will lead to the rough equality a + k = 1 − c. Suppose the short-run level of capacity utilization is above normal, so that k begins to slowly rise. From the point of view of the short-run adjustment process, k has risen to a new higher level. This rise may initially stimulate effective demand and raise a. But as the new short-run center of gravity is established, a will fall to accomodate the new higher short term level of k. Thus, an acceleration in the the growth of capacity will end up decelerating the growth of actual production, *so that the capacity utilization level will tend to fall back toward normal (or even past it).* This tendency is in striking contrast to the knife-edge instability usually found in conventional effective demand models. It is, on the other hand, implicit in most classical and Marxian analyses of accumulation. To formalize it, differentiate the expression u = $(1/r_n)$ P/Kf given in equation (26), recalling that $\dot{P}/P = ma = m(1 - c - k)$ from equations (6) and (25), respectively, while by definition $\dot{Kf} = I$ and I/P = k,

$$\dot{u}/u = \dot{P}/P - \dot{Kf}/Kf = ma - (I/P)(P/Kf) = m(1 - c - k) - (r_n)ku$$

$$(28) \qquad\qquad \dot{u}/u = m(1 - c) - mk - (r_n)ku$$

Equations (27) and (28) define a system of two nonlinear differential equations representing the slow adjustment process through which the level of capacity utilization reacts back on the rate of accumulation in fixed capital, and vice versa.

The above long-run adjustment process has the striking property that it is stable around the normal capacity utilization level u = 1 (see proofs in the Appendix). This critical point is the only stable one. Its stability holds for all positive values of the reaction coefficient g and is oscillatory for all plausible values of g, as long the system is at all profitable. This means that for any single displacement, the system tends to oscillate back toward the normal level of capacity utilization. More importantly, in the face of random shocks representing a multitude of concrete factors and disturbances, the system tends to cycle endlessly, alternately overshooting and undershooting the normal level of capacity utilization. Note that since the adjustment of the fixed investment share is denominated in time units *T*, while that of the circulating investment share is denominated in some shorter time unit *t*, it follows that the period of the fixed investment cycle is likely to be greater than that of the circulating investment cycle. Figure 3 below shows the simulation results for capacity utilization u in relation to the normal level u = 1. Figure 4 shows the corresponding behavior of profit on actual production and of profit on normal capacity production (profit on "warranted" output).

* * *

Figure 3. **Capacity Utilization.**

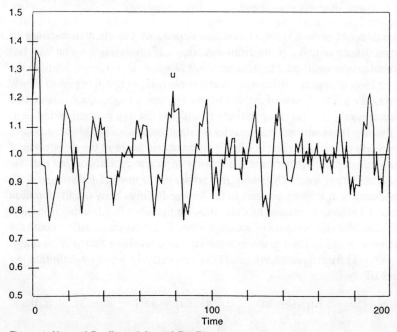

Figure 4. **Normal Profit and Actual Profit.**

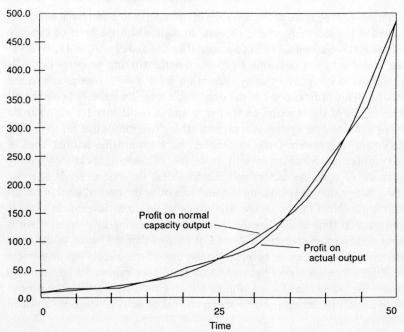

The aim of this chapter has been to present a new approach to the question of the role of effective demand in accumulation. The first step in this direction was an attempt to create a simple framework which was general enough to encompass the essential differences between Marxian, Keynesian and Kaleckian approaches to this issue. Issues which are not central to the above approaches (such as the effects of workers' savings, of the adjustments in inventory and money stocks, or of the difference between short-term and long-term debt) were ignored, while others which did play a central role in one or the other of the main approaches (such as the constancy of prices, wages, and interest rates in Keynesian and Kaleckian [KK] theory, or the link between investment in circulating capital and output growth in Marxian theory) were retained. Since Marx's schemes of reproduction abstract from aggregate borrowing or hoarding (Bleaney 1976, 106–7), while KK theories are crucially dependent on the assumption that finance is "freely available" at a constant rate of interest (Asimakopulos 1983), it was particularly important to retain this latter assumption in order to establish that it was not a decisive factor in distinguishing the two sets of approaches. What did turn out to be decisive were the crucial links between accumulation expenditures, finance, bank credit, and the burden of debt.

But the question of credit is only half of the story. An equally important difference arises in the analysis of accumulation. Dynamic analysis, as in Marx and Harrod, tends to see growth as an inherent aspect of production and investment plans, so that it is their trend which is seen as reacting to market feedback. In contrast to this, both Keynes and Kalecki adopt a notion of essentially passive firms aiming at attaining a given level of output. Production plans are implicitly static, and it is the level of production (rather than its trend) which is taken to respond to feedback.[4] Mathematically speaking, Marx's (and Harrod's) reaction functions tend to be formulated in terms of proportions or rates of growth, whereas those of Keynes and Kalecki tend to be cast in terms of absolute levels of variables. This is a difference which becomes quite crucial in the analysis of macroeconomic growth.

In latter part of this chapter, the above considerations were used to develop a simple but powerful macroeconomic model of cyclical growth. The proportion of potential profit devoted to expansion of output was assumed to respond positively to the level of excess demand and negatively to the burden of debt service payments. This was shown to give rise to persistent short-run cycles centered around expanded reproduction in the Marxian sense. Over the longer run, the proportion devoted to expansion of capacity was assumed to rise when capacity utilization was above normal (and fall in the opposite case); this simple assumption was found to lead to persistent long-run cycles centered around normal capacity utilization (the Harrodian warranted path). The overall model thus generates two distinct cycles which oscillate around a growth trend ultimately regulated by the intrinsic profitability of the system. Unlike most modern approaches, no recourse is made to external factors such as technological change or population growth in order to explain the basic growth trend,[5] and there is no presumption that the system tends to achieve the full employment of labor (as opposed to the normal utilization of fixed capital). In this sense, the model presented here is a concretization of the theory of effective demand implicit in the classical/Marxian tradition (see Shaikh 1978).

Many aspects of this approach remain to be developed. For instance, the introduction of sustained government deficit spending introduces a new factor, in that it seems to give rise to a corresponding sustained excess demand. This seems to suggest a formal basis for a link between deficit spending and inflation, at least under conditions of normal growth. Similarly, a falling potential rate of profit seems to produce qualitatively new behavior, in that the stable growth cycles analyzed here are eventually undermined and turn unstable at the point where the mass of profit-of-enterprise becomes stagnant. Both of these results are very suggestive of classical and Marxian arguments. Lastly, it is possible to generate deterministic limit cycles instead of the stochastic ones explored here by specifying slightly different functional forms for the two accumulation reaction functions. The important thing is that the general approach adopted in this paper seems to provide a very fruitful and dynamic alternative to traditional theories of effective demand.

Appendix: Analysis of Stability

Stability of the Fast Adjustment Process

The fast adjustment process is characterized by equations (23)-(24) above. Defining $z = e - b$, they can be rewritten as

$$(29) \qquad\qquad \dot{e} = - hie + h(1+i)z$$

$$(30) \qquad\qquad \dot{z} = - (1+i)e - (md - i)z - mez$$

where m = the constant profit margin

      i = the interest rate

      d = 1 − (c+k), in which c = the constant propensity to consume out of profits

      k = the constant-in-the-short-run rate of accumulation in fixed capital

      h = the reaction coefficient for the circulating capital accumulation function

and m, i, c, k, and h are positive by definition, and d is positive as long as the average short-run rate of return on fixed investment, $r = md/k$, is positive (see the discussion following equation [25]).

The above system has two critical points:

$e = z = 0$ and
$me = (1 + i)/i - (1+md)$, $mz = -1 - (1 + md)i/(1 + i)$.

Its Jacobian J is

$$J = \begin{bmatrix} -hi & h(1 + i) \\ -(1 + i) - mz & -(md - i) - me \end{bmatrix}$$

Linearizing around the second critical point shows that its determinant reduces to Det J2 $= -h(1+2i+mdi) < 0$, since i,m,d are all > 0. This means that the second critical point is unstable. On the other hand, linearizing around the first critical point e $= z = 0$, gives

$$TR\ J1 = - [hi + (md - i)]$$

$$DET\ J1 = hi(md - i) + h(1 + i)(1 + i) = h[1 + 2i + mdi]$$

Since h, m, d and i > 0, DET J1 > 0. Then a sufficient condition for (local) stability is md $\geq$ i, because this ensures that TR J0 < 0 (Hirsch and Smale 1974, 96). What is more, it can be shown that the discriminant of this system is negative for all plausible values of the reaction coefficient h (e.g., for i between .02 and .20 and md between i and 3i, any value of h between .027 and 144 will yield a negative discriminant), so that convergence will generally be oscillatory. Lastly, the phase diagram of ᴜᴜs system of equations (omitted for brevity) indicates that the basin of attraction of the stable point is very large, since it encompasses both the positive e-space and the positive z-space. Only for initial points in which both e and z are sufficiently negative will the model exhibit instability.

Now consider the economic content of the stability condition md $\geq$ i. From equation (25), the short-run regulating rate of accumulation a $=$ d and from equation (20) ma $=$ $\dot{P}/P$, thus the stability condition becomes $\dot{P}/P > = i$. Now consider the funds that businesses reinvest in their own operations. It has been assumed that dividends R are proportional to potential profits (surplus value) P, so that retained earnings RE $= P - R = P(1-x)$, where x $=$ the dividend payout rate. The corresponding net incremental return to these reinvested funds is the increase in profits $\dot{P}$ minus the increase in payouts of dividends $\dot{R}$ and finance charges $\dot{F}$. But since b $= 0$ at the critical point in question, accumulation is self-financing on average, and $\dot{F}=0$ at the critical point. Thus the incremental rate of return on reinvested funds is

$$r^* = (\dot{P} - \dot{R})/(P - R) = \dot{P}(1 - x)/P(1 - x) = \dot{P}/P$$

It follows that the stability condition md $\geq$ i is equivalent to the basic economic requirement that the funds reinvested in business earn a rate of return greater than or equal to the interest rate.

Stability of the Slow Adjustment Process

The structure of the slow adjustment process is given by equations (27)-(28). These are reproduced below in slightly different form.

$$\text{(31)} \qquad \dot{k} = - gk + gku$$

$$\text{(32)} \qquad \dot{u} = m(1 - c)u - mku - (r_n)ku^2$$

Here, k and u are the variables, and all the others are positive constants:

g   = the reaction coefficient for the rate of accumulation in fixed capital
m   = the profit margins on costs
r_n = the rate of profit on fixed capital at normal capacity (the normal fixed capital rate of profit)
c   = the capitalists' propensity to consume out of potential profits < 1

Once again, there are two critical points:

u = 1, k = k* = [m(1 − c)]/[m+r_n] > 0 and
u = 0, k = 0.

Forming the Jacobian of this system,

$$J = \begin{bmatrix} g(u - 1) & gk \\ -[m + r_n]u & m(1 - c - k) - 2(r_n)ku \end{bmatrix}$$

Linearizing around the second critical point u = k = 0, the system is found to be locally unstable, since Det J2 $= - gm(1 - c) < 0$. On the other hand, in the vicinity of the first point u = 1, k = k*, since k*[m+rn] = m(1 − c), the Jacobian, its trace and and its determinant reduce to

$$J1 = \begin{bmatrix} 0 & gk* \\ -[m + r_n] & -r_nk* \end{bmatrix}$$

TR J1 $= - r_nk* < 0$, DET J1 $= gk*[m + r_n] > 0$

which implies that the first critical point is locally stable. Moreover, the convergence implied by this stability is generally oscillatory, because plausible values of m, c, and r_n yield a negative discriminant for all but the very smallest values of the reaction coefficient g (e.g., for all m, c, r_n between .1 and .5, a reaction coefficient g > .05 is more than sufficient to guarantee oscillatory behavior).

Since capacity utilization cannot be negative, u ≥ 0. The corresponding phase diagram of this system (omitted for brevity) shows that any trajectory in the positive quadrant will converge on the first critical point u = 1, k = k*. The slow adjustment process is then stable around the warranted path.

Notes

1. Strictly speaking, net investment is the difference between gross fixed investment and current retirements IR_t, rather than current depreciation allowances DEP_t. But the difference between the latter two is not important here.

2. Bleaney points out that Marx abstracts from all credit and hoarding, which means that an increase in investment must be financed by a corresponding decrease in some other form of demand, such as capitalist consumption. This explains why there is no multiplier in Marx's analysis of the schemes of reproduction, even when investment changes to accommodate the transition from simple to expanded reproduction, etc. From this, Bleaney leaps to the conclusion that the introduction of credit into the Marxian schema would "lead logically to the Keynesian solution" (Bleaney 1976, 107). Our analysis makes it clear that his conclusion is quite unwarranted.

3. In Marxian expanded reproduction, supply equals demand and borrowing equals zero for each of the departments of production, and hence also for the aggregate. Here, we focus solely on the aggregate.

4. Only in an aside on Harrod does Kalecki modify his basically static focus to try to account for "an expanding economy." But the analysis is very awkward and seems largely designed to support Kalecki's earlier conclusions concerning the inherent static tendency of accumulation in the absence of external factors such as technical change (Kalecki 1962).

5. Kalecki (1965) relies on technical change and external markets to explain growth; Goodwin (1986) relies on exogenous population growth and technical change; while Foley (1985) relies on the growth in the exogenous money supply.

References

Asimakopulos, A. 1983. "Kalecki and Keynes on Finance, Investment, and Saving." *Cambridge Journal of Economics* 37(Sept./Dec.).
Bleaney, M. 1976. *Underconsumption Theories*. New York: International Publishers.
Bureau of Economic Analysis (BEA). 1980. *Definitions and Conventions of the 1972 Input-Output Study*. Washington, D.C. (July).
Chipman, J. S. 1951. *The Theory of Inter-Sectoral Money Flows and Income Formation*. Baltimore: John Hopkins Press.
Duménil, G. 1977. *Marx et Keynes Face á la crise*. Paris: Économica.
Foley, D. 1983. "Say's Law in Marx and Keynes." Mimeo.
————. 1984. "Money, Accumulation, and Crises." Mimeo.
————. 1987. "Liquidity-Profit Rate Cycles in a Capitalist Economy." *Journal of Economic Behavior and Organization* 8(3):363–77.
Garegnani, P. 1979. "Notes on Consumption, Investment and Effective Demand: a Reply to Joan Robinson." *Cambridge Journal of Economics* 3:181–87.

Goodwin, R. M. 1986. "Swinging Along the Turnpike with von Neumann and Sraffa." *Cambridge Journal of Economics* 3:203-10.

Hirsch, M. W., and S. Smale. 1974. *Differential Equations, Dynamical Systems, and Linear Algebra*. Orlando: Academic Press.

Kalecki, M. 1939. *Essays in the Theory of Economic Fluctuations*. London: Allen and Unwin.

————. 1962. "Observations on the Theory of Growth." *Economic Journal* (March):135-53.

————. 1965. *The Theory of Economic Dynamics*. New York: Monthly Review.

Kenway, P. 1980. "Marx, Keynes, and the Possibility of Crisis." *Cambridge Journal of Economics* 4(1): 23-36.

Keynes, J. M. 1939. *The General Theory of Employment, Interest, and Money*. New York: Harcourt, Brace, and World. 1964.

Marx, K. M. 1967. *Capital*. New York: International Publishers.

Minsky, H. 1982. *Can "It" Happen Again?: Essays on Instability and Finance*. Armonk, New York: M.E. Sharpe, Inc.

Mullineaux, A. W. 1984. *The Business Cycle after Keynes: A Contemporary Analysis*. New Jersey: Barnes and Noble.

Robinson, J., and J. Eatwell. 1973. *An Introduction to Modern Economics*. London: McGraw-Hill.

Shaikh, A. 1978. "An Introduction to the History of Crisis Theories." *U.S. Capitalism in Crisis*. New York: Union for Radical Political Economics: 219-41.

————. 1984. "The Transformation from Marx to Sraffa." *Ricardo, Marx, Sraffa*. Ernest Mandel, ed. London: Verso.

Taylor, L. 1985. "A Stagnationist Model of Economic Growth." *Cambridge Journal of Economics* 9(4): 383-403.

The Real and Financial Determinants of Stability: The Law of the Tendency Toward Increasing Instability

Gérard Duménil and Dominique Lévy

The primary aim of this chapter is to present a theory of business cycles and their secular evolution, which is elaborated within a dynamic model of capitalist production. We will show that this model, described below, can produce a number of distinct "regimes" such as balanced growth, overheating, stagnating growth, or crises. The business cycle will be interpreted as a short-run sequence of such regimes. This theory allows for differentiation between various stages in the actual evolution of business cycles in the history of capitalism, from the traditional nineteenth century pattern to the contemporary phenomena observed today. This ability to make historical differentiations is a major advance over previous attempts to model the business cycle which have treated every historical stage in the evolution of the business cycle as equivalent. Finally, this evolution of the business cycle is linked to Marx's law of the tendency for the rate of profit to fall and a corollary to this law is formulated which will be called "the law of increasing instability."

Although the analysis of crises presented below is not directly derived from the work of Smith, Ricardo, or even Marx, we nevertheless contend that it is classically inspired in the sense that it is based on a dynamic model whose assumptions are classical, and because it clarifies many aspects of Marx's view of business cycles in relation to the law of the tendency for the rate of profit to fall. In

A preliminary version of this study has been published in the *Economic Forum*, University of Utah, Winter 1986–87. We thank M. Glick for his aid in the translation of this text into English.

particular, it provides an answer to the difficult question, "Why does profitability matter?"

Our framework of analysis was developed in a previous study of the classical analysis of competition and the formation of prices of production (Duménil and Lévy 1983, 1987a). The framework of these original studies was multi-commodity (two or three commodities). However, in the present study, a single-commodity approach is utilized for the sake of simplicity. Although this can be interpreted to mean a switch from a micro to a macro approach, the basic principles and the model remain unchanged.

An important aspect of the present study is that the *financial determinants of the cycle are also analyzed*: the issuance of money, repayments of loans and interest, business failures, and monetary policy. In addition, the relative impact of real and financial determinants is discussed.

This chapter will consist of four parts:

• *Real Stability and Instability*. In this part, the model which underlies the business cycle analysis will be presented. Minimum reference will be made to monetary and financial factors. Nevertheless, the fundamental aspects of the analysis can be derived independently of monetary considerations.

• *Financial Stability and Instability*. This part introduces a macroeconomic model with money and the specific results obtained in relation to the treatment of money are established.

• *Business Failures and Stagflation*. In this part, some elaboration is added to the model with money, in particular a treatment of firm and bank responses to situations of tight liquidity. Business failures are also explicitly incorporated into the model.

• *Historical Tendencies*. This part attempts a formulation of a theory of the forms of business cycles, from its early forms in the nineteenth century to the contemporary patterns of events in contemporary capitalism. Following this formulation, the relationship of the theory of business cycles with the law of the tendency for the rate of profit to fall is introduced.

Real Stability and Instability

The object of this first section is to define a minimum framework of analysis in which the issue of the stability of capitalist production can be analyzed. The fundamental principles which govern what we call *disequilibrium microeconomics* are presented, along with the results obtained in a macroeconomic model derived directly from this microeconomics.

Disequilibrium Microeconomics

Our research stems from the attempt to reinterpret the analysis of the competitive process by the classics (Smith 1776; Ricardo 1817; Marx 1863).[1] In the classical view, economic agents react to the observation of disequilibrium. Capitalists seeking maximum profitability for their capital, for example, move a fraction of it if they notice that the rate of profit is superior in other industries. This profitability differential is what we call "the evidence of disequilibrium."

Observation of disequilibrium → Modification of behavior

Therefore, the formalization of the classical analysis relies on the *modeling* of the behavior of the agents in a situation of disequilibrium.

This approach to the analysis of economic activity (although quite natural and evident in many literary commentaries on economic activity) is ignored by mainstream economic theory, with very little exception. In the traditional perspective, the behavior of economic agents is modeled with the assumption that equilibrium always prevails. We will denote this perspective "equilibrium microeconomics," which can be counterposed to "disequilibrium microeconomics."

This latter paradigm was applied by the classical economists to three types of situations:

1. The observation of differences between rates of profit induces the mobility of capital among industries.
2. The observation of the inequality of supply and demand leads to the modification of prices. Excess supply is an inducement to diminish prices, and the reverse applies for excess demand.
3. The observation of the inequality between supply and demand also leads to the direct adjustment of outputs, without waiting for the classical indirect transmission:

Modification of prices → Change in profitability → Migration of capital → Modification of the output

This direct mechanism, which we called "direct control of quantities," was emphasized by Ricardo (1817, ch. 4).

These adjustments are not made by an auctioneer prior to real economic activity, as in the Walrasian paradigm of the *tatonnement*. Instead, classical adjustment occurs in the course of real economic life (production, transactions, consumption, etc.). Two types of agents participate in these adjustments. First, enterprises decide the level of outputs and the modifications of prices. Second, the mobility of capital is insured by the "centers for the allocation of capital." In real capitalism, such centers exist under a number of forms. Enterprises engaged in the production of several products are one example of such agents, while holding companies, banks, and individual investors are other examples.

The evidence of disequilibrium is always assessed individually, not globally, on the basis of limited information. For example, enterprises become aware of excess supply or demand through the levels of their inventories.

When fixed capital is explicitly treated in the modeling of the above behaviors, two variables play a crucial role: the ratio of capacity utilization of fixed capital (denoted u) and the ratio of inventories to outputs (s). The behavior of enterprises tends to stabilize the value of these two variables. However, enterprises do not strive to obtain full capacity utilization or zero inventories. In a world fraught with uncertainty, enterprises attempt to reach certain values of the two ratios which they consider optimal. We call these values "normal values." The normal value of the ratio of capacity utilization (for example, 80%) is denoted, $\bar{u}$, and the normal value of the ratio of the inventory to output (for example, one month of output) is denoted $\bar{s}$.

Two further points are added to the three points made by the classics and described above:

4. Enterprises do not necessarily use funds in the exact amounts which are allocated to them by the centers. The level of investment which corresponds to the full use of the allocated funds is what we call "normal investment." However, depending on the level of their ratio of capacity utilization of fixed capital, they can only use part of these resources or, to a certain extent, may overstep the limitations of the allocation.

5. In an extended model which will be presented below, a treatment of the issuance of money will be incorporated. The behavior of the agent which assumes this function is analyzed in a similar manner reacting to the observation of disequilibrium. The issuance of money is adjusted on the basis of two variables:

• Disequilibrium in the ratio of capacity utilization of enterprises (excess or underutilization of capacity) which expresses the desire on the part of enterprises to demand financial resources.

• Inflation.

On the basis of such foundations, we have built several models. The first model of this type demonstrated the relevance of the classical analysis of competition (Duménil and Lévy 1983). An analytical treatment of this model with two commodities and no fixed capital was provided in that study. A number of further developments were proposed in Duménil and Lévy (1987a). In particular, a treatment of two centers for the allocation of capital and the existence of two processes of production for the same commodity in one industry were added. In

Duménil and Lévy (1986a), we provided an analytical treatment of the stability of classical long-term equilibrium with any number of centers and enterprises. The existence of fixed capital was taken into account in a number of other contributions which we will refer to throughout the present study:

1. The so-called "micro model." Three industries are considered which produce the elements of fixed capital, the elements of circulating capital, and consumption goods, respectively. There are 13 variables in this model (originally 15, which can be reduced to 13 as a result of the homogeneity of the equations). This analysis was done by computer simulation (Duménil and Lévy 1985b). An analytical treatment of a similar model with 10 variables was given in Duménil and Lévy (1986b).

2. The "macro model." This model is a replication of the micro model for one commodity. The mechanisms related to the mobility of capital among industries are abstracted from. Therefore, only two variables exist: u and s. An analytical treatment of this model is presented in Duménil and Lévy (1987b).

3. The "macro model with money." This development of the previous model embodies the explicit treatment of money. The number of variables is now equal to four, u and s, and two new financial variables (the ratio of the stock of money of the enterprise to the sum of its productive capital and inventories, denoted m, and the equities of the bank, also divided by the sum of the productive capital and inventories of the enterprise, denoted e). The main results will be introduced below.

It is apparent that these basic models can be the basis for a large number of further developments some of which will be reported below. It is possible to endogenously determine an exogenous parameter or to add a constraint, depending on the demonstration made. For example, business failures can be explicitly treated in the macro model with money, the rate of interest can be given or determined endogenously, the supply of labor can be limited, etc.

The study of a dynamic model of this type implies the formulation of a relation of recursion which defines how the values of the variables in one period can be derived from their values in the previous period. For example, the "macro model" above leads to the determination of:

$$\mathbf{u}_{t+1} = U(\mathbf{u}_t, \mathbf{s}_t)$$
$$\mathbf{s}_{t+1} = S(\mathbf{u}_t, \mathbf{s}_t)$$

The functions U and S depend on the parameters which define the technology, the functions of reactions of the agents, and the ratio of accumulation in each period. Two issues must be investigated, the existence of equilibria and their stability. In the mathematical sense of the term, an equilibrium is a set of values of the variables $(\mathbf{u}^*, \mathbf{s}^*)$ such that:

$$\mathbf{u}^* = U(\mathbf{u}^*, \mathbf{s}^*)$$

$$\mathbf{s}^* = S(\mathbf{u}^*, \mathbf{s}^*)$$

Such equilibria can also be called "stationary states." This concept in a growth model corresponds to that of "homothetical growth." The issue of the stability of an equilibrium is more complex. Do we find convergence toward this equilibrium when the computation defined by the recursion is initiated with given values of the variables $(\mathbf{u}_0, \mathbf{s}_0)$ and repeated until infinity? Stability usually depends on the value of the parameters and the initial values of the variables. The convergence region (also called the "region of attraction") is the set of all initial values of the variables for which convergence can be obtained.

If several such equilibria exist and are stable, then this means that the economy described by this model can display different types of stationary states, which can be called "regimes."

The Equilibria, The Pitchfork

The primary property of these models is that they can, under certain circumstances, lead to convergence toward a situation which we call "normal equilibrium" (N). This is important because it corresponds to the competitive outcome described by the classics. When several industries are considered, the classical notion that the rates of profit are equalized in the long-run is achieved. The ratios of capacity utilization of fixed capital, as well as the ratios of inventory to output, attain their normal values.[2]

A second property of these models is that other equilibria, in addition to the normal equilibrium, can exist and can be stable:

1. Overheating (O). In this situation, the ratio of capacity utilization is above normal, and the ratio of inventory to production is inferior to normal. The rate of growth is also above normal. Inflation also characterizes a situation of overheating.

2. Stagnating growth, or a Keynesian situation (K). In this regime, the ratio of capacity utilization and the rate of growth are below normal, while the ratio of inventory to production is above normal. Prices are decreasing (except in situations of stagflation, which will be considered below).

3. Depression (D). In a depression, the economy collapses toward zero if nothing prevents the dramatic decline.

The stability of these equilibria and the configuration of their region of attraction is primarily conditioned by the value of a parameter which models the behavior of enterprises. This parameter is denoted ϵ and measures the intensity of the reaction to scale up or down the level of capacity utilization, in response to the change in inventories (ϵ measures this intensity only in a vicinity of normal equilibrium).

In the macro model without money, the existence and stability of the equi-

Figure 1. **Existence and Stability of the Equilibria: The Macro Model without Money.**

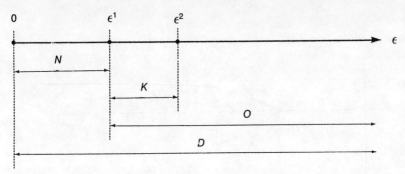

The existence and stability of the equilibria are primarily determined by, ϵ, a parameter which measures the intensity of the reaction of enterprises to disequilibria in the ratio of their inventories to outputs. The equilibria which exist and are stable in the corresponding intervals of the values of ϵ are indicated in the figure: Normal Equilibrium (N)—Overheating (O)—Stagnating growth, or Keynesian situation (K)—Depression (D).

libria depend on the values of ϵ in the following manner (see Figure 1):

1. Depression exists and is an equilibrium for all values of ϵ.
2. When ϵ inferior to a given value ϵ^1, normal equilibrium exists and is stable. In this situation, the convergence region is large. Thus, only a major disturbance can change the economic course toward another equilibrium (depression).
3. For ϵ between ϵ^1 and ϵ^2, both overheating and Keynesian equilibria exist and are stable. Their convergence regions are limited in one direction. This means that in spite of the size of the region, in general, it can be easily destabilized when a shock pushes the economy in one particular direction.
4. For ϵ higher than ϵ^2, Keynesian equilibrium is no longer stable. For these values of ϵ, only overheating remains stable (abstracting from depression).

In the micro model without money, ϵ can not be too small. Below a certain threshold, the adjustment of relative prices and of the proportions of outputs will not be achieved.

A further aspect of the relationship between equilibria and ϵ is that, in Keynesian equilibria and situations of overheating, the equilibrium values of the ratio of capacity utilization and ratio of inventory to outputs, depend on the value of ϵ. For example, comparing two situations of overheating reached for different values of ϵ, the ratios of capacity utilization will be different. A higher ϵ will produce a higher ratio of capacity utilization. Therefore, it is possible to plot this relationship between ϵ and the corresponding equilibrium value of **u** or **s**. The results are presented in Figure 2. This figure clearly illustrates the existence of a bifurcation for $\epsilon = \epsilon^1$. The configuration obtained is that of a pitchfork (see Guckenheimer and Holmes 1983).

Figure 2. **The Pitchfork: The Macro Model without Money.**

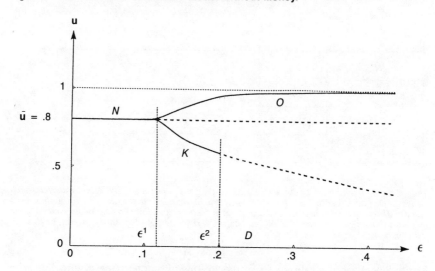

This is an extension of Figure 1. The equilibria are represented by their value in **u**. *A similar fig-ure could be presented for* **s**. *The configuration obtained is that of a pitchfork.*

The classics, especially Marx, have never contended that capitalism is globally stable, in spite of the role played in their paradigms by the formation of prices of production. This former view would be an extreme form of an apology for capitalism and corresponds to the old but still influential free-market conten-tion—*laissez faire, laissez passer*. In other words, an equilibrium exists and when disturbed, it will be autonomously restored, provided that no perverse behavior (for example, rigidities) interferes.

Capitalism is only partially stable, and the degree of stability depends on given circumstances. *N* globally stable would be equivalent to the impossibility of crises. *N* always unstable would be equivalent to the irrelevance of the classical analysis of the formation of prices of production. The existence of various regimes and the limited character of stability (nonglobal stability) is, in our opinion, a fundamental characteristic of capitalism. The pattern of equilibria which has been revealed must be considered as a powerful device for the analysis of capitalism. The remainder of this study is an attempt to support this proposi-tion.

The fact that several regimes exist and are surrounded by given regions of attraction shows that the economy can switch from one regime to another, as a result of shocks to the variables or changes in the values of the parameters (reactions functions, technique, etc.). The study of these movements introduces a theory of business cycles. Business cycles correspond to specific chains of regimes which switch from one to the other.

Before elaborating on the theory of business cycles described above, we will articulate the monetary and financial aspects of the analysis and then treat the issues which are related to liquidity squeezes.

Financial Stability and Instability

In the above investigation, the analysis focused on the *real* determinants of stability as opposed to the monetary and financial dimensions of the analysis. This second part now deals with the latter issues. The monetary and financial framework of analysis embodied in the model (macro model with money) are presented, followed by a discussion of the forms of interaction between the real and monetary determinants of stability.

Money and Finance in the Model

In the workings of a real economy, as well as in the model, many transactions require the use of money. For example, purchases and sales on the commodities market are settled through transfers of money. But, money is also necessary in order to realize financial transactions: the migration of capital among industries, the payment of wages and interest, the distribution of dividends, and the repayment of debts. Moreover, since the economy is growing, the quantities of money which are required for such purposes must also increase. For this reason, the issuance of money must be incorporated as a necessary component of the model with money.

We define two agents in the "macro model with money," one enterprise which produces the only commodity, and a bank. Since this bank is unique, it must simultaneously be conceived as an ordinary bank and a central monetary institution, such as the Federal Reserve. The money which is created by this bank is comprised of paper money and deposits accessed by transfers or checks. However, we will not distinguish between the two types of monetary assets. We assume that no interest is paid on deposits in the banks. We further abstract from reciprocal loans among enterprises (since only one enterprise is considered), as well as loans to and from households and the state. Money is exclusively issued by the bank and never originates from other sources, such as private treasuries or foreign exchange.

When considering the issue of money, the only sound method of analysis is through the balance sheets of enterprises and banks. Two sides of the balance sheet are implied in the expression "money and finance." Money refers to the asset side and finance refers to the liability side. The balance sheets of the enterprise and of the bank in our model are presented in Figure 3.[3] The notation is as follows:

Figure 3. **Balance Sheets of the Enterprise and of the Bank:
Stock of Money Held by Final Consumers.**

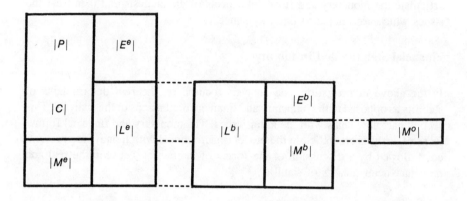

/P/ Stock of productive capital   /C/ Stock of commodity capital
/M^e/ Stock of money capital   /E^e/ Equities of the enterprise
/L^e/ Loans received by the enterprise   /L^b/ ≡ /L^e/ Loans by the bank
/E^b/ Equities of the bank
/M^o/ Stock of money outside   /M^b/ ≡ /M^e/ + /M^o/ Stock of money
     of the circuit of capital   issued by the bank
/P/ + /C/ + /M^e/ is "Total Capital"   /P/ + /C/ is "Engaged Capital"

$$ m = \frac{Stock\ of\ money\ of\ the\ enterprise}{Engaged\ capital} \qquad e = \frac{Equities\ of\ the\ bank}{Engaged\ capital} $$

The enterprise must decide on price, the capacity utilization of its stock of fixed capital, and its level of investment. Prices and capacity utilization are decided in the manner described in the first part of this chapter. Prices are modified on the basis of the level of involuntary inventories. The ratio of capacity utilization is fixed on the basis of its previous value and the level of involuntary inventories.

The decision concerning the ratio of utilization (decision to produce) only depends on the ''real'' variables. This decision is not a function of the availability of money, except in situations of extreme liquidity squeezes, when the enterprise is rationed and cannot execute its plan for production (even with zero investment) because of a lack of money.

On the contrary, the *decision to invest* is made on the basis of the funds available for investment. After production has been decided and the necessary purchasing power secured, the remaining amount of money determines the ability to invest (we abstract here from precautionary behavior which would induce enterprises to conserve stocks of money in order to honor future commitments).

This chain of events can be made more explicit by the following sequence of actions which begins at the opening of the market:

1. The inputs are purchased, as well as the elements of fixed capital corresponding to the new investment, and wages are paid. Money flows back to the enterprise.
2. The enterprise repays its debts which have matured, both principal and interest.
3. The enterprise pays dividends. Specifically, by this transaction we mean the net balance of the payment of dividends and the purchase of newly issued shares by dividend receivers.
4. New loans are issued by the bank to the enterprise. The new money is added to the already existing stock held by the enterprise.
5. The enterprise decides on its level of utilization of fixed capital and purchases the inputs necessary to set in motion the existing fixed capital (prior to the new investment) at the decided level of capacity utilization.
6. The enterprise decides on the level of new investment on the basis of the size of the remaining stock of money.

The three first transactions are mandatory actions taken by the enterprise. Only the fourth event is voluntary and depends on the initiative of the enterprise. The demand for loans affects their total volume. The supply of loans on the part of the bank is not limited by the availability of resources, since only one form of money exists which can be created by the bank. However, the issuance of money must be limited in some way. It is very difficult to conceive of an *ex ante* control procedure. One method might be that the bank would estimate an amount of ''normal'' transactions in some sense, and thus compute the value of the stock of money exactly corresponding to these transactions. Such a procedure would lack realism, however. For this reason, the issuance of money is controlled *ex post* in our model, as explained earlier. In the decision to issue money, the two indicators of disequilibrium are the eagerness of the enterprise to borrow, based on its ratio of capacity utilization, and the evidence of inflation (or deflation).

Parameter τ is the debt-equity ratio for the enterprise. The rate of change of the price level is j. The decision to issue money through credit is governed by:

$$\tau_{t+1} = \tau_t g_j(-j_t) g_u(\mathbf{u}_t - \bar{\mathbf{u}})$$

in which g_j and g_u are two strictly increasing functions of their arguments and are equal to one when their arguments are equal to zero.

The main results which can be obtained in this model are the following:

1. It is possible to reach equilibrium by the simultaneous convergence of real and financial variables.

Figure 4. **The Macro Model with Money: Convergence toward Normal Equilibrium.**

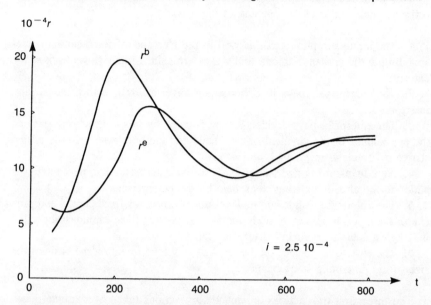

This figure presents the convergence of the two rates of return on equity: enterprise r^e, and bank r^b, toward equality at a level greater than the rate of interest. This rate of profit is the rate of profit over the real components of capital /P/ + /C/, if the stock of money out of the circuit of capital is equal to zero.

2. A variety of regimes can be obtained as in the previous model which excluded money: normal equilibrium, overheating, stagnating growth or Keynesian situations, depression (if we abstract from business failures).

In normal equilibrium, the financial variables defined in the first part stabilize to specific values. In overheating situations, m is superior to its value in normal equilibrium, and e is lower. In the Keynesian regime, the situation is inversed. Moreover, it is interesting to note that the rate of profit over equity of the bank is equalized to that of the enterprise, as shown in Figure 4.

This last result represents an important finding concerning the relationship between the rate of profit and the rate of interest. *The rate of profit is not equal to the rate of interest paid on loans.* This result is not due to a specific assumption of the model but is a necessary feature of a financial system in which money can be issued by private agents and in which the interest charged on loans is greater than the interest paid on deposits. First, the rate of interest on deposits is smaller than the rate charged on borrowings (it is assumed to be equal to zero in the model). Second, $/M^b/$ is the sum of notes and all deposits (checking, saving, etc.); interest is paid only on some of these elements.

Consider the balance sheet of the bank. The income of the bank is the interest paid. If i is the rate of interest, this income is equal to $i\,/L^b/$. The rate of return on equity is therefore:

$$r^b = i\frac{/L^b/}{/E^b/}$$

The rate of return on equity for the enterprise is r^e, and its rate of profit over engaged capital is r. When equilibrium prevails and the stock of money out of the circuit of capital is zero, $r^b = r^e = r$, thus:

$$i = r\frac{/E^b/}{/L^b/} \text{ and } i < r \text{ if } /M^b/ > 0$$

The mere existence of money (issued by a capitalist institution) implies that the rate of interest is inferior to the rate of profit by an amount determined by the relative quantity of money required within the circuit of capital.

Real and Monetary Determinants of Stability

A crucial result, in what has been presented so far, is that the inclusion of money and finance in the model does not alter its basic properties. This finding stresses the primary importance of production and the real aspects of the workings of capitalism. However, this feature does not imply that money is "neutral." In this section, we will briefly investigate some dimensions of the relationship between real and monetary determinants, as revealed by the model.

Money and Finance as Triggers

In a model with regimes, the sequence of economic events can be altered by the influence of "shocks." When money is integrated in such a model, one important form of shock is a monetary shock. Therefore, money can propel the economy from one regime to another.

An example of such monetary influence concerns the rate of interest. Consider an economy in an overheating situation—a regime in which the convergence region is very limited in one direction. A sudden rise in the rate of interest can destabilize the system and propel it into a recession, bounded by a Keynesian situation, or a collapse. Both real and monetary determinants play a role in this phenomenon. The "real" aspect of the mechanism defines the underlying configuration on which the impact of the movement of the rate of interest can be analyzed. The propensity of capitalist production to generate endogenous reductions in productive activity constitutes the fundamental factor. Money only acts as a trigger. This type of determination certainly played a role in the nineteenth century and still represents an important aspect of contemporary capitalism.

The shock which triggers the switch may also concern the monetary aggregates (sharp curtailment of the issuance of money, or sudden reflation) rather than the rate of interest. The change in monetary policy in the U.S. economy since 1979 clearly illustrates the crucial role played by such events.

Money and Finance and the Value of The Reaction Parameters

A second and more complex aspect of the interaction between real and monetary determinants is the effect of a number of interrelations which are excluded from the model. We will consider only one example where the parameter ϵ is dependent on the value of the rate of interest.

Parameter ϵ measures the intensity of the enterprise reaction to scaling up or down its activity when its inventories differ from their normal value. It is easy to understand that this type of reaction is influenced by the rate of interest. A high rate of interest is an inducement for enterprises to manage their inventories tightly (high ϵ). Short-term borrowing is costly, and conversely, excess liquidity can be deposited in order to yield a considerable return (in real life, not in the model). Similarly, a low rate of interest, in relation to the cost of scaling down activity, is an inducement to ignore rising inventories and to wait for the restoration of demand.

Financial Instability

Another important aspect of the interaction between real and financial determinants is their possible divergent paths. While the model can be stable from the point of view of the real mechanisms, it can be disrupted by the influence of the financial mechanisms. This general idea will only be briefly sketched on the basis of Figure 5. In the first part of the experiment described in this figure, the rate of interest is low. The normal equilibrium is stable. As we increase the rate of interest (but keeping it below the rate of profit), normal equilibrium becomes unreachable and the economy begins to decline and is driven downward. In our opinion, the result of this experiment is not a common pattern of events in advanced capitalist countries; however, it may correspond to the situation of many third world countries where the burden of debt is becoming unbearable.

Business Failures and Stagflation

This part of the study introduces a group of possible developments of the model related to the reactions of the enterprise and the bank to a situation of liquidity squeeze within the productive system. It also develops a number of ideas concerning business failures which were raised in the first part. The various reactions which can be associated with the squeeze are presented, followed by an explana-

Figure 5. **The Macro Model with Money: Financial Instability.**

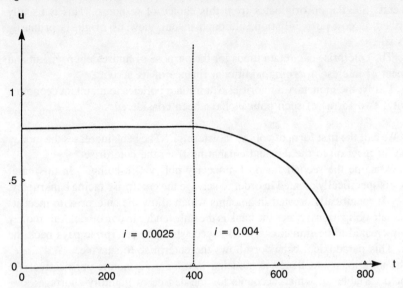

In the first part of the experiment described in this figure, the rate of interest is low. The normal equilibrium is stable. In the second part of the experiment the rate of interest is higher. Normal equilibrium can now no longer be reached, and the economy is declining.

tion of the way in which business failures are accounted for in the model. Next, an important aspect of contemporary economic policy is analyzed: the trade-off between inflation and business failures under stagflation.

Liquidity Squeeze

As a result of borrowing, the enterprise is committed to paying back its debt with interest. This obligation is proportional to the amount of debt incurred. In the model, the enterprise must pay out at each step, a given fraction, δ, of its total debt with the interest, i.e., a total $/L^e/(i + \delta)$. This quantity must be compared at each period with the stock of money which is held. If the stock is deficient, then the enterprise goes bankrupt.

As long as the stock of money is clearly larger than the commitment to pay, the behavior of the enterprise can be as described earlier. However, if the situation becomes tighter, specific responses can be initiated by the enterprise and the bank. Three such reactions have been modeled:

1. The enterprise modifies its behavior concerning the determination of prices. Its sensitivity to stockpiling is maintained, but an element of rigidity is introduced and inflation is created. The enterprise tends to alleviate the financial pressure by increasing prices. It has a choice between diminished activity (which

would be avoided by diminished prices) and the inability of honoring past commitments. Stagflation originates from this choice of response. This is usually described as cost-push inflation, although in our view its origin is primarily financial.

2. The enterprise can retain funds for the purpose of future debt payment and payment of interest, forgoing additional finance of its activity.

3. Lastly, the monetary authorities can initiate policies to maintain economic activity. Two forms of such policies have been considered:

- We call the first form of policy "bolstering." The bank increases the money supply in reaction to the demand emanating from the enterprise.
- We name the second form of monetary policy "rescuing." In this case, money is specifically created in order to salvage the enterprise facing bankruptcy. Money is specifically created in amounts which allow the enterprise to meet its immediate obligations. Since the bank is the only lender in our model, this money is only created to be immediately destroyed when the enterprise pays back the bank. This paradoxical behavior allows the enterprise to survive.

The inflationary tendency is modeled in a macroeconomic perspective. We define a variable, v, which accounts for the degree of liquidity shortage:

$$v = \frac{/M^e/}{/L^e/(i + \delta)}$$

A limit value exists, $\bar{v}$ of v, below which at least one share of the economy is confronted with liquidity problems. The equation which defined the determination of the price by the enterprise was:

$$p_{t+1} = p_t g(\bar{s} - s_t)$$

It is now modified by the addition of a second function:

$$p_{t+1} = p_t g(\bar{s} - s)h(\bar{v} - v_t)$$

in which h is an increasing function of its argument for the positive values of this argument, and $h = 1$ for the negative values of its argument.

In a similar manner, the issuance of money, modified to include the "bolstering" policy, is determined by:

$$\tau_{t+1} = \tau_t g_j(-j_t)g_u(\mathbf{u}_t - \bar{\mathbf{u}})h_v(\bar{v} - v_t)$$

in which h_v possesses the same properties as h_v above.

To model the "rescuing" policy requires the development of a further framework of analysis which will be developed below.

Business Failures

In a model in which only one enterprise is considered, it is difficult to study a phenomenon such as bankruptcies. Normally, an analysis of bankruptcy would require the existence of a large number of enterprises, since once a unique enterprise in a one enterprise model is bankrupt, the analysis ends. In the present study, we will conserve the macroeconomic framework of analysis and consider *the* enterprise in the model, as the *average* of a large set of enterprises which differ in regard to *l*, their *ratio of indebtedness*:

$$l = \frac{/L^e/}{/P/ + /C/ + /M^e/}$$

First, the computation of the flows of money necessary for the payment of debt and interest is made. Then the share of the enterprises capable of paying is determined, depending on the distribution of enterprises in *l*. The model is built in such a way that it is impossible for all enterprises to default simultaneously. The assets and liabilities of the proportion of enterprises which fail are deleted from the economy.[4] The loans which are not repaid are computed as losses for the bank and diminish its equities.

The fraction of the system with high indebtedness violently disappears in this process. As a result, the financial structure of the economy tends to be restored.

The consideration of business failures introduces an important complement to the general pattern of the equilibria presented in the first part of this study (the pitchfork). A new regime appears as an inferior situation in which the system is sustained by the constant devaluation of capital. We denote this regime *F* (see Figure 6).

Policies, The Inflation/Failures Trade-Off

Previously, two reactions of the bank to a situation of liquidity squeeze were introduced: "bolstering" and "rescuing." The effects of these policies on the pattern of the equilibria can be described on the basis of the representation of the pitchfork in Figure 6. Both policies are successful to a limited extent since the lower branch of the fork is shifted upward.

If enterprises react to a liquidity squeeze by a tendency to increase prices, as described before, stagnating growth and inflation can coexist on the lower branch of the fork. This situation corresponds to "stagflation." Under such circumstances, policies of bolstering or rescuing operate in an inflationary context. *Monetary policy must be neither too restrictive, nor too loose.* A strict control increases the bankruptcies or might create a collapse, while a loose policy accelerates inflation.

The issuance of money is controlled in the model by the parameters of reaction

Figure 6. **The Macro Model with Money and Failures: Bolstering and Rescuing.**

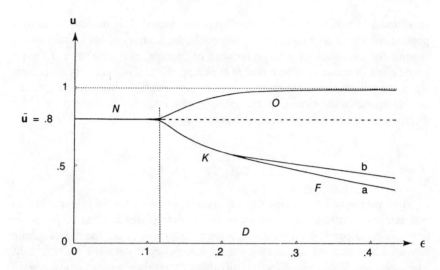

Same as the legend of Figure 1, plus: Inferior situations with business failures. The effect of bolstering and rescuing is to shift this branch upward from (a) to (b).

for the bank. If we vary the parameter which measures the sensitivity of the bank's reaction to monetary difficulties for a given degree of aversion to inflation, we obtain a trade-off between inflation and failures, as shown in Figure 7.

Historical Tendencies

In this last part, a theory of the historical evolution of the business cycle in relation to Marx's law of the tendency for the rate of profit to fall is formulated. First, the relationship between Marx's law of the tendency for the rate of profit to fall and the framework presented above is sketched. This analysis provides an interpretation of the various forms of the business cycle in the history of capitalism. In this context, the relationship between the evolution of capitalism and the development of economic theory is presented.

The Law of the Tendency toward Increasing Instability

In this study, we will not discuss either the factual (Duménil, Glick, and Rangel 1987a) or theoretical controversy (Okishio 1961) around Marx's law of the tendency for the rate of profit to fall. The purpose of this section is to establish the following thesis:

A tendency toward a stricter management of capital (an increasing parameter

Figure 7. **The Inflation/Failures Trade-off.**

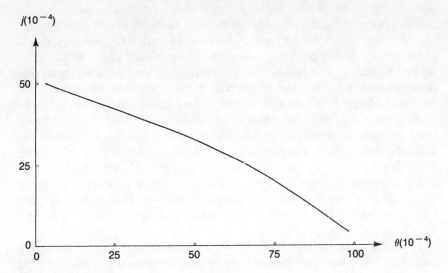

In the macro model with money and failures, the impact of policies of bolstering and rescuing in a stagflationist environment are shown. Varying the intensity of the policy, a trade-off between inflation and failures is created. j is the rate of inflation, and θ the proportions of enterprises which go bankrupt at each period.

ϵ) *can be associated with the historical tendency for the rate of profit to fall. This stricter management results in a tendency toward increased instability. Moreover, most countertendencies to the falling rate of profit can not offset this propensity toward instability (this movement of* ϵ*), but instead are the expression of this modification in the functioning of capitalism.*

Actually, two parameters exist in the present form of the model. They both account for the intensity of the reaction of enterprises to the evidence of disequilibria. The first concerns enterprise reactions to stockpiling, the second measures the reaction to the degree of capacity utilization. High levels of these ϵs correspond to swift and strong reactions to the evidence of bloated or deficient inventories, or excessive or inferior levels of capacity utilization. These strong reactions indicate a form of "tight" management. This strict concern becomes a necessary feature of the management of enterprises as the rate of profit tends to decline. The combination of a diminished rate of profit with a relatively high rate of interest implies the transformation of management in the direction of controlling costs and minimizing the quantities of money $/M^e/$, inventories $/C/$, and productive capital $/P/$, necessary for their operations. This transformation of management is a crucial aspect of the evolution of capitalism (the consequences concerning the class structure are not addressed here).

Intensive utilization of fixed capital plus strict management of inventories and liquidities are important countermeasures to the falling rate of profit. They offset considerably the fall in profitability, as can be shown empirically. But the crucial point to understand in this regard is that these countermeasures *do not restore the stability of capitalism*. On the contrary, they are responsible for what we called in previous work the "instability in dimension" (Duménil and Lévy 1985b). When enterprises manage their inventories more carefully, promptly cutting production in response to excess levels of inventories, they contribute to the restoration of their profitability. However, such actions jeopardize the general stability of the system, since any downward signal is transmitted to the whole system (diminished purchase of inputs, diminished wages, etc.). This type of epidemic can either develop into crises or stabilize the economy at inferior levels of capacity utilization.

It is important to recall that Marx associated the tendency for the rate of profit to fall with *accelerated* accumulation—not stagnation—and with *increasing* instability (Duménil 1977). The model provides a theoretical justification for this view.

It must also be stressed here that these forms of management have very positive effects concerning the control of the proportions of prices and outputs in capitalist economies. In this sense, individual interests coincide with the general interest. But, this same capacity to efficiently react to disequilibrium is responsible for the instability of capitalism in dimension. For this reason, *capitalism is very stable in "proportions" and unstable in "dimension."*

This property explains why the free-market perspective concentrates its attention on proportions which are the positive aspect of capitalism. Equilibrium microeconomics in a general equilibrium model rules out any possibility of deficient demand, and this explains why the Keynesian revolution was necessary. Keynes disregarded the issue of proportions and only considered the problem of dimension in a macroeconomic framework of analysis in which Say's law is rejected. This property also explains why two paradigms exist in Marx's analysis, that of stability, at the beginning of Volume III of *Capital* where the convergence of prices toward prices of production is analyzed (as well as the adjustment of outputs), and that of instability, in recurrent references to crises throughout his work.

This formulation of a law of the increasing instability of capitalism, in relation to the reaction parameters of enterprises and the tendency for the rate of profit to fall, introduces a theory of the historical evolution of the forms of the business cycle, an issue which will be addressed now.

The Forms of the Business Cycle

The pitchfork analysis which has been presented in this study stresses a number of basic features concerning the origin of business cycles. Moreover, it suggests the existence of different forms of the business cycle corresponding to successive stages of capitalism. We will consider four such forms: the nineteenth century, the between-two-wars, the nineteen-fifties, and contemporary configurations.

The Business Cycle as a Succession of Regimes

Figure 8 presents four possible configurations of the business cycle. In the first case, figure (a), the value of ϵ insures the stability of normal equilibrium. After an important shock, the economy progressively moves back to normal equilibrium. In the case of (b), the economy switches from normal equilibrium to overheating, then is destabilized toward a Keynesian state, and moves back to normal equilibrium. This latter chain requires a change in ϵ or a lateral shift of the pitchfork. In the case of (c), the value ϵ is again given, as in the first instance, but at a higher level (beyond the bifurcation). The level of activity flips from overheating to a Keynesian state and vice versa. In the last case, (d), it is a Keynesian state which is destabilized. Beginning from a situation of stagnating growth (instead of the traditionnal overheating as in (b), a recession occurs.

The model which is presented in this study is not a model of the business cycle. However, it is possible to develop this model to obtain endogenous switches from one regime to another (for example, ϵ can be transformed into an endogeneous variable).

The Nineteenth Century Configuration

If one considers the profile of economic activity in nineteenth century England (Gayer, Rostow, and Jacobson-Schwartz 1953), it is easy to distinguish two subperiods. The first period, which can be called "Ricardian," is characterized by a steady growth which is only interrupted by limited and short lived stages of recession (cf. Figure 8 [a]). Ricardo referred to these as states of "distress." A second period might be called "Marxian." In this period a fullfledged business cycle appears and recurs reliably (cf. Figure 8 [b]).

The traditional pattern of the business cycle, as described by Marx, corresponds to a repetitive chain of events which requires about ten years to thoroughly unfold. The economy is drawn from one stage to the other in a specific scenario. Beginning in the trough, the recovey ushers in a phase of balanced growth which lasts several years. Then a phase of overheating is initiated and lasts approximately a few months or more. Suddenly the economy is destabilized and declines at high speed, only to stagnate at low levels of activity. Capital is devalued in the recession and the whole circuit is reinitiated. There is very little inflation, on average, during the entire process. It is easy to reinterpret this pattern of events on the pitchfork. The story goes from a Keynesian state, to normal equilibrium, to overheating, and into a collapse which stabilizes in the Keynesian situation. The cycle can be presented as a succession of switches from one regime to the other. In other approaches to the study of business cycles, the circuit is directly

108

Figure 8. **Four Configurations of the Business Cycle.**

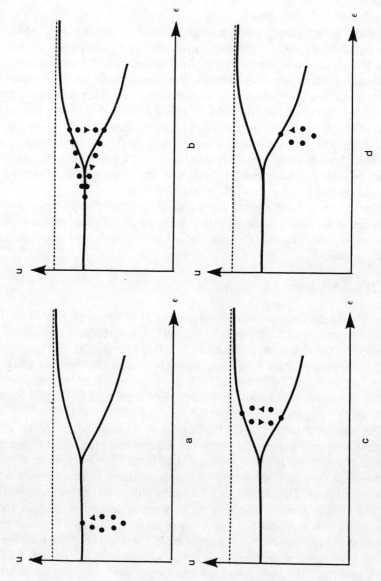

This figure illustrates the fact that the business cycle can be analyzed (using the pitchforks presented in Figures 2 or 6) as a succession of switches from one regime to another. Various configurations can, thus, be obtained.

Figure 9. **Business Cycles: The Nineteenth Century Configuration.**

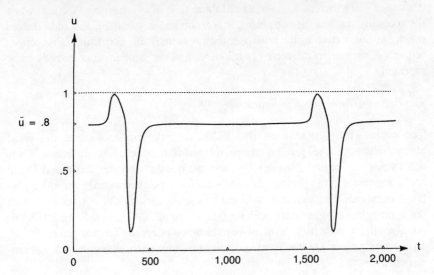

In this traditional form of the cycle, the value of ϵ is usually smaller than ϵ^1. Only during limited periods, as a result of the effect of a shortage or a bottleneck, such as deficient labor power, ϵ will increase and the economy will switch from normal equilibrium to overheating. During this regime, the economy is destabilized and collapses. It stagnates for a limited period of time, but eventually the constraint is relaxed and ϵ restored. The economy moves back to normal equilibrium, and so on.

described in relation to a single mechanism; this constitutes an important methodological difference between our approach and others.[5] In this theory of the succession of regimes, inflation is also zero in the average (zero in normal equilibrium, inflation in overheating, deflation in Keynesian situations).

Since normal equilibrium lasts several years, the value of ϵ is usually inferior to ϵ^1. High values are only cyclically reached when the economy encounters a constraint which affects the behavior of enterprises. When the constraint becomes effective, the consequence is an increase of ϵ (stricter management). This is the process which Marx describes in Vol. III of *Capital*, where he discusses the overaccumulation of capital, as well as in the study of the reserve army in Vol. I. In the analysis of overaccumulation, the rate of profit falls as a result of an increase in wages. Another constraint is the inability of the credit system to adjust to the growth of production. In such a case, the rate of interest increases and ϵ rises temporarily.

The cyclical movement of ϵ can be modeled without specifying the nature of the constraint. In the example in Figure 9, we assume that the economy is confronted with such a constraint. The rate of growth of the constrained variable is inferior to that of the economy in normal equilibrium. The existence of this restriction has two consequences. First, ϵ is sensitive to the pressure created by the constraint and varies according to the distance between the actual situation and the limit produced by the constraint. When the economy moves closer to the constraint and ϵ increases, it switches to a regime of overheating. Second, when the economy reaches the constraint, it is autonomously destabilized and tumbles down. At the bottom of the collapse, the pressure of the constraint is no longer felt and ϵ is restored, the recovery initiated, and the same process is ready to be repeated.

The Between-Two-Wars Configuration

The cycle which occured in the 1920s is very similar to that described above, although the general magnitude of the process is different. Over that cycle, ϵ increased considerably, and the overheating was sharp and lasted for a relatively long period. The depression was exceptional when the collapse occurred. The monetary and economic authorities did not respond with the appropriate expansionary policies (see Duménil, Glick, and Rangel 1987b). As a result, a very high level of bankruptcies occured. *Laissez faire, laissez passer* was an attitude that carried disastrous consequences under such circumstances.

The Nineteen-Fifties Configuration

Any student of the post-World War II business cycle can not help but notice that the character of the cycle was highly modified. During the fifties, normal equilibrium does not appear attainable. Instead, the economy is constantly moving from excessive spurts of growth to recessions, producing cycles of very short duration. This new situation can be easily interpreted as a new range in the variation of ϵ. As a result of the transformation undertaken during the war, ϵ is now superior to ϵ^1 and fluctuates in this new range but does not recover to its previous values in normal equilibrium. The cycle corresponds to constant switches from overheating to Keynesian state and vice versa (cf. Figure 8 [c]).

These circumstances produce a *stop and go* situation, with zero inflation on the average. Demand policies appear to be very effective and well adapted to the new economic conjuncture. However, the economic authorities seem incapable of defining the right measure of the therapy (a right measure does not exist).

The result of a series of such shocks in the model are presented in Figure 10, and thus, a new form of cycle is generated. In this simulation, the shocks upward or downward are automatic and their intensity depends on the size of the discrepency between the actual and the normal value of the ratio of capacity utilization.

In the first half of the sixties, the ratio of capacity utilization soars. Strong and steady growth is restored temporarily, and the business cycle seems to

Figure 10. **Business Cycles: The Fifties Configuration.**

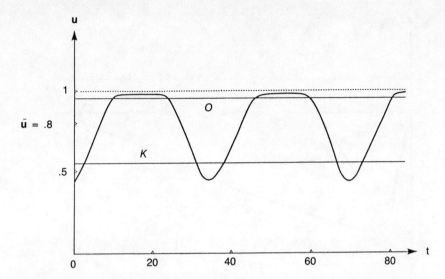

The value of ε is fixed, and demand shocks (budget deficits) are autonomously generated depending on the difference between the actual ratio of capacity utilization and its normal value. The characteristic pattern of the stop and go is reproduced.

disappear permanently. Autonomous stability is combined with stabilizing policy. Figure 11 compares two reversions back to normal equilibrium following a strong disruption of equilibrium. Stabilizing policies in a context of autonomous stability are very effective.

We will now consider the course of events which accompanies the new—and dramatic—fall in profitability in the second half of the sixties.

The Contemporary Configuration

With the decrease in profitability of the late sixties, a new shift forward in the value of ε occurs. In this situation, the economy is constantly attracted by an inferior regime (with approximately zero industrial growth). Movements take place around this inferior equilibrium. There are recurrent upsurges which can never be consolidated, as well as recessions which are not preceded by phases of overheating. Three important features of this period must be outlined:

1. A high ratio of business failures is a constant feature of the economy (above the minimum level necessary for the adjustment of the proportions of prices and outputs in capitalism).
2. The survival behavior described above leads to inflation (see the Liquidity Squeeze discussion).

Figure 11. **Demand Policy.**

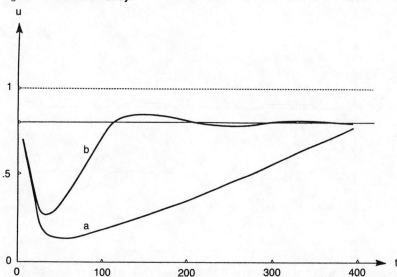

The underlying conditions are those of normal equilibrium. The economy has been the victim of a strong perturbation of equilibrium. The two curves in the figure allow the comparison of the autonomous return to equilibrium (a) and the return accompanied by a systematic demand adjustment (b). The efficiency of the policy is clearly exemplified.

3. The inferior level of economic activity in which the economy is confined is constantly sustained by economic policy. Therefore, the inflation/failure trade-off described before is a basic element of the description of the economy.

Under such circumstances, the configuration of the business cycle is again different. The economy stagnates in a sustained inferior state of activity (with inflation). It is destabilized downward by a demand shock, without the phase of overheating, and then recovers to the same inferior regime (cf. Figure 8 [d]).

Economic Theory and the Forms of the Business Cycle

In the above section, a theory of the evolution of capitalism in relation to the tendency for the rate of profit to fall and the analysis of the cycle has been established. A distinction between different stages of the evolution of the business cycle was made, and in each stage, the specific configuration of the particular cycle was examined. In the present section, we will use this previous analysis to briefly suggest a relationship between the evolution of the business cycle and the history of economic theory. Schematically, each stage discussed above can be associated with a corresponding stage in the development of economic thinking:

1. A characteristic feature of the cycle in the nineteenth century is that the economy remains in normal equilibrium for a number of years. Therefore, normal equilibrium is actually perceived by the economic agents as a natural

course of events. The other episodes are dramatic, usually of short duration, and are considered as "exceptions" or "accidents." In fact, most of the ideological representations associated with the Walrasian paradigm of equilibrium corresponds to normal equilibrium. In this simple view, an equilibrium exists and is stable. Only perverse behavior on the part of some economic agent can prevent the rapid return to equilibrium. With the exception of money (mentioned by Walras), state intervention is unjustified. In spite of their violent character, crises appear as episodes of restoration. Normal equilibrium in the nineteenth century thus displays all the components of the free-market creed. However, the episode of the 1930s shows very clearly how the defense of this conception can be disasterous outside of its sphere of applicability (i.e., when the conditions for normal equilibrium are not met).

2. Stabilizing policies (budget deficits), corresponding to the Keynesian paradigm of the boosting of the economy, are actually shocks. They have a positive influence under many circumstances when the switch from one regime to the other is desired. These policies are effective in a situation of normal equilibrium which has been disturbed, although they are not absolutely necessary. These same policies can also obstruct a movement toward depression. However, their effect is circumscribed by the particular equilibria which exist and are stable. This is clearly evidenced by the stop and go configuration, which we introduced to describe the fifties, in which the fine tuning can never be achieved. In spite of the difficulties of the stop and go policy, demand policy appears very effective to the policy makers, and the fact that they constantly overshoot the target confirms this effectiveness. For this reason, the postwar period was fertile ground for the rise of the Keynesian view in the U.S. when normal equilibrium was restored in the first half of the sixties. The miracle seemed at hand and fine tuning was put on the agenda. This period coincided with the final triumph of Keynesianism in the U.S.

3. In the seventies, a new revolution in economic thinking was accomplished. Attention became focused on monetary policy. This view coincided with the new situation in the economy. The only available economic alternative offered was between a very distant overheating, which was historically accepted only during war periods,[6] and the present sustained inferior state of affairs. Demand policy is no longer adequate. The aim of policy was no longer to provoke a switch from one regime to the other, but to sustain stagnating growth within "tolerable" levels. The nature of the situation is well represented by the failures/inflation trade-off which has been presented. *It defines the program of monetarism.* Keynesian demand policy does not have any impact on the trade-off between failures and inflation. In the analysis of monetarism, the criticism of Keynesianism and the emphasis on monetary policy must not be confused with the decision to make the fight against inflation the number one priority (as decided in 1979). Similarly, the interpretation of this theoretical revolution as something related to the new factual situation is not a validation of the theory itself, just as its success in the sixties does not prove the truth of the Keynesian theory.

* * *

In conclusion, it is possible indeed to build a theory of crises and business cycles on the basis of the classical analysis of competition. The same mechanisms which account for the ability of capitalism to manage its "proportions," i.e., to determine adequate relative prices and outputs, are responsible for the fragile structure of capitalism concerning its dimension (the general level of economic activity). Prompt reaction to the signals of disequilibrium, when they indicate the necessity of moderating activity, can initiate a backward spiral of decreasing demand from within the productive system (an endogenous diminishing of demand). This propensity to recession is conditioned by the level of profitability, in relation to the rate of interest and more generally by the constraint that the financial system applies to enterprises. High pressure (low profitability and financial constraint) implies strict management on the part of enterprises, and thus, instability.

This view has a lot in common with Marx's analysis of crises in *Capital*. First, in both cases, the problem of crisis is approached in terms of instability. The situation of the reserve army or financial factors are presented as possible mechanisms which trigger the destabilization of the system. Second, the movement of the rate of profit is the crucial factor which determines the fundamental conditions for stability in both analyses.

Concerning the interaction between monetary and financial factors, it appears that the real determinants of stability are fundamental. Monetary factors can play a role, which under certain circumstances can determine the future of the system. However, such mechanisms must be understood on the basis of an analysis of the primary determinants of stability.

Following our interpretation, Marx's law of the tendency for the rate profit to fall can be extended. The law of the tendency toward increasing instability is a natural completion of the former law. A crucial point in this analysis is that increasing instability cannot be avoided by the operation of many of the counter-tendencies which, to a large extent, offset the fall in profitability. On the contrary, increased instability is the product of these countertendencies. Therefore, it appears clear that the present difficulties of contemporary capitalism can still be viewed as new forms of the expression of its inner contradictions.

It is possible to be more specific in the presentation of this thesis, since successive stages in the forms of the "instability problem" can be identified. Four such stages have been described in this chapter, the nineteenth century, the between-two-wars period, the fifties and sixties, and contemporary capitalism. Each configuration justifies a different economic perspective: free-market nonintervention, Keynesian demand policies, and monetary polices.

Notes

1. See Duménil and Lévy (1983, 1985a, 1985b, 1987a).
2. Depending on the model studied, this result has been demonstrated either analytically or using computer simulations.

3. See Duménil (1977).
4. Marx called this the "devaluation of capital."
5. See Kalecki (1935), Samuelson (1939), Goodwin (1951), Semmler (1984), and Foley (1985).
6. Specifically, overheating was accepted during the two world wars. It justified measures which were opposed to the free-market ideology during World War II.

References

Duménil, G., M. Glick, and J. Rangel. 1987a. "The Rate of Profit in the United States; From the Turn of the Century to the Nineteen Eighties." *Cambridge Journal of Economics* 11(4):331–60.

————. 1987b. "Theories of the Great Depression: Why did Profitability Matter?" *The Review of Radical Political Economics* 19(2).

Duménil, G. and D. Lévy. 1983. "La Concurrence capitaliste: Un processus dynamique," J.P. Fitoussi and P. A. Muet, eds. 1987.

————. 1985a. "The Classicals and the Neoclassicals, A Rejoinder to Frank Hahn." *Cambridge Journal of Economics* 9:327–45.

————. 1985b. "Stability and Instability in a Dynamic Model of Capitalist Production" (abridged version). W. Semmler, ed., pp. 132–69. 1986.

————. 1986a. *The Stability of Long-Term Equilibrium in a General Disequilibrium Model.* Working paper 8717. Paris: CEPREMAP.

————. 1986b. *The Analytics of the Competitive Process in a Fixed Capital Environment.* Paris: CEPREMAP. Forthcoming in *Manchester School* 57 (1):34–57.

————. 1987a. "The Dynamics of Competition: A Restoration of the Classical Analysis." *Cambridge Journal of Economics* 11(2): 133–64.

————. 1987b. "The Macroeconomics of Disequilibrium." *Journal of Economic Behavior and Organization* 8: 337–95.

Duménil, G. 1977. *Marx et Keynes face à la crise.* Paris: Économica.

Fitoussi, J. P., and P. A. Muet, eds. 1987. *Macrodynamique et déséquilibres.* Paris: Économica.

Foley, D. 1985. *Liquidity Profit Rate Cycles in a Capitalist Economy.* New York: Barnard College.

Gayer, A. D., W. W. Rostow, and A. Jacobson-Schwartz. 1953. *The Growth and Fluctuations of the British Economy (1790–1850).* Oxford: Oxford Clarendon Press.

Goodwin, R. M. 1951."The Nonlinear Accelerator and the Persistence of Business Cycles." *Econometrica* 19(1):1–17.

Guckenheimer J., and P. Holmes. 1983. *Nonlinear Oscillations, Dynamical Systems, and Bifurcations of Vector Fields.* New York, Berlin: Springer-Verlag.

Kalecki, M. 1935. "A MacroDynamic Theory of Business Cycles." *Econometrica* 3(3):327–44.

Marx, K. 1863. *Capital.* Vol. 3. New York: First Vintage Book Edition. 1981.

Okishio, N. 1961."Technical Change and the Rate of Profit." *Kobe University Economic Review* 7: 86–99.

Ricardo, D. 1817. *The Principles of Political Economy and Taxation.* London: Dent and Son Ltd. 1960.

Samuelson, P. A. 1939."Interactions between the Multiplier Analysis and the Principle of Acceleration." *Review of Economic Statistics* 21(2):75–78.

Semmler W. 1984. *On Stability and Instability in Classical Economics.* New York: New School for Social Research.

Semmler, W., ed. 1986. *Competition, Instability, and Nonlinear Cycles Lecture, Notes in Economics and Mathematical Systems.* No. 275. Berlin: Springer-Verlag.

Smith, A. 1776.*The Wealth of Nations.* London: Dent and Son Ltd. 1964.

II

Stabilization Policy in Nonlinear Dynamical Models with Money and Finance

Comparative Monetary and Fiscal Policy Dynamics

Richard H. Day

According to the dynamic Keynesian story, rising employment and capacity utilization during the upswing of the business cycle lead eventually to rising interest rates due to the crowding out on money markets as the transactions demand for money rises. This eventually causes a fall in investment and declines in aggregate demand, employment and interest rates. Although the latter will tend to stimulate investment and consumption, recovery can take some time because of excess capacity.

Using the standard Hicksian model of this process but with supply adjustments on commodity markets, Day and Shafer (1985) have shown that such fluctuations will persist with either a periodic or nonperiodic character when induced investment is strong enough. In a subsequent study (1987), they prove that erratic cycles can occur with positive measure, i.e., they can be "observable" in principle. In that case, GNP behaves like a stationary stochastic process even though the model is deterministic. Day and Lin (in preparation) have shown that all of these possiblitities are consistent with the normal qualitative properties of demand and are robust for parameter values that fall within the ranges that have emerged in various econometric discussions.

One of the salient findings of this work is the complex response that macro behavior exhibits in response to a change in parameter values. As the intensity of induced investment changes, or as the multiplier and monetary effects vary, a stable stationary state can shift into or out of a cycle that can be strictly periodic,

This paper was begun at the Industrial Institute of Economic and Social Research, Stockholm, in the summer of 1983, continued at The Netherlands Institute for Advanced Study in Wassenaar the following year, and completed at the Modelling Research Group, Department of Economics, USC, Los Angeles, 1985. The simulations and computer graphics were prepared by T. Y. Lin. The final draft was prepared at Deer Harbor, Washington, in July 1987.

have periodic turning points with random amplitude, or have both randomly fluctuating turning points and amplitudes.

What implications do these findings have for considerations of monetary and fiscal policy? This chapter shows how changes in the money supply (M), government expenditure (G), or the average tax rate (τ) can trigger the economy into or out of stable stationary, periodic or nonperiodic behavior. Moreover, the change of a policy parameter in a given direction can have switching directions of influence. For example, a steady increase in government expenditure could shift the economy from a stable stationary state through cycles of varying periods, nonperiodic fluctuations, and back into a stable stationary state.

This fact introduces a source of uncertainty that arises not from the erratic nature of political and other "exogenous" influences, but entirely from intrinsic, nonlinear interactions of the financial and real sectors. It provides a new hypothesis concerning the notorious difficulty of anticipating the real world effects of given monetary or fiscal changes.

Obviously, it will be necessary to explore this hypothesis in more general models where the special assumptions used here are relaxed. But when the general price level is changing rather modestly, when output, employment, interest rates and investment are changing relatively rapidly, and when the phenomenon of crowding out on money markets during a regime of tight money is evidently at play, the present analysis should be relevant, even if only as a crude, first approximation under these very special conditions. Certainly, it exhibits some features of the overall picture, and it seems worthwhile to investigate the issues in a tractable theoretical setting. The analysis is familiar to every economist and requires a minimum of mathematical and computational machinery.

It has become common in recent years to examine questions of macro policy within the context of intertemporal equilibrium in overlapping generations (OG) models. It is now well known that such models can also produce nonperiodic cycles as shown in Benhabib and Day (1981, 1982) and elaborated in Grandmont (1985). The former show that fluctuations can persist with constant monetary growth, and the latter shows that government policy can stabilize chaotic cycles. In constrast, the present analysis is conducted in a disequilibrium context, which, in spite of limitations, has some features that are possibly closer to reality than the OG approach, at least under some conditions. In particular, its ingredients of consumption, investment, and monetary demand have been looked at empirically, and something is known about the signs and the range of values specific parameters should have.

The Model

The standard linear demand for money is

(1) $$D^m(r, Y) = L^0 - \lambda r + kY$$

where L^0, k, and λ are parameters. Given a fixed supply of money, M, and immediate money market clearing, $r = r' + (k/\lambda)(Y - Y^{**})$, where $Y^{**} = (M + \lambda r^0 L^0)/k$ is the income level at which the interest rate is equal to r^0. If we assume that this value bounds interest from below then,

(2)
$$r = L^m(Y; M): = \begin{cases} r^o & , 0 \leq Y \leq Y^{**} \\ r^o + (k/\lambda)(Y - Y^{**}) & , Y^{**} \leq Y \leq M/k. \end{cases}$$

In what follows, assume that $r^0 = 0$. In Keynesian terms, the interval $(0, Y^{**})$ is the liquidity trap where changes in aggregate income have little impact on interest rates. Above Y^{**}, the interest rate is sensitive and the crowding out effect of the transactions demand for money drives interest rates upward.[1]

The linear investment function is

(3)
$$I = I^0 + \beta Y - \gamma r.$$

It should also be augmented by a nonnegativity constraint if disinvestment is not important in the short run. It then takes the form

(4)
$$I(r,Y): = \max \{0, \beta(Y - Y') - \gamma r\}.$$

If Y' is positive, it is a threshold below which excess capacity is so great that orders for investment goods are zero even though interest rates may be very low. Above the threshold Y', income has a stimulating effect.[2]

Although all of the above is quite conventional, it is at this point that we introduce a crucial novelty. Substituting (2) into the investment function so as to eliminate the interest rate yields an "IY" relation that incorporates both accelerator and monetary crowding out effects. The resulting investment-income function has 3 or 4 branches depending on the strength of the monetary interaction.

The first branch occurs in the range $0 \leq Y \leq Y'$ when induced investment is zero because of excess capacity. (Autonomous investment may still be positive.) The second branch occurs for incomes between the investment threshold Y' and Y^{**} where interest is at its lower bound, but the stimulating effect of income on induced investment is operating. The slope here is β. The third branch occurs after the transactions demand pushes the interest rate up out of the liquidity trap, and the interest depressing effect of interest comes into play. The slope here is σ: $= \beta - k\gamma/\lambda$, so it must be less than the slope in the earlier regime. If σ is positive, the monetary effect is weak. The investment function will look like Figure 1a. If σ is negative, then the monetary effect is strong. The picture is shown in Figure 1b. In this case, the rise in interest rates required to clear the money market depresses investment, overpowering the stimulating effect of income increases. This crowding out is enhanced by increases in k or γ or by decreases in λ or β, or if the ratio of interest rate effects γ/λ is greater than the ratio of income effects β/k. It implies that eventually investment is driven to zero when income reaches the point Y^*: $= [(k\gamma/\lambda)Y^{**} - \beta Y']/\sigma$, where $Y^{**} = (M\text{-}L^0)/k$. For incomes above this point, induced investment is eliminated and only autonomous investment remains.

This analysis deals solely with the case in which the monetary effect is strong as shown in Figure 1b. In this situation, the investment function can be written

$$(5) \qquad I = H(Y): = \begin{cases} 0, & 0 \le Y \le Y' \\ \beta(Y - Y'), & Y' \le Y \le Y^{**} \\ \sigma(Y^* - Y), & Y^{**} \le Y \le Y^* \\ 0, & Y^* \le Y \le Y^u \end{cases}$$

The regime switching character of the IY function is a consequence of the linear forms for money and investment demand (1) and (3). It could be thought of as approximating a smooth function where the marginal income effect is fairly stable over wide ranges but changes more rapidly in certain critical regions. The interval $[0,Y']$ approximates a situation where investment is very low due to extreme excess capacity. The "liquidity trap" range of income $[0,Y^{**}]$ approximates a region where the interest rate changes very little with changes in Y; the range $[Y^{**},Y^*]$ corresponds to a region where the interest rate is sensitive to growing money demand; the range above Y^* is the area where endogenous investment is reduced severely because of high interest rates. Day and Lin (1985) show that the approximation is good and that the qualitative behavior of the general and the piece-wise linear models are similar.

The model is completed by the consumption function and the components of autonomous demand. Let the former be

$$(6) \qquad C = C^0 + aY, \text{ where } a = (1-\tau)\alpha$$

in which α is the marginal propensity to consume (MPC) and τ is the average tax rate. Define the constant expenditure term $A = I^0 + C^0 + G$, where I^0 and C^0 are autonomous consumption and investment, and G is government expenditure. Also, let μ be an intensity parameter that enables us to vary exogenously the importance of induced investment in aggregate demand or to explore proportional changes in the parameters of investment and monetary demand. This parameter can also be thought of as a speed of adjustment in investment.

Assuming a one-period adjustment lag, the difference equation for GNP is obtained,

$$(7) \qquad Y_{t+1} = \Theta(Y_t): = \begin{cases} A + aY_t, & 0 \le Y_t \le Y' \\ A - \beta Y' + [a + \mu\beta]Y_t, & Y' \le Y_t \le Y^{**} \\ A + \sigma Y^* - [a + \mu\sigma]Y_t, & Y^{**} \le Y_t \le Y^* \\ A + aY_t, & Y^* \le Y_t \le Y^u \end{cases}$$

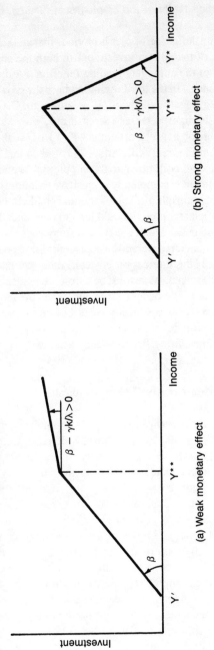

Figure 1. **The IY Function with Intrinsic Monetary Effect.**

(a) Weak monetary effect

(b) Strong monetary effect

The bound Y^u is the smaller of full employment income, full capacity income or M/k.

From (7) and the definition of σ, it is obvious that an increase in μ enhances the stimulating effect of income on investment in both the second and third "branches" or regimes of the aggregate income function. (A decrease, of course, has the opposite influence.) In the third regime, where the crowding out effect plays a role, the slope of aggregate demand is $(1 - \tau)\alpha + \mu\sigma$. Given $\sigma = \beta - (\gamma/\lambda)k$, an increase of μ can be interpreted as increasing β, γ or k, or decreasing λ.

The implication for aggregate demand $\Theta(Y)$ of weak and strong monetary effects are shown in Figure 2. Of course, if $\mu = 0$ so that induced investment is unimportant, the model boils down to the simple stable multiplier process. If γ is zero, so that investment is completely insensitive to interest rates, the same can be said except that the multiplier involves the marginal effect of income on investment. If this is sufficiently high, it could lead to unbounded divergences from the simple stationary state (in which the system supposedly would break down). But if $\gamma > 0$, then the monetary interaction is present; these possibilities are shown in the two diagrams. If the interaction is weak, then the usual multiplier stability analysis can be undertaken. (One must be careful to determine in which regime or regimes the stationary state occurs.) It is only when the monetary effect is strong that all the complex dynamics briefly described in the beginning of the chapter can come into play. It is in this situation that the comparative static analyses can no longer be assumed to suffice. Instead, a comparative dynamic analysis is necessary.

Bifurcation and Comparative Policy Dynamics

The methodology for a comparative dynamic analysis, nonetheless, is similar. In comparative statics, one studies how stationary states change in response to shifts in a parameter. Such stationary states, if stable, give the asymptotic behavior of the dynamic model. If the stationary states are unstable, they will not represent asymptotic behavior. Instead, model trajectories will converge to a set of points called an *attractor*. This set will be finite if the asymptotic behavior is a strictly periodic cycle; it will be uncountable if the behavior is chaotic, and it will be an uncountable set with positive measure if the asymptotic behavior is ergodic. In the latter case, the model will behave like a stationary stochastic process. Sometimes these trajectories have periodic turning points but random amplitudes; sometimes both their turning point periods and amplitudes are random. Two remarkable features of nonlinear dynamic models that have been understood with rapidly growing precision in the past two decades are (a) the robustness of these behaviors, that is, their occurrence for "large" sets of parameter values, and (b) the intricately complex dependence of attractors on parameter variations: models shift from stationary states through cycles of various orders into and out of chaotic and ergodic regimes. The

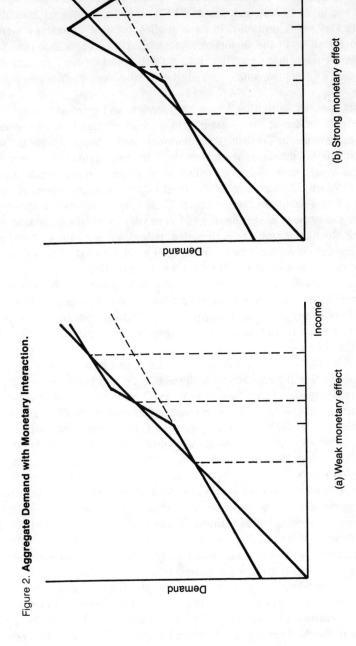

Figure 2. **Aggregate Demand with Monetary Interaction.**

(a) Weak monetary effect

(b) Strong monetary effect

method used to obtain the critical values of parameters where the qualitative behavior of a model changes, described in terms of its attractors, is called bifurcation analysis. A detailed exegesis of the method and complete analytical results are given in Day and Shafer (1987). Detailed numerical examples are given in Day and Lin (1989). In those studies, bifurcation analyses were performed for shifts in the importance of induced investment demand. Similar analyses for shifts in the traditional macro policy instruments, government expenditure, G, the tax rate, τ, and the money supply, M, are presented here.

First, consider shifts in government spending and refer to Figure 3a. The parameter G influences the constant term representing autonomous expenditure in aggregate demand. There are three stationary states. Suppose GNP is "stuck" on the smallest of the three, and it is stable. Therefore, a small increase in G will have the usual stable multiplier effect shifting the stationary state gradually upward. When the total exceeds the level G^2, the aggregate demand curve 2 results. Here a qualitative jump occurs. There is now only one stationary state. Because the slope of aggregate demand is negative with absolute value greater than one, fluctuations must be perpetuated. Indeed, using the theory developed in the references cited, it can be seen that after a brief period of growth, ergodic fluctuations occur and GNP will follow a stationary stochastic process. Further increases in G will be associated with changing long-run distributions of GNP, and irregular fluctuations will continue to occur. If G is increased enough, the unstable stationary state will disappear. Then a stable stationary state is reached and further measures in expenditure will again be associated with the usual stable multiplier processes.

Assume GNP is stuck at the stationary state, and G is at a very high level. Decreases in G will be associated with stable decreases in stationary GNP until the point G^3 associated with the demand curve 3 is reached. After this, stochastic fluctuations will appear. If G is decreased continuously, these will persist until G^0 is reached and the stable multiplier process will re-emerge. Note that changes in G have entirely different impacts on the qualitative behavior of GNP in the range (G^0, G^3) than for values outside this range. These values, therefore, are critical bifurcation points.

Next, consider changes in the tax rate. Such changes tilt aggregate demand by changing the slope of the aggregate consumption function. Beginning with the same base situation as before, critical bifurcation points for τ are readily identified, as shown in Figure 3b. Again, the attractors shift from stable stationary states reached by the usual multiplier process to ergodic sets associated with nonperiodic fluctuations that are stationary stochastic processes.

Finally, consider changes in the money supply. The switching points Y^{**} and Y^0 depend on the money supply parameter but not on the slopes of the aggregate demand segments. Changes in M, therefore, induce parallel shifts in aggregate demand in the third regime, as shown in Figure 3c. Two bifurcation points are

127

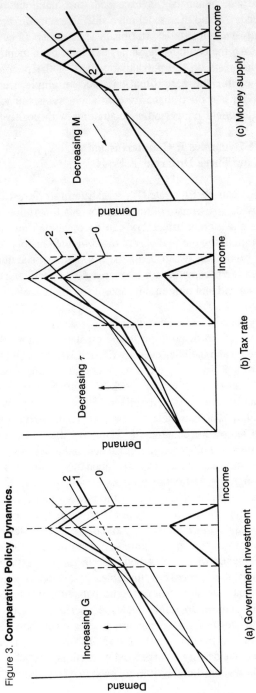

Figure 3. **Comparative Policy Dynamics.**

(a) Government investment

(b) Tax rate

(c) Money supply

readily identified. When M² is exceeded, the maximum value of aggregate demand exceeds Y^u and the model must shift to a non-Keynesian regime. When $M < M^0$, only a single, stable, stationary state exists. In between these values, chaos reigns. All the complex dynamics that have been mentioned can occur. Of course, all this rests on the particular values of the parameters of aggregate demand chosen for the base situations. As we emphasized above, however, ergodic behavior is robust: there are continuous ranges of values for the policy instruments that yield nonperiodic fluctuations with positive measure.

Comparative Dynamics I: Counterfactual Simulations for Three Different Periods

These findings can be illustrated by constructing bifurcation diagrams. Such diagrams provide an estimate of the attractor as a function of a given parameter. Given a base situation, a trajectory can be computed and the values of GNP plotted. By eliminating the first part of the computed history, say, the first fifty or one hundred points, an estimate of the asymptotic behavior of the trajectory remains. Then the parameter can be increased or decreased slightly and a new trajectory computed and plotted, and so on, for the range of parameter values of interest.

In the paper cited above, Day and Lin provide three examples for the parameters of this model corresponding to the great depression (Period I), the early sixties (Period II) and the late seventies (Period III). In each case, the parameters are the same except for γ, the interest effect on investment, which is adjusted to reflect the accumulation of capital stock. Of course, A (which contains G), Y', Y^*, Y^{**}, L^0 and M are adjusted to reflect shifts in autonomous expenditure and in the money supply. The parameters are shown, their derivation is discussed, and the estimated aggregate demand functions are illustrated in their paper. The general appearance of all three aggregate demand functions is like that of Figure 2b, except that succeeding functions are much bigger, reflecting the growth of the economy through the half century involved.

Using these as the base situations, three sets of bifurcation diagrams were computed, one for changes in G, one for changes in τ, and one for changes in M. These are reproduced in Figures 4, 5, and 6. First, consider changes in government expenditures as shown in Figure 4. For all three periods the computations show the emergence of complex behavior in the range (G^0, G^2). Within this range, the multiplier process is unstable. In Period I, shown in Figure 4a, persistent fluctuations shift from ergodic behavior, where GNP is distributed throughout an interval, to stable cycles, to periodic cycles that have random amplitudes and back to ergodic behavior. The patterns shown in the shading give an indication of how the density of GNP values vary with changing G. Where the shading is dark, the density is larger and where it is light, the density is smaller.

Period II shows a strikingly different pattern of response. Throughout most of

Figure 4. Comparative Dynamics on Government Expenditure (or Autonomous Investment and Consumption).

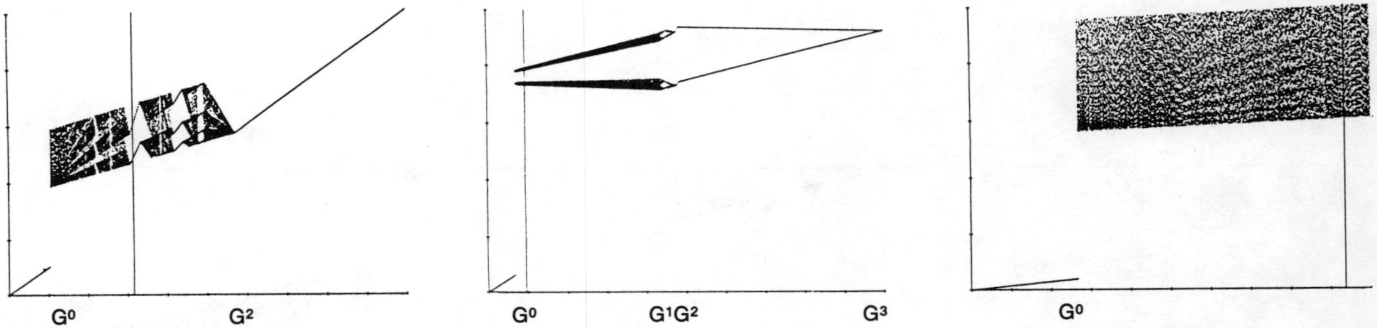

(a) I: 1930–34

(b) II: 1961–65

(c) III: 1975–78

130

Figure 5. **Comparative Dynamics on the Tax Rate (or the Marginal Propensity to Consume).**

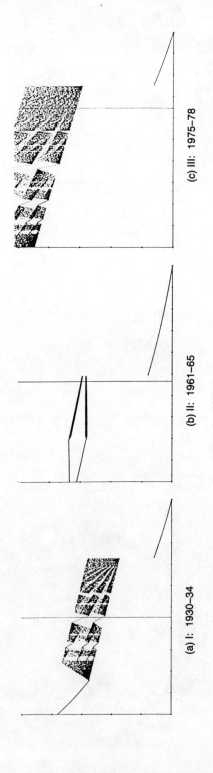

(a) I: 1930–34

(b) II: 1961–65

(c) III: 1975–78

the expenditure range, a fluctuation with two-period turning points occurs. Between G^0 and G^1, this cycle has a random amplitude, whereas, from G^2 to G^3, behavior is strictly periodic. Notice that the amplitude of the cycle increases from G^0 through G^2 and decreases to G^3, where a stationary state emerges. Notice also that in the short interval (G^1, G^2), four and probably higher order cycles exist, although these are not easily seen because of the scale.

Period III displays GNP values which beyond G^0 distribute themselves throughout an interval which changes very little with further changes in expenditure. Except for extremely low expenditure levels where a very high unemployment stationary state prevails, fluctuations are influenced only in the details of their frequency distribution.

Next, consider tax policy. The bifurcation diagrams for the three examples are shown in Figure 5. As before, each diagram is strikingly different. In Period I, the complex change in the qualitative behavior of GNP in response to increases or decreases in the tax rate are evident. In Period II, a small increase in the tax rate could have caused a drastic, discontinuous fall in GNP. Decreases in the tax rate would have had only a gradual impact on average GNP, with slowly growing then declining fluctuation amplitudes. In Period III, the qualitative effect of tax rate changes is more like that in Period I.

In Figure 6, the three bifurcation diagrams are given for changes in the money supply. Again, the qualitative influence of policy change is strikingly different in the three examples.

The vertical line gives the money supply used in the base period siumlation.

Qualitative Dynamics

In order to get a better understanding of the complex macroeconomic response to policy changes, a closer look at the relationship between the qualitative behavior of GNP and the parameters of demand is needed. For this purpose, six parameter sets will be used that represent widely varying estimates reported in the literature. These parameters are described in the Appendix at the end of the chapter. All lie within the ranges of values discussed in the literature.

The aggregate demand functions are shown in Figure 7. For Cases 1 through 5, there is a single stationary state, while for Case 6, there are three. In Cases 1 and 2, when $\mu = .25$, the stationary state is stable. In Cases 3 through 5, however, it is unstable, and in Case 6, the smallest one is stable, but the other two are unstable. This is seen in column 4 of Table 1 of the Appendix which gives $c = \Theta'(Y^m)$, where Y^m is the largest stationary state.

If the parameters are those of examples 1 and 2, then irregular fluctuations could be propagated only in the presence of exogenous, random shocks. This is the situation usually assumed by macroeconomists to hold in the real world. In examples 3 through 6, the situation is different: fluctuations persist because

132

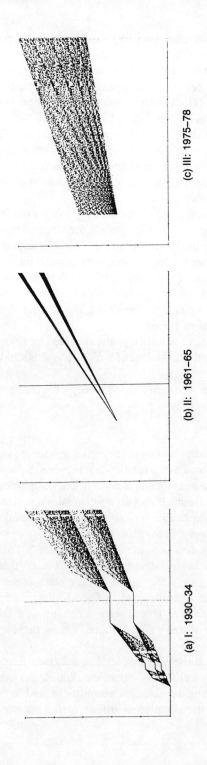

Figure 6. **Comparative Dynamics on the Money Supply.**

(a) I: 1930–34

(b) II: 1961–65

(c) III: 1975–78

Figure 7. **Aggregate Demand for Alternative Values of** α **and** μ.

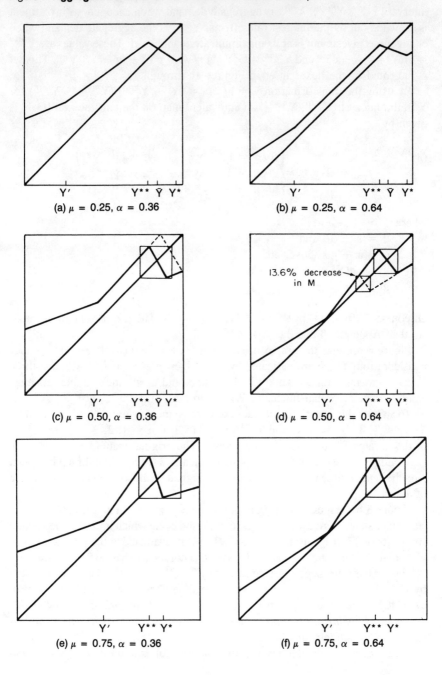

(a) $\mu = 0.25,\ \alpha = 0.36$

(b) $\mu = 0.25,\ \alpha = 0.64$

(c) $\mu = 0.50,\ \alpha = 0.36$

(d) $\mu = 0.50,\ \alpha = 0.64$

(e) $\mu = 0.75,\ \alpha = 0.36$

(f) $\mu = 0.75,\ \alpha = 0.64$

Y^m is unstable. All trajectories must lead into a trapping set. This set is the interval $[Y^{min}, Y^{max}]$. Y^{min} is aggregate demand when endogenous investment is crowded out by the interest rate effects. Y^{max} is the aggregate demand when endogenous investment is at its maximum attainable level. These values are $Y^{min} = \Theta(Y^*) = A + aY^*$ and $Y^{max} = \Theta(Y^{**}) = A - \beta Y' + (a + \mu\beta)Y^{**}$. This set is indicated by the boxes inset in Figures 1c through 1f.

By using the transformation $y = g(Y)$: $= (Y - Y^{min})/(Y^{max} - Y^{min})$ for Y in the interval $[Y^{min}, Y^{max}]$, an equivalent map on the unit interval $[O,1]$ is given by

(8)
$$y_{t+1} = T(y_t): = \begin{cases} f(y): = 1 - by^{**} + by, & y \in [0, y^{**}] \\ g(y): = 1 + xy^{**} - cy, & y \in [y^{**}, y^*] \\ h(y): = - ay^* + ay, & y \in [y^*, 1] \end{cases}$$

where $a = (1 - \tau)\alpha$
  $b = a + \mu\beta$ and
  $c = a + \mu\sigma$ above, and
  $y^* = g(Y^*) = y^{**} + 1/c$
  $g(y^{**}) = y^{**}$.

Of course, $T(0) = 1 - by^{**}$ and $T(1) = a(1 - y^*)$. The parameters are summarized in Appendix Table 3.

Figure 8 presents the graphs of equation (8) for the unstable examples under consideration. These are indicated by solid lines in each figure. All have three linear segments with the same tilted-z shape, and as all are unstable, all must exhibit trajectories that fluctuate. Where do these trajectories go?

To answer this question, consider the iterated maps where $T^n(y)$ is defined by $T^0(y) \equiv y$, $T^1(y) \equiv T(y)$ and $T^{n+1}(y) = T(T^n(y)$, $n = 1, 2, 3, \ldots$ In Figure 8, the iterates T^n, $n = 1, 2, 4$ are shown. The original map $T^1 = T$ has three segments. Successive maps have more segments as if the original map had been stretched, then folded to give a sequence of jagged teeth, somewhat like the blade of a saw.

Figure 8 corresponds with example 3 when $\sigma = .36$. In addition to Y^m, the stationary state, there exists a unique two-period cycle which is determined by the fix points of T^2. It is unstable because $dT^2(y)/dy$ evaluated at the periodic points y^{m21} and y^{m22} is $-bc = -1.86$. T^3 (which is not shown) has no fix points except y^m, but T^4 has four fix points in addition to y^m, y^{m21} and y^{m22}. These are denoted by y^{m4i}, $i = 1, \ldots 4$, which are stable because $dT^4(y)/dy = -\alpha b^2 c \sim -.70$ evaluated at the periodic points y^{m4i}, $i = 1, \ldots 4$. *In a world described by this example, a regular predictable four-period business cycle would emerge unless perturbed by random shocks.*

Figure 8b shows the iterates one, two and four for example 4 when $\mu = .5$ and

Figure 8. **Successive Iterated Maps on the Trapping Set.**

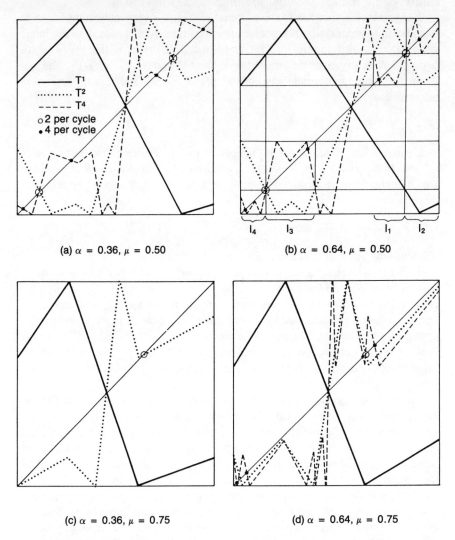

(a) $\alpha = 0.36$, $\mu = 0.50$

(b) $\alpha = 0.64$, $\mu = 0.50$

(c) $\alpha = 0.36$, $\mu = 0.75$

(d) $\alpha = 0.64$, $\mu = 0.75$

a = .64. The second iterate, like that for example 3, has an unstable two-period cycle. But now T^4 has become steeper, not flatter, which also possesses four additional fix points. Indeed, T^4 is *expansive* over the entire interval [0,1], that is, its derivative, wherever it is defined, is greater than unity in absolute value. Such maps generate nonperiodic, or chaotic, trajectories that can be characterized by probability functions or cumulative distributions (Day and Shafer 1985, 1987). Although cycles of every order 4n, n = 1, 2, 3. . . exist, *they are unstable and irregular fluctuations emerge for almost all initial conditions, i.e., with probability one for initial conditions drawn at random from [0,1].*

A closer look at the map T^4 shows that it possesses a very interesting property in addition to expansivity. It possesses four invariant sets indicated by the intervals I^i, $i = 1, \ldots 4$ in Figure 8b. This means that $T^4(I^i) = I^i$, so that every fourth period, a trajectory visits the same invariant set. Moreover, $I^{i+1} = T(I^i)$. The sets I^i can, therefore, appropriately be called "periodic sets" and have the following interpretation. If

(9) $y_t \in I^i$ then $y_{t+j} \in I^{(i+j) \, mod \, 4}$, $j = 1, 2, \ldots$

Examples 5 and 6 are shown in Figures 8c and 8d. The first of these possesses a stable two-period cycle, while the second possess stable periodic sets within which fluctuations are erratic, as in example 4. If I^i, $i = 1, 2$ are the periodic sets, then if

(10) $y_t \in I^i$ then $y_{t+j} \in I^{(i+j) \, mod \, 2}$, $j = 1, 2, \ldots$

has the same stochastic-like character noted for example 4.

To put it another way, examples 4 and 6 reveal a kind of periodic fluctuation with more-or-less random amplitudes, but where the latter are confined to well-defined, predictable sets. The amplitudes are not random in the usual stochastic sense that they are determined by random shocks, but rather in the sense that for predictions farther and farther into the future, calculations based on the known, immediate past value become more and more hazardous; tiny errors due to round-off are amplified explosively so that exact prediction is possible only in the set-valued sense.

Although it is extremely difficult to derive analytical expressions for the density functions characterizing the ergodic property exhibited by examples 4 and 6, they can be approximated by computation. In Figure 9 the numerical histograms for the examples 3 through 6 are shown based on 10,000 iterates of equation (8). In the stable periodic Cases 3 and 5, all of the density is piled up on the intervals containing the periodic points; whereas for examples 4 and 6, contrastingly, the density is distributed throughout the invariant periodic sets. Within these sets, GNP has a nonperiodic character, wandering close to periodic cycles of various orders but always wandering away from them in an unpredictable way. Of course, random shocks which allow impulses of sufficiently large magnitude would upset even this degree of predictability.

Comparative Policy Dynamics II:
Policy Effect Reversals

Using the information from the preceeding section, it will be shown how the profile of aggregate demand is modified within the trapping set by changes in the

Figure 9. **Density Distributions for Trajectories in Cases 3–6.**

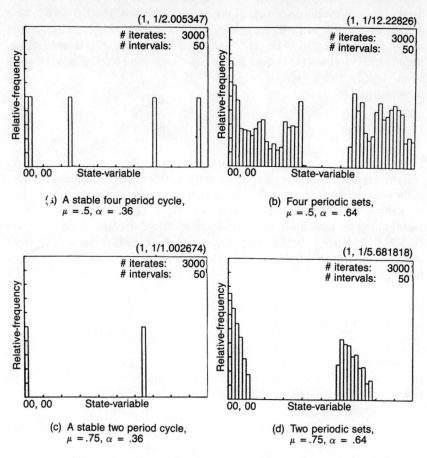

(a) A stable four period cycle,
$\mu = .5$, $\alpha = .36$

(b) Four periodic sets,
$\mu = .5$, $\alpha = .64$

(c) A stable two period cycle,
$\mu = .75$, $\alpha = .36$

(d) Two periodic sets,
$\mu = .75$, $\alpha = .64$

policy instruments. The four unstable cases of the preceeding section will be used as examples. First, consider monetary policy as represented by an exogenous change in the money supply M. In order for aggregate demand to have the tilted-z shape shown in Figure 8, it can be shown that the following expression must hold:

$$(11) \qquad Y^{min} < Y^{**} < Y^* < Y^{max}.$$

Let Δ_m indicate the change in the variable it precedes caused by a change in the money supply, which we denote ΔM. Then it is easy to see

$$(12) \qquad \begin{aligned} \Delta_m Y^{min} &= a\eta\Delta M \\ \Delta_m Y^{**} &= (1/k)\Delta M \\ \Delta_m Y^* &= \eta\Delta M \\ \Delta_m Y^{max} &= (b/k)\Delta M \end{aligned}$$

where $\eta = k\mu/(\lambda\sigma)$ and $b = a + \mu\beta$ as before. The parameters Y', a, b, and c are unaffected. As noted in section 2, a change in the money supply involves a parallel shift in the third segment of the aggregate demand function in (7), now defined in the interval $[Y^{**} + \Delta_m Y^{**}, Y^* + \Delta\sigma_m Y^*]$. This corresponds to a shift in the segment $g(y) = 1 + c^{**} - cy$ when the trapping set is transformed to the unit interval. For (11) to hold for the new money supply $M + \Delta M$, we must have

$$(13) \qquad \begin{aligned} Y^{min} + \alpha\eta\Delta M &< Y^{**} + k^{-1}\Delta M \\ &< Y^* + \eta\Delta M < Y^{max} + bk^{-1}\Delta M. \end{aligned}$$

For any ΔM satisfying this set of inequalities, the qualitative dynamics described in the previous section are unchanged. Of course, the exact amplitudes of the periodic cycle in example 3 or the range of amplitudes in the periodic sets of example 4 will be modified so that monetary policy can have the effect of exacerbating or attenuating the business cycle. More interesting, however, are changes that violate (13). If the last inequality on the right is reversed or replaced by an equality, the tilted-z shape gives way to single-peaked shape determined by two regimes:

$$(14) \qquad y_{t+1} = T_1(y_t): = \begin{cases} f(y_t): = 1 - by^{**} - by_t, \ y_t \in [0, y^{**}] \\ g(y_t): = 1 + cy^{**} - cy_t, \ y_t \in [y^{**}, 1] \end{cases}$$

where $y^{**} = 1 - 1/c$. Note that if b and c are greater than unity, T_1 is expansive. On the other hand, if the left-most inequality in (13) is reversed or changed to an equality, then the tilted-z gives way to a "check mark" shape defined by

$$(15) \qquad y_{t+2} = T_2(y_t): = \begin{cases} g(y_t): = 1 - cy_t, \qquad y_t \in [0, y^*] \\ h(y): = -ay^* + ay_t, \ y_t \in [y^*, 1] \end{cases}$$

where $y^* = 1/c$. Because $0 < a < 1$, T_2 is not expansive. It is easy to show that if $a^k c > 1$ for some k, then there may exist an expansive map of order k. If $ac < 1$, then no iterate is expansive. (See Day and Shafer, 1987). For the switch from (8) to (14) to occur, set

$$(16) \qquad \Delta M = (Y^{max} - Y^*)/(\eta - bk^{-1}).$$

If $\eta > 0$, a sufficient *increase* in the money supply will cause the switch, while if $\eta < bk^{-1}$, a sufficient *decrease* will cause the switch. (Of course, if $\eta = bk^{-1}$, monetary policy cannot bring about the switch in question.) In either of these cases, a large enough change in M shifts aggregate demand from a nonexpansive tilted-z form to an expansive, single-peak form, given that both b and c are greater than unity as they are for examples 3 and 4. *The effect of such policy changes is, therefore, to trigger the economy from a stable cycle (examples 3 and 5) or a set periodic chaos (examples 4 and 6) to a chaotic behavior in which nonperiodic, and more or less random fluctuations in amplitudes are spread throughtout the entire trapping set.* In the former, there is perfect predictability and in the latter the set, predictability is lost.[3]

In example 3, an *increase* in the money supply of 6.6% is sufficient to cause the destabilizing switch from a stable four-period cycle to turbulent fluctuations. In example 4 where we have set periodicity, the switch occurs for a *decrease* in the money supply of at least 13.6%.[4] Figure 10 shows the new empirical density functions (histograms) for these two examples. Panels a and b correspond to panels 9a and 9b, respectively. Changes in a policy instrument can eliminate, or at least reduce, chaos in the sense of reduced variance of GNP, as can be seen by beginning with these new situations and then changing the money supply. But again, changes in control which are opposite in sign are required to have this stabilizing effect given the difference in parameter values.

With regard to fiscal policy, changes in government expenditure cause changes in A.

$$(17) \qquad \begin{aligned} \Delta_g Y^{min} &= Y^{min} + \Delta G \\ \Delta_g Y^{**} &= 0 \\ \Delta_g Y &= 0 \\ \Delta_g Y^{max} &= Y^{max} + \Delta G. \end{aligned}$$

Using these in the inequality expression (11) in a way analogous to the discussion of changes in M, increases in government expenditures such that

$$(18) \qquad \Delta G \geq Y^{**} - Y^{min}$$

switch the economy to the T_2 type (Equation 15), while decreases such that

$$(19) \qquad \Delta G \leq Y^* - Y^{max}$$

switch it to T_1 (Equation 14). When the economy is periodic as in Case 3, increases in expenditure satisfying (18) simply reduce the amplitudes of the periodic cycle, while decreases satisfying (19) bring about ergodic, strictly turbulent fluctuations.

When the economy is originally set periodic, as in example 4, periodic chaos is changed to turbulent, nonperiodic fluctuations by decreases satisfying (19), while increases satisfying (18) can cause either periodic cycles or chaotic

Figure 10. **Density Distributions Induced by Changes in the Money Supply.**
(panel a compares with Figure 3a, panel b with Figure 3b)

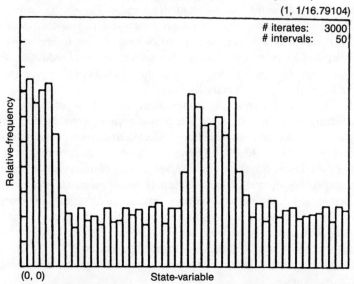

(a) Distribution of GNP values induced from a stable four period cycle by an *increase* in the money supply (Case 3).

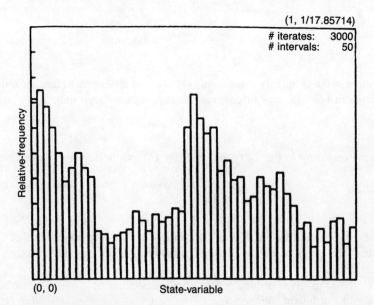

(b) Distribution of GNP values induced from a stable set-periodic cycle by a *decrease* in the money supply (Case 4).

behavior depending on the values of a and c.

Recall that α is the marginal propensity to consume unadjusted for the average income tax, i.e., $a = (1 - \tau)\alpha$. A change in the tax rate in amount $\Delta\tau$ induces a change in the adjusted marginal propensity to consume of $-\alpha\Delta\tau$. Therefore,

(20)
$$Y^{min} = (1 - \alpha\Delta\tau)Y^*$$
$$Y^* = 0$$
$$Y^{**} = 0$$
$$Y^{max} = (1 - \alpha\Delta\tau)Y^{**}.$$

Now changes in the tax rate can cause switches in the qualitative dynamics, perhaps pushing the economy into or out of a chaotic, set periodic, or strictly turbulent regime. The possibilities in the several examples can readily be derived in a manner exactly analogous to the discussion of monetary or expenditure policy.

* * *

Although the calculations have been tedious, some striking new insights have emerged:

(1) Policy changes can trigger drastically different patterns of reponse depending on their pre-existing levels and their direction.

(2) A policy may have no effect for small changes and then, after a higher or lower threshold is reached, trigger great changes in behavior.

(3) Changes in autonomous expenditure, prices, and capital accumulation must bring with them great changes in the qualitative response of GNP to policy changes, even when all the other parameters are fixed.

(4) Complex dynamics occur for a wide range of behavioral parameter and instrumental variable values.

Evidently, policymakers may have even more to contend with in attempting to guide an economy than has already been recognized by macroeconomists. Comparative policy analysis may need to be concerned not just with the effects of monetary and fiscal parameters on the long-run level of output and employment. It may also need to recognize the potential ability of policy changes to shift output adjustments into cyclical or nonperiodic fluctuations, or contrastingly, to stabilize such instabilities when they emerge. It may also need to recognize the disconcerting possibility that the direction of influence on the economy of a given policy instrument under one set of conditions may be in the opposite direction under another set of conditions.

A better understanding of these possibilities in more general dynamic models where some of the restrictive assumptions of the present one have been relaxed would seem to be an important priority for further research.

There are still many questions with incomplete answers. Does the economy possess a structure that can be unstable when prices adjust to excess supplies and demands, when capital accumulates, and when consumption and investment decisions respond over a considerable period of time to unfolding and anticipated conditions? Can this instability be moderated by appropriate fiscal and monetary policies? Answering these questions is what macroeconomics is all about. It is an unfinished task. Hopefully, the potential importance of nonlinear structural relationships as a source of macroeconomic trouble has been demonstrated here, a source relatively neglected in the years that have intervened since Hick's, Goodwin's, and Kaldor's seminal contributions to the subject.

Appendix

Hall (1977) estimated the adjusted marginal propensity to consume to be a = .36. Some discussants argued for a still lower value, but several others, notably Gramlich and Klein, suggested a much higher value. (Hall, 121.) Branson (1979) gives a value of .72, while Morley (1983, 67) gives a value of .65. Both of these imply a negative value for autonomous consumption in 1977, the year for which Hall's data were calculated. For a = .64, this is not a problem, so we use that value.

For the investment function, Hall estimated the base values $\alpha = 1.36$ and $\gamma = 83.8$. He considered alternative values representing possible fractions of complete adjustment possible within a given year as derived from Jorgensonian investment considerations. This is similar in the present context to a choice of values of μ between zero and one. Hall presented evidence for a value of $\mu = .25$. Gramlich and Klein, however, (op cit., p. 121) suggested a much higher value. We shall use .50 and .75 to represent this alternative view. Klein asserted (see Hall, op. cit., p. 121) that it was an econometrically established fact that the marginal effect of income on aggregate demand, which in our notation would be a $+ \mu\beta$, was roughly 1.5. Given a = .36 and $\beta = 1.36$, then $\mu \sim .84$. Or, using a = .64, $\mu \sim .63$. Thus, the figure of .5 is moderate and the value .75 is not extreme. Sims' argument (Hall, op. cit., p. 105) for a positively sloped IS curve is, in effect, also an argument for a large value for μ. The parameters describing marginal effects are completed by the demand for money which Hall estimated to be k = .135 and $\lambda = 2.0$. These possibly proved to be the most controversial of all. Modigliani, for example, argued for parameter values many times lower (op. cit., p. 111) and Goldfeld suggested lower values too, though not by so exaggerated an amount (op. cit., p. 119). In the present piece-wise linear version of the standard model, these parameters enter aggregate demand only in the interest sensitive regime, but this regime will be badly represented if data for only a narrow range of interest rates were available. (For a discussion of this point see Day and Lin).

Although Hall addressed what are essentially dynamic issues, he used a traditional, comparative static analysis based on local linearity in the neighborhood of the Keynesian disequilibrium which he assumed was stable. For these reasons he only had to consider marginal effects of policy variables. But (7) need not be stable. In order to obtain its solutions, we have to estimate the threshold or "kink" parameter Y', Y**,

Table 1

Marginal Income Effects for Alternative Values of a and μ

Case	(1) a	(2) μ	(3) b = a + $\mu\beta$	(4) c = a + $\mu\sigma$
1	.36	.25	.70	.71
2	.64	.25	.98	.43
3	.36	.50	1.04	1.79
4	.64	.50	1.32	1.51
5	.36	.75	1.38	2.86
6	.64	.75	1.66	2.58

Table 2

Level Parameters for Alternative Values of a and μ

Case	C^0	A	Y'	Y**	Y*	Y^{max}	Y^{min}
1	379	661	424	1276	1545	1410	1218
2	0	282	424	1276	1545	1388	1273
3	379	661	733	1276	1447	1489	1183
4	0	282	733	1276	1447	1467	1209
5	379	661	836	1276	1415	1569	1170
6	0	282	836	1276	1415	1547	1187

Table 3

Parameters of the Transformed Map*

	b	c	a	Y**	Y*	T(0)	T(1)
Case 3	1.04	1.79	.36	.304	.863	.684	.047
Case 4	1.32	1.51	.64	.260	.922	.657	.045
Case 5	1.38	2.86	.36	.266	.615	.633	.139
Case 6	1.66	2.58	.64	.247	.634	.590	.235

*The parameter of aggregate demand for the four unstable cases are transformed to the unit interval.

and Y* because of its non-linearity. To do this we must estimate the "level" parameters L^0 and C^0 that enter the demand for money and demand for goods functions.

The relevant data in real terms for 1977 were Y = 1350, C = 865, I = 210, G = 282, M = 232 and r = 5%. To estimate C^0, we use equation (6). Then A = C^0 + G. To estimate L^0, assume we are not in the liquidity trap, so L^0 = M + λr − kY. From (4), I^0 = − βY' = I − βY + π. Dividing by − β gives Y'. From Y** = (M − L^0)/k and using (4), we get Y* = [(τ k/λ)Y** − βY ']/σ.

The resulting parameters are shown in Tables 1 and 2.

Notes

1. When income exceeds M/k, the model breaks down. A switch in regime would be necessary then to explain how changes in the price level, the transaction velocity, or the money supply take place so as to permit continued functioning of the system. In this study, attention is confined to parameter values that avoid this problem.

2. If Y' is negative, then $I^0 = -\beta Y'$ is positive and can be thought of as autonomous investment. If $Y^{**} > Y'$, then investment has an interest sensitive range. For this to happen, we must have $Y^{**} = (M + \lambda r^m - L^0)/k > Y'$ or given that $r^m = 0$, $M - L^0 > kY'$. In what follows we assume that this is true.

3. Actually, changes in policy instruments can lead to a breakdown in the trapping set. Then trajectories can "escape" the bounds given by Y^{min} and Y^{max} with GNP declining to the smallest stationary state. This actually happens in example 6 when we try to duplicate the comparative dynamic analysis carried out for example 4. The result is that when the money supply is reduced sufficiently, fluctuations eventually die out, and GNP declines to the smallest, stable stationary state.

4. In the latter case, increases in the money supply would simply expand the domains of the periodic sets and, hence, the range of amplitudes of the four-period, erratic fluctuations. In the former case decreases in the money supply will eventually cause a switch in regime to the inverted-peak profile. Because $\alpha c < 1$, expansivity is not induced, and the monetary effect is simply to reduce the amplitude of the strictly periodic cycle. In this sense, the economy is stabilized but at the cost of higher average unemployment and excess capacity.

References

Benhabib, J., and R. Day. 1981. "Rational Choice and Erratic Behavior." *Review of Economic Studies* 48:476-95.

————. 1982. "A Characterization of Erratic Dynamics in the Overlapping Generations Model." *Journal of Economic Dynamics and Control* 48:459-72.

Branson, W. 1979. *Macroeconomic Theory and Policy.* 2nd ed. New York: Harper and Row.

Day, R., and T.Y. Lin. 1987. "A Keynesian Business Cycle," in: E. Nell and W. Semmler (eds), N. Kaldor and Mainstream Economics, Festschrift for N. Kaldor forthcoming. London: Macmillan Press.

Day, R., and W. Shafer. 1985. "Keynesian Chaos." *Journal of Macroeconomics* 7:277-95.

————. 1987. "Ergodic Fluctuations in Deterministic Economic Models." *Advances in Dynamic Economics.* A. Medio, ed. (Special Issue). *Journal of Economic Behavior and Organization* 9.

Grandmont, J. 1985. "On Endogenous Competitive Business Cycles." *Econometrica* 53:995-1045.

Hall, R. 1977. "Investments, Interest Rates, and the Effects of Stabilization Policies." *Brookings Papers in Economic Activity* 1:61-121.

Morley, S.A. 1983. *Macroeconomics.* Chicago: The Dryden Press.

Monetary Stabilization Policy in a Keynes-Goodwin Model of the Growth Cycle

Toichiro Asada

Why do periodical alternations of booms and slumps occur in a capitalist economy? A classical answer to this question is a Marxian theory of the business cycle, which is based on the notions of industrial reserve army and class struggle.[1] According to this theory, the rate of profit is determined by the "rate of exploitation," and the latter is determined by the relative bargaining power of capitalists and workers. It may be said from the macro-economic point of view that the rate of exploitation approximates to the profit-wage ratio which reflects the relative share of profit in national income. This theory supposes that workers' bargaining power is *inversely* proportional to the rate of unemployment. That is to say, when the rate of unemployment is low, workers' bargaining power is relatively strong so that the relative wage share increases, which implies that the rate of profit decreases. The decrease of the rate of profit induces the decrease of the rate of accumulation, so that the rate of unemployment increases. An increasing rate of unemployment weakens workers' bargaining power, which implies a recovery of profitability so that accumulation is activated. Hence, according to this theory, a mechanism of an endogenous business cycle is embedded in the capitalist economy through the changes in the relative bargaining power of capital and labor.

It is well known that Goodwin (1967) formalized this Marxian business cycle idea. According to Goodwin, the above mentioned mechanism can be described by the following system of dynamical equations.

This is a revised version of the paper which was published in *The Hitotsubashi Review* 91 (3) (March 1984) in Japanese.

(i) $\qquad \dot{Z}/Z = f_1(E); f_1' > 0, f_1(E^*) = 0, 0 < E^* < 1$

(ii) $\qquad \dot{E}/E = f_2(Z); f_2' < 0, f_2(Z^*) = 0, 0 < Z^* < 1$

where E is the rate of employment (1 minus the rate of unemployment), and Z is the relative wage share in national income. Formally, this is equivalent to the famous Volterra-Lotka system of "predator and prey" in mathematical biology, and the solution curves of this system become closed orbits around the equilibrium point as in Figure 1.[2]

Although Goodwin's formulation is quite exciting and useful, his original model is insufficient to incorporate some characteristics of modern capitalist economies, because it has some classical or anti-Keynesian flavors.

First, this model neglects the presence of the government sector. Second, it *presupposes* the full utilization of the capital stock, so that it excludes by assumption the Keynesian unemployment due to insufficient effective demand. Third, the existence of the investment function—which is independent of the saving function—is not allowed for. Fourth, money and financial assets are not incorporated into the model explicitly.

In this chapter, we explicitly incorporate the monetary sector and a Keynesian investment function into Goodwin's growth cycle model, and investigate the implications of the government's monetary stabilization policy. This modification adds some Keynesian flavors to Goodwin's classical model, so that the model may be called the Keynes-Goodwin model of the growth cycle.[3]

The Model

The simplifying assumptions of the model are:
1. It is a one sector model.
2. Capital depreciation is neglected.
3. Economic agents are divided into two classes, i.e., capitalists and workers. Workers spend all of their disposable income, and capitalists save a part of their disposable income.
4. The goods market and money market are always cleared.
5. The population of workers and labor productivity grow exponentially at the exogenously given rates. The output-capital ratio in the case of full capacity utilization of capital is constant.[4]

The variables in the model are defined as follows:

X = real output.
K = real capital stock.
I = real investment demand.
G = real government expenditure.
$g \equiv \dot{K}/K$ = rate of capital accumulation.

Figure 1

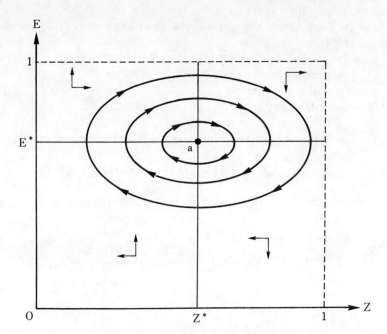

δ = capacity utilization ratio of capital stock $(0 \leq \delta \leq 1)$.

L = labor employment.

L^s = labor supply.

$n_1 \equiv \dot{L}^s/L^s \equiv$ constant = growth rate of workers' population.

$E \equiv L/L^s$ = rate of employment $\equiv 1 -$ rate of unemployment $(0 \leq E \leq 1)$.

w = money wage rate.

p = price level.

$\omega \equiv w/p$ = real wage rate.

$\pi \equiv \dot{p}/p$ = rate of price inflation.

π^e = expected rate of price inflation.

$\delta\bar{x} \equiv X/K$ = output-capital ratio $(\bar{x} \equiv$ constant = output-capital ratio in case of full capacity utilization of captial).

$\delta v \equiv L/K$ = labor-capital ratio $(v$ = labor-capital ratio in case of full capacity utilization of capital).

$\ell \equiv L/K \equiv v/\bar{x}$ = labor-output ratio (reciprocal of labor productivity).

$n_2 \equiv -\dot{\ell}/\ell \equiv$ constant = rate of technical progress.

t_w = average tax rate on wage income.

t_r = average tax rate on profit income $(0 \leq t_w \leq t_r < 1)$.

s_r = capitalists' average propensity to save $(0 < s_r \leq 1)$.

$Z \equiv w L / p X \equiv \omega\ell$ = relative share of pre-tax wage in national income $(0 \leq Z \leq 1)$.

$Z_n \equiv (1-t_w) \, w \, L \, / \, p \, X \equiv (1-t_w) \, \omega\ell$ = relative share of after-tax wage in national income ($0 \le Z_n \le 1-t_w$).

$r \equiv (p \, X - w \, L) \, / \, p \, K \equiv \delta(\bar{x} - \omega v) \equiv \delta\bar{x} \, (1 - \omega\ell) \equiv \delta\bar{x} \, (1-Z)$ = pre-tax rate of profit.

$r_n \equiv (1-t_r) \, (pX - wL) \, / \, pK \equiv (1-t_r) \, \delta\bar{x} \, (1-Z) \equiv (1-t_r) \, \delta\bar{x} \, \{1 - Z_n / (1-t_w)\}$ = after-tax rate of profit.[5]

ϱ = nominal rate of interest.

M = nominal money supply.

The equilibrium condition for the goods market is expressed as follows:

(*) $X = (1-t_w) \, \omega L + (1-s_r) \, (1-t_r) \, (X - \omega L) + I + G$

Dividing both sides of this equation by K and rearranging terms, we have

(**)
$$\delta\bar{x} \, [1 - (1-s_r)(1-t_r) - \frac{s_r(1-t_r) + (t_r - t_w)}{1-t_w} \, Z_n]$$

$$= g + h; \; g \equiv I/K, \; h \equiv G/K.[6]$$

Now, assume the following investment function, which can be derived from Tobin's version of Keynesian investment function (the so called "q theory" of investment).[7]

(***) $g = g(r_n, \varrho - \pi^e); \; g_1 \equiv \partial g / \partial r_n > 0, \; g_2 \equiv \partial g / \partial (\varrho - \pi^e) < 0$

Substituting this equation into eq. (**), we have the following IS equation:

(1)
$$\delta\bar{x}[1 - (1-s_r) \, (1-t_r) - \frac{s_r(1-t_r) + (t_r - t_w)}{1-t_w} \, Z_n]$$

$$= g(\delta\bar{x} \, (1-t_r) \, (1 - \frac{1}{1-t_w} \, Z_n), \, \varrho - \pi^e) + h$$

Next, the equilibrium condition for the money market (LM equation) may be formulated as

(****) $M/p = X \cdot \phi(\varrho, \pi^e); \; \phi_1 \equiv \partial\phi / \partial p < o, \; \phi_2 \equiv \partial\phi / \partial\pi^e \le 0,$

where $\phi(\varrho, \pi^e)$ is the "Marshallian k" (the reciprocal of the velocity of circulation of money). Dividing both sides of equation (****) by K, we have

(2) $$m = \delta\bar{x}\,\phi(\varrho, \pi^e);\ m = M/(pK).$$

The other basic equations in our model are as follows:

(3) $$\dot{w}/w = f(E) + \pi^e;\ f'(E) > 0$$

(4) $$E \equiv L/L^s \equiv \delta\ell\bar{x}K/L^s$$

(5) $$Z_n \equiv (1 - t_w)wL/pX \equiv (1-t_w)w\,\ell/p$$

(6) $$\pi \equiv \dot{p}/p$$

(7) $$g(\delta\bar{x}(1-t_r)\,(1 - \frac{1}{1-t_w}\,Z_n),\ \varrho-\pi^e) = \dot{K}/K$$

(8) $$\dot{L}^s/L^s = n_1;\ n_1 \equiv \text{constant}.$$

(9) $$\dot{\ell}/\ell = -n_2;\ n_2 \equiv \text{constant}.$$

Equation (3) is an "expectation-augumented" Phillips curve. This equation says that workers' bargaining power reflects the rate of employment.

Equations (4) through (6) are the definitions of the rate of employment, after-tax wage share, and the rate of price inflation, respectively. Equation (7) implies that the investment contributes to the increase of capital stock. Equations (8) and (9) say that the rates of increase of the labor force and labor productivity are given exogenously.

Thus, there are nine independent equations and twelve endogenous variables $(E, Z_n, p, w, \pi, \pi_e, \varrho, K, L^s, \ell, \delta$ and $M)$. Therefore, "three degrees of freedom" remain in this system.

Goodwin-type Growth Cycle

If we close the system by adding the following set of equations, the system bears a Goodwin-type growth cycle.

(10) $$\delta = 1$$

(11)
$$\pi^e = \pi$$

(12)
$$\dot{M}/M = \mu + \alpha(\varrho - \bar{\varrho}); \; \alpha \geq 0$$

Equation (10) implies that the full capacity utilization of capital stock is always attained. Equation (11) is the so called perfect myopic foresight hypothesis of inflation expectation. It says that "every current price rate of change is known with certainty" (Burmeister 1980, 85). Equation (12) formalized the government's monetary policy rule. The rule with $\alpha = 0$ is called a monetarist rule which fixes the rate of growth of the money supply. The rule with $\alpha > 0$ is called an activist or Keynesian rule which subcribes to change the rate of growth of the money supply proportionally to the change of the nominal rate of interest.

Equations (1) through (12) can be reduced to the following more compact system,

(13)   (i) $H(Z_n) = \tilde{g}(Z_n, \varrho - \pi) + h$

          (ii) $m = \bar{x}\phi(\varrho, \pi)$

          (iii) $\dot{m}/m = \mu + \alpha(\varrho - \bar{\varrho}) - \pi - \tilde{g}(Z_n, \varrho - \pi)$

          (iv) $\dot{Z}_n/Z_n = \dot{w}/w - \pi - n_2 = f(E) - n_2$

          (v) $\dot{E}/E = \tilde{g}(Z_n, \varrho - \pi) - (n_1 + n_2)$

where $H(Z_n) \equiv \bar{x} [1 - (1 - s_r)(1 - t_r) - \{s_r(1 - t_r) + (t_r - t_w)\} Z_n/(1 - t_w)]$, $\tilde{g}(Z_n, \varrho - \pi) \equiv g(\bar{x}(1 - t_r) \{1 - Z_n/(1 - t_w)\}, \varrho - \pi)$ and the endogenous variables of this system are Z_n, E, m, ϱ and π.

The classical nature of this system is evident. In the short-run, Z_n, E and m are given, and the short-run equilibrium values of ϱ and π are determined by equations (13) (i) and (13) (ii). It follows from equation (13) (i) that if Z_n is given, the level of the rate of investment (g) which assures the full capacity utilization of capital stock is determined uniquely, and this investment level is attained by the adjustment of the real rate of interest ($\varrho - \pi$). In other words, the real rate of interest is determined in the goods market independently of the money market. This is a fundamental feature of the classical macro model. Furthermore, the postulate of classical dichotomy applies to this system. Namely, in this system, the movements of main real variables are determined independently of the money market. Now, let us prove this assertion.

First, solving equation (13) (i) with respect to $\varrho - \pi$, we have

(14) $\varrho - \pi = \Phi(Z_n); \; \Phi'(Z_n) = \{H'(Z_n) - \tilde{g}_1\}/\tilde{g}_2,$
$$\begin{matrix} & (-) & \quad (-) \; (-) \end{matrix}$$

where $\tilde{g}_1 \equiv \partial\tilde{g}/\partial Z_n$ and $\tilde{g}_2 \equiv \partial\tilde{g}/\partial\,(\varrho-\pi)$. If the sensitivity of investment with respect to the change of the rate of profit is so small that $|\,g_1\,|$ is small enough, then we have $\Phi'\,(Z_n) > 0$. From this point, we shall assume that $\Phi'\,(Z_n) > 0$.

Substituting equation (14) into equation (13) (ii), we obtain

(15) $$m = \bar{x}\phi[\Phi(Z_n)+\pi,\ \pi].$$

Solving this equation with respect to π, we have

(16) $$\pi = \pi(Z_n, m);\ \pi_1 \equiv \partial\pi/\partial Z_n = -\ \phi_1\Phi'/(\phi_1 + \phi_2) < 0,$$
$$\pi_2 \equiv \partial\pi/\partial m = 1/\bar{x}(\phi_1 + \phi_2) < 0.$$

From equations (14) and (16) we also obtain

(17) $$\varrho = \Phi\,(Z_n) + \pi\,(Z_n, m) \equiv \varrho\,(Z_n, m);$$
$$\varrho_1 \equiv \partial\varrho/\partial Z_n = \phi' + \pi_1 = \phi_2\phi'/(\phi_1 + \phi_2) \geq 0,$$
$$\varrho_2 \equiv \partial\varrho/\partial m = \pi_2 < 0.$$

Substituting equations (13) (i) into equation (13) (v), and substituting equations (16) and (17) into equation (13) (iii), we have the following fundamental dynamical system:

(S_A) (i) $\dot{Z}_n = \{f(E) - n_2\}\,Z_n \equiv F_1\,(Z_n, E)$

          (ii) $\dot{E} = \{H(Z_n) - (h + n_1 + n_2)\}\,E \equiv F_2(Z_n, E)$

          (iii) $\dot{m} = [\mu + \alpha\,\{\varrho(Z_n, m) - \bar{\varrho}\} - \pi\,(Z_n, m)$
                           $- H(Z_n) + h]\,m \equiv F_3\,(Z_n, m)$

It can be seen by inspection that equations (S_A) (i) and (S_A) (ii) in this system form a subsystem which is independent of equation (S_A) (iii). This feature of the system can be visualized in Figure 2. In this figure, arrows show the directions of causalities. This figure clearly shows that paths of the rate of employment and wage share are independent of the money market. Moreover, a subsystem which consists of equations (S_A) (i) and (S_A) (ii) is the same as Goodwin's (1967) growth cycle model. Hence, the working of the system can be analyzed by utilizing Goodwin's method.

First, the stationary solution (long-run equilibrium) of the system (S_A) (i)–(ii) is given as

(18) $$Z_n{}^* = H^{-1}(h + n_1 + n_2)\ \text{and}$$

(19) $$E^* = f^{-1}(n_2).$$

Figure 2. **Directed graph of (S$_A$).**

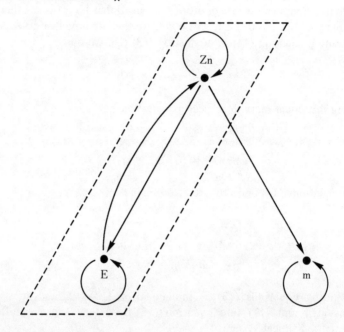

Assume that $0 < Z_n^* < 1-t_w$ and $0 < E^* < 1$. In this case, the phase diagram of the system becomes like Figure 3.

Goodwin (1967) showed that the solution curve of this system corresponding to the given initial condition $[Z_n(0), E(0)]$ becomes a closed orbit around the equilibrium point as follows.

From equations (S_A) (i) and (S_A) (ii), we have

(20)
$$dE/dZ_n = \frac{\{H(Z_n) - (h+n_1+n_2)\}E}{\{f(E)-n_2\}Z_n}$$

or

(21) $\{H(Z_n) - (h+n_1+n_2)\} (dZ_n/Z_n) = \{f(E-n_2\} (dE/E).$

Integrating this equation we obtain

(22) $\varphi(Z_n) \equiv \int \{H(Z_n)/Z_n\}dZ_n - (h+n_1+n_2) \log Z_n$
      $= \int \{f(E)/E\} dE - n_2 \log E + C \equiv \Psi(E)$

where C is the integral constant.

From this equation, it can be seen that

Figure 3

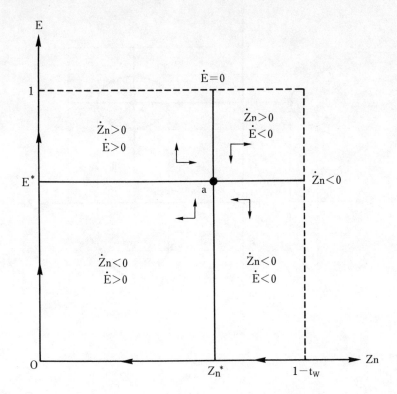

(23) $\varphi'(Z_n) = \{H(Z_n) - (h + n_1 + n_2)\}/Z_n$
$$\gtreqless 0 \leftrightarrow Z_n \lesseqgtr Z_n^*$$

and

(24) $\Psi'(E) = \{f(E) - n_n\}/E \gtreqless 0 \leftrightarrow E \gtreqless E^*.$

As Figure 4 shows the amplitude of the cycle depends on the initial condition $[Z_n(0), E(0)]$. The more remote the initial condition is from the equilibrium point, the greater is the amplitude. The time patterns of the rate of employment (E), the after-tax wage share (Z_n), and the real rate of interest ($\varrho - \pi$) in this model are illustrated in Figure 5.[8]

Now, it is evident in this model that the monetary policy of the government is ineffective in stabilizing the real variables, but, it is effective in stabilizing the monetary variables such as m, π or ϱ. Next, this assertion is proven.

The stationary solution of the system ($\dot{S}_A$) (i)–(iii) can be written as

Figure 4

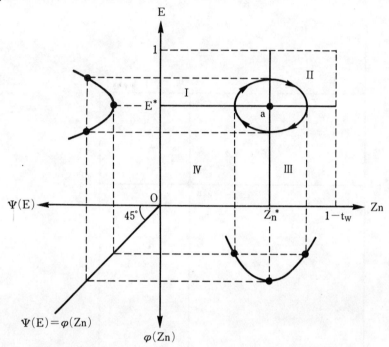

Figure 5

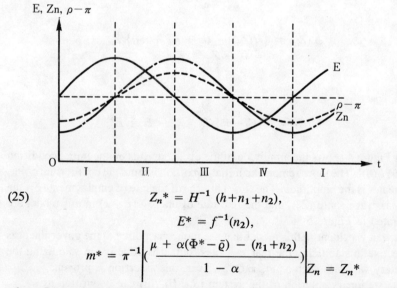

$$(25) \qquad Z_n^* = H^{-1} (h + n_1 + n_2),$$

$$E^* = f^{-1}(n_2),$$

$$m^* = \pi^{-1} \left| \left(\frac{\mu + \alpha(\Phi^* - \bar{\varrho}) - (n_1 + n_2)}{1 - \alpha} \right) \right|_{Z_n = Z_n^*}$$

where $\Phi^* \equiv \Phi(Z_n^*)$.[9] Linearizing the system (S_A) around the equilibrium point (Z_n^*, E^*, m^*), gives

$$(26) \quad \begin{bmatrix} \dot{Z}_n \\ \dot{E} \\ \dot{m} \end{bmatrix} = \begin{bmatrix} 0 & F_{12}{}^* & 0 \\ F_{21}{}^* & 0 & 0 \\ F_{31}{}^* & 0 & F_{33}{}^* \end{bmatrix} \begin{bmatrix} Z_n - Z_n{}^* \\ E - E^* \\ m - m^* \end{bmatrix}$$

where, $F_{12}{}^* \equiv f'(E^*)Z_n{}^* > 0$, $F_{21}{}^* \equiv H'(Z_n{}^*)E^* < 0$, $F_{31}{}^* \equiv [\alpha \varrho_1{}^* - \pi_1{}^*$
$$\underset{\begin{array}{c}(+ \text{ or} \\ 0 \ )\end{array}}{} \quad \underset{(-)}{}$$

$- H'(Z_n{}^*)] \, m^*$, and $F_{33}{}^* \equiv (\alpha \varrho_2{}^* - \pi_2{}^*)m^* \equiv (\alpha - 1)\pi_2{}^* \, m^*$.
$$\underset{(-)}{} \qquad\qquad \underset{(-)\;(-)}{} \qquad\qquad \underset{(-)}{}$$

The characteristic equation of this system is

$$(27) \quad \Delta(\lambda) \equiv \begin{vmatrix} \lambda & -F_{12}{}^* & 0 \\ -F_{21}{}^* & \lambda & 0 \\ -F_{31}{}^* & 0 & \lambda - F_{33}{}^* \end{vmatrix}$$

$$= \quad (\lambda - F_{33}{}^*) \; (\lambda^2 - F_{12}{}^* F_{21}{}^*) = 0.$$

Hence, the characteristic roots are

$$(28) \quad \lambda = F_{33}{}^*, \pm \sqrt{F_{12}{}^* F_{21}{}^*}$$

$$= (\alpha - 1) \, \pi_2{}^* \, m^*, \pm i \sqrt{- H'(Z_n{}^*) f'(E^*) Z_n{}^* E^*}$$
$$\underset{\quad(-)\qquad(+)}{}$$

where $i \equiv \sqrt{-1}$. Therefore, the solution of the system (26) can be expressed as follows.

$$(29) \qquad \text{(i)} \quad Z_n(t) = Z_n{}^* + B_1 \cos (\theta t + \epsilon_1)$$

$$\qquad\qquad \text{(ii)} \quad E(t) = E^* + B_2 \cos (\theta t + \epsilon_2)$$

$$\qquad\qquad \text{(iii)} \quad m(t) = m^* + A \, e^{\lambda_1 t} + B_3 \cos (\theta t + \epsilon_3)$$

where $\lambda_1 \equiv (a - 1) \, \pi_2{}^* \, m^*$ and $\theta \equiv \sqrt{-H'(Z_n{}^*) f'(E^*) Z_n{}^* E^*} > 0$.
$$\underset{(-)}{} \qquad\qquad \underset{(-)\;(+)}{}$$

In addition, the values of the constants A and B_j ($j = 1, 2, 3$) depend on the initial condition $[Z_n(0), E(0), m(0)]$.

Equation (29) can be considered to be an approximate solution of the system (S_A) near the equilibrium point. It is clear from equation (29) that if the monetarist rule of money supply ($\alpha = 0$) is adopted, $\lambda_1 > 0$, so that the movements of m get to be explosive, and in this case the rate of inflation (π) also moves explosively.[10] The government can minimize this sort of price instability by adopting an activist money supply rule. In fact, if $\alpha > 1$, the explosive factor in equation (29) (iii) vanishes. But, even in this case, the cyclical movements of monetary variables caused by the "real" factors are inevitable.

The period of the cycle (T) in equation (29) is given as

(30) $$T \equiv 2\pi/\theta = T(|H'(Z_n{}^*)|, f'(E^*), Z_n{}^*, E^*);$$
$$\partial T/\partial|H'| < 0, \ \partial T/\partial f' < 0, \ \partial T/\partial Z_n{}^* < 0, \ \partial T/\partial E^* < 0$$

where,

(31) $$|H'| = \bar{x}[s_r(1-t_r) + (t_r - t_w)]/(1-t_w).$$

Hence, the greater the senitivity of wage change with respect to the change of employment (f') and capitalists' propensity to save (s_r), the shorter is the period of the cycle.

Variable Propensity to Save

The workings of the real variables in the previous section's model are the same as those of the original Goodwin (1967) growth cycle model in spite of the fact that the monetary sector and the independent investment function are introduced. As is well known, Goodwin's growth cycle model is "structurally unstable in the sense that small variations in the parameters will alter the properties of the system" (Desai 1984, 256).[11]

In this section, this proposition is exemplified by performing a particular perturbation in the previous section's model.

Now, assume that

(32) $$s_r = s_r(\pi^e); \ s_r{}'(\pi^e) < 0$$

and keep all of the other assumptions of the model intact. Equation (32) implies that the increase of the expected rate of price inflation, (π^e), induces the increase of capitalists' propensity to consume from the present income $(1-s_r)$, since the increase of π^e implies the acceleration of the decrease of the expected purchasing power of money income.[12]

In this case, the system (13) in the previous section is modified as

(33)   (i) $H(Z_n, \pi) = \tilde{g}(Z_n, \varrho - \pi) + h$

(ii) $m = \bar{x}\phi(\varrho, \pi)$

(iii) $\dot{m}/m = \mu + \alpha(\varrho - \bar{\varrho}) - \pi - \tilde{g}(Z_n, \varrho - \pi)$

(iv) $\dot{Z}_n/Z_n = f(E) - n_2$

(v) $\dot{E}/E = \tilde{g}(Z_n, \varrho - \pi) - (n_1 + n_2),$

where

(34)
$$H(Z_n, \pi) = \bar{x} [1 - (1 - t_r) \{1 - s_r(\pi)\}$$

$$- \frac{(1 - t_r) s_r(\pi) + (t_r - t_w)}{1 - t_w} Z_n];$$

$$H_1 \equiv \partial H / \partial Z_n = - [x(1 - t_r) s_r(\pi) + (t_r - t_w)]/(1 - t_r) < 0,$$
$$H_2 \equiv \partial H / \partial \pi = - \bar{x}(1 - t_r) [1 - Z_n/(1 - t_w)] s_r'(\pi) < 0 \text{ (if } Z_n < 1 - t_w).$$

From equation (33) (ii) we have

(35)
$$\varrho = \varrho(m, \pi); \quad \varrho_1 \equiv \partial \varrho / \partial m = 1/(\bar{x} \phi_1) < 0,$$
$$\varrho_2 \equiv \partial \varrho / \partial \pi = - \phi_2/\phi_1 \leq 0.$$

Substituting this equation into equation (33) (i), we have

(36)
$$H(Z_n, \pi) = \tilde{g}[Z_n, \varrho(m, \pi) - \pi] + h.$$

Solving this equation with respect to π, we obtain

(37)
$$\pi = \pi(Z_n, m); \quad \pi_1 \equiv \partial \pi / \partial Z_n = (H_1 - \tilde{g}_1)/[g_2(\varrho_1 - 1) - H_1],$$
$$ (-) \ (-) \ \ (-) \ (-) \ \ \ \ (-)$$

$$\pi_2 \equiv \partial \pi / \partial m = \tilde{g}_2 \varrho_1 / [H_2 + \tilde{g}_2(1 - \varrho_2)] < 0.$$
$$ (-) \ (-) (-) \ \ (-) \ \ \ (-)$$

Again in this case, $\pi_1 < 0$ if the sensitivity of the investment with respect to the rate of profit $|\tilde{g}_1|$ is relatively small. From now on, we shall assume that $\pi_1 < 0$.

Substituting equation (37) into equation (35), we obtain

(38)
$$\varrho = \varrho(m, \pi(Z_n, m)) \equiv \tilde{\varrho}(Z_n, m);$$
$$\tilde{\varrho}Z_n \equiv \partial \tilde{\varrho} / \partial Z_n = \varrho_2 \pi_1 \gtreqless 0,$$
$$ (- \text{ or }) (-)$$
$$ 0$$

$$\tilde{\varrho}_m \equiv \partial \tilde{\varrho} / \partial m = \varrho_1 + \varrho_2 \ \pi_2 = (\frac{1}{\bar{x}} - \phi_2 \ \pi_2) \ /\phi_1.$$
$$ (-) \ (- \text{ or }) (-) \ \ \ \ \ \ \ \ \ (- \text{ or }) (-) (-)$$
$$ 0 0$$

Now, assume that $\tilde{\varrho}_m < 0$. This assumption will be rationalized if the sensitivity of money demand with respect to the change of expected rate of inflation $|\phi_2|$ is relatively small.

Substituting equations (37) and (38) into equation (33) (i), and further substituting equation (33) (i) into equations (33) (iii) and (33) (v), the following "fundamental dynamical system" results.

(S_B) (i) $\dot{Z}_n = \{f(E) - n_2\}\, Z_n \equiv F_1(Z_n, E)$

    (ii) $\dot{E} = \{H[Z_n, \pi(Z_n, m)] - (h + n_1 + n_2)\}\, E \equiv F_2\,(Z_n, E, m)$

    (iii) $\dot{m} = \{\mu + \alpha[\tilde{\varrho}(Z_n, m) - \bar{\varrho}] - \pi(Z_n, m)$
            $- H[Z_n, \pi(Z_n, m)] + h\}m$
            $\equiv F_3(Z_n, m)$

In this system, the classical dichotomy no longer holds, because there is a feedback effect from the monetary sector to the real sectors so that the system ceases to be "decomposable" (see Figure 6).

Now, the (local) stability of the system is investigated by assuming that an economically meaningful stationary solution (long-run equilibrium) exists.[13]

The Jacobian matrix (J^*) evaluated at the long-run equilibrium point of the system (S_B) can be written as

$$(39) \qquad J^* \equiv \begin{bmatrix} 0 & F_{12}{}^* & 0 \\ F_{21}{}^* & 0 & F_{23}{}^* \\ F_{31}{}^* & 0 & F_{33}{}^* \end{bmatrix}$$

where $F_{12}{}^* \equiv f'(E^*)\, Z_n{}^* > 0$, $F_{21}{}^* \equiv \underset{(-)\ (-)(-)}{(H_1{}^* + H_2{}^* \pi_1{}^*)}\, E^*$, $F_{23}{}^*$

$\equiv \underset{(-)\ (-)}{H_2{}^*}\, \pi_2{}^*\, E^* > 0$, $F_{31}{}^* \equiv [\alpha\tilde{\varrho}_{zn}{}^* - \underset{(-)\ (-)}{(1 + H_2{}^*)\pi_1{}^*} - \underset{(-)}{H_1{}^*}]m^*$,
$\qquad\qquad\qquad\qquad\qquad \underset{\substack{(+\ \mathrm{or}\ ) \\ 0}}{}$

and $F_{33}{}^* \equiv [\underset{(-)}{\alpha\tilde{\varrho}_m{}^*} - \underset{(-)\ (-)}{(1 + H_2{}^*)\, \pi_2{}^*}]m^*$.

The characteristic equation of this system is

$(40)\quad \Delta(\lambda) \equiv |\lambda I - J^*|$

$$\equiv \begin{vmatrix} \lambda & -F_{12}{}^* & 0 \\ -F_{21}{}^* & \lambda & -E_{23}{}^* \\ -F_{31}{}^* & 0 & \lambda - F_{33}{}^* \end{vmatrix}$$

$$\equiv \lambda^3 + a_1\lambda^2 + a_2\lambda + a_3 = 0,$$

Figure 6. **Directed graph of (S_B).**

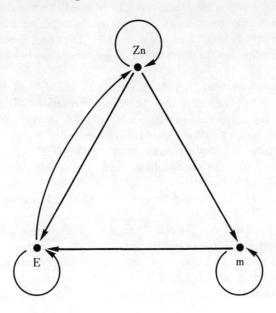

where

(41) $a_1 \equiv -F_{33}^*,\; a_2 \equiv -F_{12}^*F_{21}^*,\; a_3 \equiv F_{12}^* (F_{21}^* F_{33}^* - F_{23}^* F_{31}^*).$
       (?)   (+) (?)   (+)   (?) (?)   (+)   (?)

The Routh-Hurwicz conditions for stable roots are given by

(42)   (i) $a_1 \equiv -F_{33}^* > 0$

            (ii) $a_3 \equiv F_{12}^* (F_{21}^* F_{33}^* - F_{23}^* F_{31}^*) > 0$
                        (+)   (+)

            (iii) $a_1 a_2 - a_3 \equiv F_{12}^* F_{23}^* F_{31}^* > 0.$
                                    (+)   (+)

These conditions are equivalent to the following set of conditions:

(43)   (i) $F_{31}^* > 0$

            (ii) $F_{33}^* < 0$

            (iii) $F_{21}^* F_{33}^* - F_{23}^* F_{31}^* > 0$

Now, the implications of these local stability conditions can be investigated. Condition (43) (i) is satisfied if $|H_2^*|$ is relatively small. This condition is satisfied also in the case when $\tilde{\varrho}_{zn} > 0$ and α is sufficiently large. The condition that $|H_2{}^*|$ is relatively small is equivalent to the condition that the sensitivity of capitalists' propensity to save with respect to the expected rate of inflation $|s_r{}'(\pi^*)|$ is relatively small (see equation [34]). The condition that α is sufficiently large implies that the government's monetary policy must be sufficiently activistic.

Now, let us suppose that $|s_r{}'(\pi^*)|$ is so small that $|H_2{}^*| < 1$. In this case, condition (43) (ii) is violated so that the system becomes locally unstable if the monetarist money suppy rule ($\alpha=0$) is adopted. But, even if $|H_2{}^*| < 1$, the government can assure the condition (43) (ii) by setting $\alpha > 0$ sufficiently large.

Finally, consider the implication of condition (43) (iii). Suppose that conditions (43) (i) and (43) (ii) are satisfied. Then, a *necessary*, condition for the inequality (43) (iii) to be satsifed is $F_{21}{}^* < 0$. If $|H_2{}^*|$ is sufficiently small (i.e., $|H_2{}^*| < H_1{}^*/\pi_1{}^*$), this condition is satisfied. Furthermore, $F_{21}{}^*$
$$(-)\ (-)$$
$F_{33}{}^* - F_{23}{}^* F_{31}{}^*$ becomes a linear increasing function of α if $F_{21}{}^* < 0$ and $\varrho_{zn}{}^*$ is relatively small, reflecting the fact that $|\phi_2{}^*|$ is relatively small. In this case, the government can assure the condition (43) (iii) by setting $\alpha > 0$ sufficiently large, even if this condition is not satisfied when $\alpha = 0$.

The result of the above analyses can be summarized as the following:

Proposition 1.
   (i) Suppose that $|s_r{}'(\pi^*)|$ is relatively small. Then, the equilibrium point of the system (S_B) becomes locally unstable when the monetarist money supply rule ($\alpha = 0$) is adopted.
   (ii) Suppose that $|s_r{}'(\pi^*)|$ and $|\phi_2{}^*|$ are relatively small. Then, the equilibrium point of the system (S_B) becomes locally stable when the monetary policy rule is sufficiently activist (i.e., α is sufficiently large).

Next, the condition for cyclical solution around the equilibrium point is investigated. The characteristic equation (40) can be rewritten as

(40)'
$$\lambda^3 + b\lambda - c = a(\alpha)(\lambda^2 + b)$$

where $a(\alpha) \equiv F_{33}{}^*$; $a'(\alpha) = \tilde{\varrho}_m{}^* m^* < 0$, $b \equiv - F_{12}{}^* F_{21}{}^*$, and
$$\underset{(+)}{}$$
$c \equiv \underset{(+)\ (+)}{F_{12}{}^* F_{23}{}^* F_{31}{}^*}$.

Suppose that $|s_r{}'\pi^*)|$ is so small that $a(0) > 0, b > 0$ and $c > 0$. Moreover, for simplicity, suppose that $\tilde{\varrho}_{zn}{}^* = 0$, so that c is independent of α. In this case, the relation of equation (40)' is illustrated in Figure 7. $U(\lambda)$ in this figure denotes the left side of equation (40)', while $V(\lambda; \alpha)$ denotes the right side when policy

Figure 7

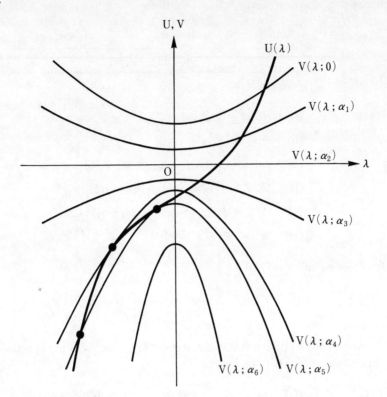

parameter α is given, where $0 < \alpha_1 < \alpha_2 < \alpha_3 < \ldots$. We can see from this figure that (i) the characteristic equation (40)' has a pair of complex roots so that the cyclical fluctuation around the equilibrium point occurs when $\alpha \epsilon$ (0, α_4) $\cup$ (α_5, ∞), and (ii) equation (40)' has no complex root so that the cyclical fluctuation around the equilibrium point does not occur when $\alpha \epsilon [\alpha_4, \alpha_5]$. These conclusions and the results of the stability analysis are summarized in Figure 8.

Adaptive Expectation Hypothesis

In this section, the perfect myopic foresight assumption of inflation expectation (equation [11]) is replaced by the following adaptive expectation hypothesis.

$$(44) \qquad \dot{\pi}^e = \gamma(\pi - \pi^e); \gamma > 0$$

In addition, for simplicity, assume that s_r is constant through time. Then, the system (13) is modified as

Figure 8

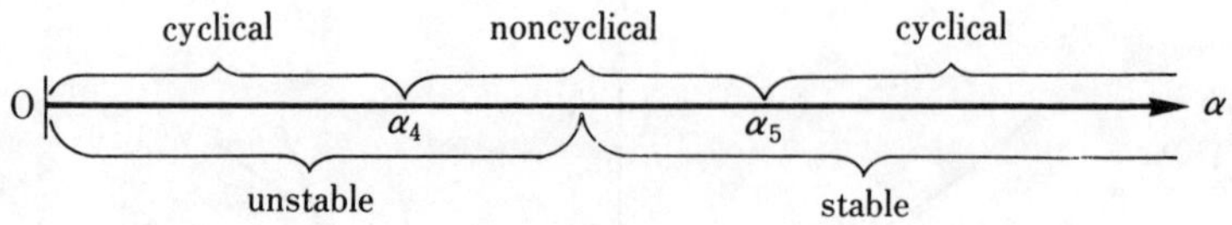

$$(45) \qquad \text{(i)} \quad H(Z_n) = \tilde{g}(Z_n, \varrho - \pi^e) + h$$

$$\text{(ii)} \quad m = \bar{x}\phi(\varrho, \pi^e)$$

$$\text{(iii)} \quad \dot{m}/m = \mu + \alpha(\varrho - \bar{\varrho}) - \pi - \tilde{g}(Z_n, \varrho - \pi^e)$$

$$\text{(iv)} \quad \dot{Z}_n/Z_n = \dot{w}/w - \pi - n_2 = f(E) + \pi^e - \pi - n_2$$

$$\text{(v)} \quad \dot{E}/E = \tilde{g}(Z_n, \varrho - \pi^e) - (n_1 + n_2)$$

$$\text{(vi)} \quad \dot{\pi}^e = \gamma(\pi - \pi^e); \ \gamma > 0.$$

From equation (45) (i) we have

$$(46) \qquad \varrho - \pi^e = \Phi(Z_n); \ \Phi'(Z_n) = \{H'(Z_n) - \tilde{g}_1\}/\tilde{g}_2.$$
$$(-) \qquad \qquad (-)(-)$$

Also in this section, it is assumed that $\Phi'(Z_n) > 0$. Substituting equation (46) into equation (45) (ii), we have

$$(47) \quad \pi^e = \pi^e(Z_n, m); \quad \pi_1^e = \partial\pi^e/\partial Z_n = -\phi_1\Phi'/(\phi_1 + \phi_2) < 0,$$
$$\pi_2^e \equiv \partial\pi^e/\partial m = 1/\bar{x}(\phi_1 + \Phi_2) < 0.$$

From equations (46) and (47), we obtain

$$(48) \qquad \varrho = \Phi(Z_n) + \pi^e(Z_n, m) \equiv \varrho(Z_n, m);$$
$$\varrho_1 \equiv \partial\varrho/\partial Z_n = \Phi' + \pi^e = \phi_2\Phi'/(\phi_1 + \Phi_2) \geq 0,$$
$$\varrho_2 \equiv \partial\varrho/\partial m = \pi_2^e < 0.$$

Then, the system (45) can be summarized as follows:

$$(S_C) \qquad \text{(i)} \quad (1/Z_n + \pi_1^e/\gamma) \dot{Z}_n + (\pi_2^e/\gamma) \dot{m} = f(E) - n_2 \equiv F_1(E)$$

$$\text{(ii)} \quad \dot{E} = \{H(Z_n) - (h + n_1 + n_2)\} E \equiv F_2(Z_n, E)$$

$$\text{(iii)} \quad (\pi_1^e/\gamma) \dot{Z}_n + (1/m + \pi_2^e/\gamma) \dot{m} = \mu + \alpha \{\varrho(Z_n, m) - \bar{\varrho}\}$$
$$- \pi^e(Z_n, m) - H(Z_n) + h \equiv F_3(Z_n, m)$$

Now, the following proposition can easily be proven (the proof is omitted).

Proposition 2.
A set of local stability conditions of the system (S_c) is given by (i) the small expectation coefficient γ and (ii) the large monetary policy parameter α.

Note that the model of this section is reduced to the model of the Goodwin-type growth cycle if the expectation coefficient is infinite, because
$$\lim_{\gamma \to +\infty} \pi^e = \lim_{\gamma \to +\infty} (\pi - \dot{\pi}^e/\gamma) = \pi.$$

* * *

The main source of instability in the models presented in this chapter stems from the money market. Suppose, for example, that the expected rate of inflation is increased. Then, the nominal rate of interest tends to increase in pursuit of the increase of the expected rate of inflation. This accelerates the increase of the velocity of circulation of money (the reciprocal of the Marshallian k) through the substitution from money to bonds. The increased velocity induces the growth of the rate of inflation, which entails higher expectations of the rate of inflation. In the Goodwin-type model, this instability is locked in the monetary sector, while in the models that follow, instability spreads to the the real sectors through the variable propensity to save or the discrepancy between expected and actual rates of inflation. To offset this instability, the monetarist money supply rule is ineffective but activist rule is required.

In the models presented in this chapter, the budget constraint of the government plays no dominant role.

The budget constraint of the government may be formulated as

$$(49) \qquad p\,G + R - T = q\,\dot{B} + \dot{M}$$

where R = nominal payment of the interest on bonds
T = nominal income tax
q = market price of the bond
B = existing bond stock

For simplicity, assume that the bond is consol type. Then, $R = B$ and $q = 1/\varrho$. In this case, we can rewrite equation (49) as follows.

$$(50) \qquad G + B/p - T/p = \dot{B}/\varrho p + \dot{M}/p$$

Although this relation also must be met in the models in this chapter, this equation does not affect the dynamics of variables such as E, Z_n or m. However, if consumption from the interest on bonds and the wealth effect on consumption are introduced, the dynamics of the system are no longer independent of equation (50), because this equation becomes another root of the transmission of instability from the monetary sector to real sectors. Obviously in this case, monetarist policy rule is ineffective to stabilize the economy, so that some sort of activistic stabilization policy rule must be required.[14]

Notes

1. See Marx (1967) Part VII and Sylos-Labini (1970) Chap. II.
2. See Hirsch and Smale (1974) Chap. 12.
3. Although the object of this chapter is somewhat similar to that of Di Matteo's (1984) paper, it was independently written and the analytical details of both are considerably different. As for the various developments of Goodwin's growth cycle model, see, for example, Balducci, Candela and Ricci (1984), Desai (1973, 1984), Desai and Shah (1981), Flaschel (1984), Glombowski and Krüger (1984, 1986), Goodwin (1983, 1984), Medio (1980), Pohjola (1981), Sato (1985), Van der Ploeg (1983, 1984), Velupillai (1979), Wolfstetter (1982) et. al.
4. This implies that the technical progress is the "Harrodian-neutral" type.
5. From the expression of r and r_n, "distribution frontiers" are drawn (see Figure F1 and Figure F2). If we assume full capacity utilization of capital, we have $r = \bar{x}(1-Z)$, which is nothing but the Sraffian equation in our model (in Sraffa's 1960 notation, $r = R(1-w)$).
6. Note that $[s_r(1-t_r)+(t_r-t_w)]/(1-t_w) > 0$ since $0 \le t_w \le t_r < 1$. By the way, equation (*) can be rewritten as $r_n = (g+h-t)/s_r$, where $t \equiv T/K \equiv [t_w \omega L + t_r(X-\omega L)]/K$. This equation relates the after-tax rate of profit (r_n) to the rate of accumulation (g), the rate of government deficit ($h-t$) and capitalists' propensity to save (s_r), which is a basis of Kaleckian theory of income distribution (see Kalecki 1971).
7. As for the proofs, see, for example, Tobin (1969) and Yoshikawa (1980).
8. Note that under the assumption $\Phi'(Z_n) > 0$, $\varrho - \pi$ moves in the same direction as Z_n (see equation [14]).
9. We assume that $\alpha \neq 1$.
10. This statement follows from equation (16).
11. As for the formal definition of the structural (in)stability, see, for example, Hirsch and Smale (1974 Chap. 16), Medio (1980) and Valupillai (1979).
12. This type of saving function was introduced by Okishio (1979).
13. Economically meaningful stationary solution implies that the stationary solution (Z_n^*, E^*, m^*) of the system (S_B) with the properties $0 < Z_n^* < 1, 0 < E^* < 1 - t_w$ and $0 < m^*$.
14. As for the formal analysis of stabilization policy in which the government's budget constraint plays an essential role, see Asada (1987).

References

Akashi, S., and T. Asada. 1986. "Money in Kaldorian Cycle Theory." *The Economic Review*. The Institute of Economic Research, Hitotsubashi University 37:169–77.

Asada, T. 1987. "Government Finance and Wealth Effect in a Kaldorian Cycle Model." *Journal of Economics (Zeitschrift für Nationalökonomie)* 47:143–66.

Balducci, R., G. Candela, and G. Ricci. 1984. "A Generalization of R. Goodwin's Model with Rational Behaviour of Economic Agents." R. M. Goodwin, M. Krüger and A.

Figure F1. **Pre-tax distribution frontier.**

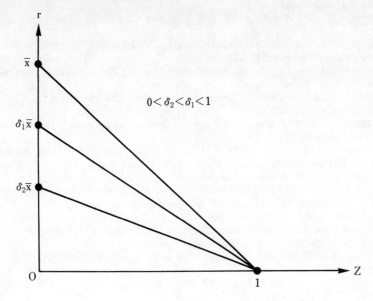

Figure F2. **After-tax distribution frontier.**

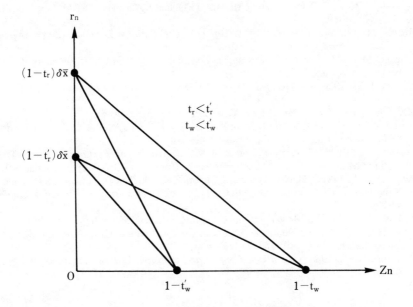

Vercelli, eds. *Nonlinear Models of Fluctuating Growth*. Berlin, Heiderberg, New York and Tokyo; Springer-Verlag.

Burmeister, E. 1980. *Capital Theory and Dynamics*. Cambridge: Cambridge University Press.

Desai, M. 1973. "Growth Cycles and Inflation in a Model of the Class Struggle." *Journal of Economic Theory* 6:527–45.

Desai, M. 1984. "An Econometric Model of the Shares of Wages in National Income: UK 1855–1965." R. M. Goodwin et. al., eds., op. cit.

Desai M., and A. Shah. 1981. "Growth Cycles with Induced Technical Change." *Economic Journal* 91:1006–10.

Di Matteo, M. 1984. "Alternative Monetary Policies in a Classical Growth Cycle." R. M. Goodwin et. al., eds., op. cit.

Dornbusch, R., and S. Fischer. 1978. *Macroeconomics*. New York: McGraw-Hill.

Flaschel, P. 1984. "Some Stability Properties of Goodwin's Growth Cycle: A Critical Elaboration." *Zeitschrift für Nationalökonomie* 44:63–9.

Flaschel, P. 1984. "The Inflation-Biased 'Natural' Rate of Unemployment and the Conflict over Income Distribution." R. M. Goodwin et. al., eds. op. cit.

Foley, D. K. 1986. "Stabilization Policy in a Nonlinear Business Cycle Model." W. Semmler, ed. *Competition, Instability, and Nonlinear Cycles*. Berlin, Heiderberg, New York and Tokyo: Springer-Verlag.

Friedman, M. 1977. *Inflation and Unemployment*. Occasional Paper No. 51. London: The Institute of Economic Affairs.

Glombowski, J., and M. Krüger. 1984. "Unemployment Insurance and the Cyclical Growth" R. M. Goodwin et. al., eds. op. cit.

———. 1986. "Some Extensions of a Classical Growth Cycle Model." W. Semmler, ed. op. cit.

Goodwin, R. M. 1967. "A Growth Cycle" C. H. Feinstein ed. *Socialism, Capitalism and Economic Growth*. Cambridge: Cambridge University Press.

Goodwin, R. M. 1983. "A Note on Wage, Profits and Fluctuating Growth Rate." *Cambridge Journal of Economics* 7:305–9.

———. 1984. "Disaggregating Models of Fluctuating Growth." R. M. Goodwin et. al., eds. op. cit.

Hirsch, M. W., and S. Smale. 1974. *Differential Equations, Dynamical Systems and Linear Algebra*. New York: Academic Press.

Kalecki, M. 1971. *Selected Essays on the Dynamics of the Capitalist Economy*. Cambridge: Cambridge University Press.

Keynes, J. M. 1936. *The General Theory of Employment, Interest and Money*. London: Macmillan.

Marx, K. 1967. *Capital* Vol. I New York: International Publishers.

Medio. A. 1980. "A Classical Model of Business Cycle." E. J. Nell, ed. *Growth, Profits and Property*. Cambridge: Cambridge University Press.

Okishio, N. 1979. "Theoretical Frame of Monetarism." *The Economic Review*. The Institute of Economic Research, Hitotsubashi University 30:289–99. (In Japanese).

Pohjola, M. T. 1981. "Stable, Cyclic and Chaotic Growth: The Dynamics of a Discrete-Time Version of Goodwin's Growth Cycle Model." *Zeitschrift für Nationalökonomie* 41:27–38.

Robinson, J. 1956. *The Accumulation of Capital*. London: Macmillan.

Rose, H. 1967. "On the Nonlinear Theory of the Employment Cycle." *Review of Economic Studies*. 34 (April):153–73.

Rowthorn, R. E. 1980. *Capitalism, Conflict and Inflation*. London: Lawrence and Wishart.

Sargent, T. 1979. *Macroeconomic Theory*. New York: Academic Press.
Sato. Y. 1985. "Marx-Goodwin Growth Cycles in a Two-Sector Economy." *Zeitschrift für Nationalökonomie* 45:21-34.
Sraffa, P. 1960. *Production of Commodities by Means of Commodities*. Cambridge: Cambridge University Press.
Sylos-Labini, P. 1970. *Problemi dello Sviluppo Economico*. Editori Laterza & Figli, Bari. Japanese edition, translated by H. Onoe, Heibonsha, Tokyo, 1973.
Tobin, J. 1969. "A General Equilibrium Approach to Monetary Theory." *Journal of Money, Credit and Banking* 1:15-29.
Van der Ploeg, P. 1983. "Predator-Prey and Neoclassical Models of Cyclical Growth." *Zeitschrift für Nationalökonomie* 43:235-56.
Van der Ploeg, F. 1984. "Implications of Workers' Savings for Economic Growth and the Class Struggle." R. M. Goodwin et. al., eds. op. cit.
Velupillai, K. 1979. "Some Stability Properties of Goodwin's Growth Cycle," *Zeitschrift für Nationalökonomie* 39:245-57.
Wolfstetter, E. 1982. "Fiscal Policy and the Classical Growth Cycle." *Zeitschrift für Nationalökonomie* 42:375-93.
Yoshikawa, H. 1980. "On the 'q' Theory of Investment." *American Economic Review* 70:739-43.

Qualitative Effects of Monetary Policy in "Rich" Dynamic Systems

Peter S. Albin

It is widely presumed that monetary policy has informational effects on business expectations as well as allocative effects. The former influence may affect system dynamics particularly, in already volatile settings. This chapter reports on on-going computer experiments aimed at isolating the qualitative informational effects of procyclical (accommodative) and countercyclical monetary interventions. The modeling approach is described first and is followed by an explanation of the associated schema for complexity classification of dynamic systems. The next section contains the specification of monetary controls. The results and interpretations are then presented. The analysis shows that intervention according to conventional rules can: a) alter the intrinsic dynamics of the system, e.g., from periodic to aperiodic (chaotic) or the reverse; b) delay natural equilibrium-seeking tendencies; c) worsen the tradeoff between approximating an aggregate target and reducing fluctuations around the target; d) worsen the tradeoff between approximating an aggregate target and achieving "selective" objectives. A "countercyclical" rule is not necessarily superior to an "accommodative" rule under these conditions nor does "finer tuning" necessarily lead to finer results. Although the models specify only myopic expectations and intervention rules, the analysis generates a strong presumptive case with respect to higher-order specifications as well.

The Experimental Setting

The experimental setting is a computer model simulating variations in the investment of individual firms who draw information on the likely path of the system from observation of the actions of their economic neighbors. The system's dynamic behavior in the absence of policy intervention is examined first. Detailed properties of the system are given in Albin (1987); its salient characteristics are summarized below.[1]

1. The economy consists of N firms organized in M industries. It is convenient to operate with 100 firms in 5-firm industries.

2. Each firm sets a *three-option investment plan* contingent on expectational information as to whether the business climate will be *unfavorable, normal,* or *favorable*. *Normal* is the firm investment level that aggregates to the level of capital formation which supports a balanced growth path in the sense of Solow (1956) and as translated to a nonlinear system by Day (1982). The *unfavorable* and *favorable* climates can be thought of as worst-case and best-case scenarios.

3. The data needed to *calculate* the three separate plan options are assumed to be price-dimensioned and obtainable by the firm without additional cost in the ordinary course of doing business. These data and the mechanics of calculating optimal plans are of standard type and are not considered here.

4. The strategic information needed to *choose* the appropriate plan option is costly and available only with some delay. The firm is assumed to base its strategic decision on "leading indicators" drawn from observation of the immediate past actions of its "economic neighbors." This is the most timely and least costly source of strategic information.

5. The "economic neighborhood" can overlap the industry but is not identical to it. Neighborhood relationships represent variously intra-industry relationships among competitors, supplier-customer relationships, and/or inter-industry input-output relationships.

6. The neighborhood is specified as an index set. Thus the index set $(-2, -1, 1, 2)$ defines for firm J the neighbors $(J-2, J-1, J+1, J+2)$. If all firms have the same index set, the system is *homogeneous* and the industry distinction is purely nominal.

7. If the neighborhood set varies according to the firm's position within its industry, the system is *heterogeneous*. Typically, one can designate one or two firms as "leaders" who draw information from outside the industry, while the remaining firms react to the leaders and within-industry competitors. Heterogeneous models can capture a variety of oligopolistic behaviors and "consonant rivalry" (Kuenne, 1979).

8. The firm selects a negative, zero, or positive increment—designated -1, 0, $+1$—to its normal investment level. The selection is made according to an algorithmic rule for reacting to the investment actions of its neighbors as observed in the immediately preceeding period. The rule is a model parameter which is varied experimentally. Since there is only a relatively small number of observable actions within the neighborhood, it is feasible to simulate all possible integer rules, thus generating the full strategy set of the firm (which set includes both meaningful and nonsensical behaviors).

9. In the simulations described here the rules are restricted to functions of

the algebraic sum of neighbor actions. In anglicized BASIC, a rule takes a form like: IF THE NET TOTAL OF NEIGHBOR ACTIONS IN THE PREVIOUS PERIOD IS 3 OR 4 THEN SELECT +1 (a positive investment increment) ELSE IF THE NET TOTAL OF ACTIONS IS −3 OR −4 THEN SELECT −1 (a negative increment) ELSE SELECT 0 (*normal* investment).

10. Firms are arrayed on a line segment and the left-most and right-most industries are treated as experimental boundaries. In the cases reported here, the boundary industries are constrained to *normal* investment at all times.

11. For convenience, firms are assumed to be approximately equal in size. In addition, the investment increment can be assumed to be of constant dollar amount for all firms. Thus SUM, the algebraic sum of firms' actions can be construed as either an ''index of business sentiment'' or with a scale transformation as a measure of ''excess aggregate investment.''

12. The system is started by distributing an initial pattern of non-zero shocks to firms selected probabilistically. Therafter, the system evolves deterministically. The distribution of shocks is varied experimentally.

Figure 1b gives representative outputs for a homogeneous, 100-firm model in which the neighborhood and pattern of initial shocks are fixed, and the rule is varied experimentally. Firms are arrayed horizontally. Above normal, normal, and below normal investment levels are displayed as black, white, and grey, respectively; and each line of patterns represents a time step of the system. To help in identifying characteristic patterns, Figure 1a gives outputs for a simpler two-state model (above normal = black; normal or below normal = white). The displays can be thought of as low-detail snapshots of the contents of a data bank giving values of a firm-level variable. The organizing principle is that found in many standard data sets: firm records organized according to industry, and industry records according to product or process adjacency (as in SIC codes). Looking ahead to Figure 2, the conventional plots to the right of the snapshots give the time series of SUM around the base line of zero excess aggregate investment.

Complexity Classification of Dynamic Behaviors

Four distinct types of dynamic behavior appear in the figures (indicated by numerals and notes). It has been determined that the same rule will consistently produce the same qualitative behavior for all nontrivial initial configurations. Each distinctive visual presentation, or *characteristic signature*, has been shown (Wolfram, 1984; Albin, 1987) to correspond to a qualitative level of computational complexity that embraces dynamic properties, statistical characteristics of generated data, and linguistic properties. The latter are critical since they determine the scale of data and computational resources needed to comprehend a system and project its future path.

171

Figure 1a. **The Four Qualitative Types in Two-state Models.**

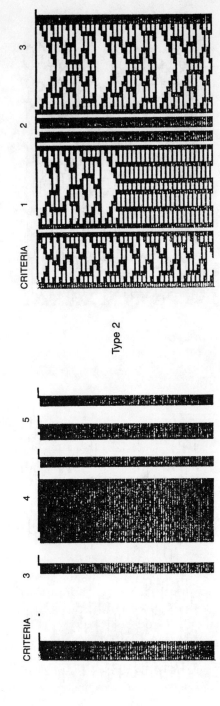

Type 1

Type 2

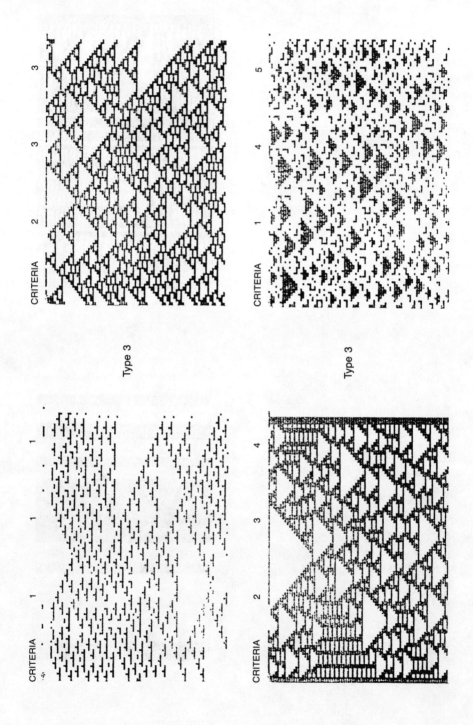

172

CRITERIA   2   3   3   3

Type 3

CRITERIA   1   1   4   5

Type 3

CRITERIA   1   1   1

CRITERIA   2   3   4

173

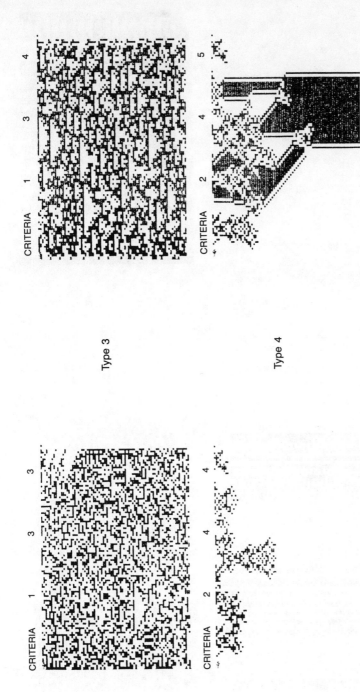

Type 3

Type 4

Notes: In each panel, values for 100 sites (firms) are printed horizontally for 80 vertical time steps. Plotted sums are not given in these panels—but see Figure 2, below. The "criteria" are rule parameters: thus "CRITERIA 1 4 5" represents the rule "print as black if 1 or 4 or 5 of your neighbors printed black in the previous time step." All cases are generated for an identical pattern of starting values which was initially produced randomly.

Note that the case on the right for type 2 is "transitional." It yields complicated cycles with periodicities that vary with the initial pattern—thus, it does not emulate a limit cycle in the strictest sense. In other topologies this rule generally produces aperiodic output. Incidentally, this rule: "print black if 1 or 2 or 3 neighbors previously printed black," is a quite plausible formulation in expectational models.

174

Figure 1b. **Qualitative Behavior of Three-state Models.**

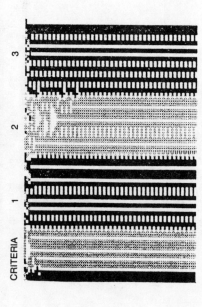

Type 2

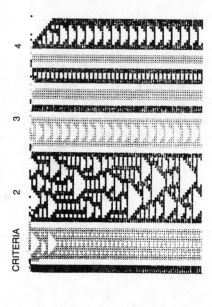

Type 3

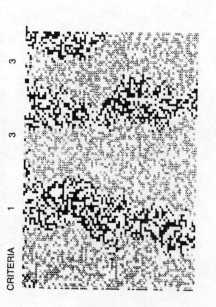

175

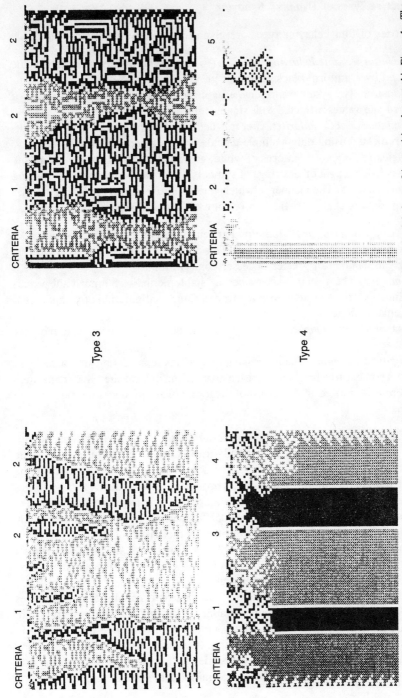

CRITERIA

2   2   1

Type 3

CRITERIA

2   2   1

Type 3

CRITERIA

2   4   5

Type 4

CRITERIA

1   3   4

Type 4

Notes: Type 1 cases (all black, white, or grey) are not shown. The case in row 1 is type 2. The case on the right in row 2 is transitional as noted in Figure 1a. The other type 3 cases display "pseudo sectors" of like activity. The case to the left in row 4 is transitional in the line-segment topology; it displays long transients with type 4 properties.

Qualitative Types of Dynamic Behavior

Properties of four behavior types are given in summary form.

1. Uniform Stable Behavior. All sites (firms) quickly assume a common value indicated by a uniform black, white or grey field.

Dynamics: The system represents a stable equilibrium with all trajectories of summed site values attracted to a single limit point.

Computational Complexity: After transients die out the system can be replicated or projected using only a simple calculator or a computer without memory.

Linguistic Category: Patterns of white, grey, and black dots representing site values can be thought of as strings of symbols which can be processed according to linguistic rules. The manner in which various initial strings are processed into uniform data is characteristic of a (Chomsky) regular language.

2. Simple Stability or Periodicity. Particular sites or local groups of sites take on constant or simply-periodic values. This behavior is observable as horizontal or vertical banding of greater or lesser complication.

Dynamics: The system is described as stable periodic. Summed site values form limit cycles. A system evolving from a finite configuration of nonquiescent sites remains finite.

Computational Complexity: The system can be simulated on a finite memory device.

Linguistic Category: The processing of symbols representing site values constitutes a context-free language—e.g., a given string of local site values regardless of where it is situated in the snapshot diagram always produces the same future strings.

3. Aperiodic Behavior. In one manifestation, the characteristic signature appears "noisy" with no apparent regularities. Closer inspection confirms the appearance of a wide variety of dot patterns in strings of arbitrary length. In the technical literature, this presentation has prompted rigorous description via ergodic theory (Are all possible strings encountered?) and entropic measurement (Do all possible dot patterns occur with equal frequency—is the system maximally disordered?). In another manifestation, the characteristic signature displays recurrent patterns, such as the self-similar "blocking triangles," and a reduced set of dot patterns. This presentation is confirmed by entropic measurements and prompts calculation of fractal dimensions.

Dynamics: The system is aperiodic and time irreversible. Summed values suggest chaotic trajectories around strange attractors. An unbounded system expands into vacant sites and "pseudosectors" with one value predominant in multistate systems may appear and persist. As noted, strings of site values may exhibit statistical regularities; these properties are unique to each generating rule (firm strategy) and are insensitive to the initial pattern of shocks.

Computational Complexity: The memory requirements for a simulating device grow without restriction. These requirements are "irreducible" also meaning that there is no "analytical" shortcut to full system emulation.

Linguistic Category: The evolution of the system is "context sensitive," meaning that a given string of site values may produce different successor strings at different locations in the snapshot diagram.

4. Irregular and Persistant Behavior. The characteristic signature consists of several irregular forms which interact in unexpected ways. Different initial patterns may produce dramatically different snapshot diagrams.

Dynamics: Depending on the initial pattern of shocks, this type of irregular system may grow, cycle, contract or die out. Intricate local structures may persist, die out, or propagate leading to intricate interactions with other local structures, and "time irreversible" systems suggest historical development. Few statistical regularities can be detected in time series of system aggregates; these may exhibit shifts which mimic structural changes.

Computational Complexity: Local structures act, in effect, as components of a universal computer. The system is computation irreducible; furthermore, limiting system behavior and statistical properties for arbitrary imput are effectively unpredictable.

Linguistic Category: The "human unpredictability" of the system is captured by the Chomsky category of "unrestricted language"—formally corresponding to the arbitrarily large simulation device required to emulate the system.

Projective Properties

For the economist, an intuitive understanding of the classification system can be gained by asking how a forecaster for a firm might decode a time series of local observations to derive a closed-form representation or to project the system and thus improve upon the current myopic rule for forming expectations. For example, there would be little problem in handling the type 1 uniform equilibrium. It is clear that one need only observe a few time slices to confirm uniformity and that this information would suffice to project the system arbitrarily far into the future. In terms of computational resources, one would need only a pocket calculator (without memory) to multiply the equilibrium value by t and so effect a growth extrapolation t years into the future.

For the type 2 periodic system, a time slice of observed data thick enough to contain the full record of a cycle would suffice for projections. These data would fit within a finite memory device. Thus, for a cycle of period p, in order to project the system to period t arbitrarily far in the future, one needs only the capacity to calculate a modular division of (t/p) and look up the corresponding value in the memory device. Perhaps, one might wish to observe more cycles to confirm the dynamics, but the principle is clear: there exists an observation of finite length on the past behavior of a determinate system that tells all that is necessary to project the future behavior of the system with simple means.

This commonly-held presumption on resource bounds for observation and extrapolation no longer holds for the third and fourth types of systems. Put one way, in order to predict the tth state of the system, the entire record to $t - 1$ is needed; put another way, there is no bounded store of data which tells all that is necessary to know about the system; put still another way, the marginal value of an additional observation does not decline. The computer needed to represent such systems must have memory that grows in size with the length of the projection; furthermore, the computer needed for the type 4 system must be without any effective restriction on its logic. The distinction between type 2 and type 3 systems is particularly important for the theory of economic expectations. In a type 2 system, an economic agent needs only to observe a full cycle of data within a restricted band of adjacent sites. Once a particular pattern of site values recurs, the whole future history of that local band can be extrapolated. In a type 3 system, the recurrence of a particular local pattern is of limited use in forming projections. The further future in the local band varies according to "context," the values at distant sites. The data and computational resources needed to project the "context sensitive" case are far greater than those needed for the "context free" setting and greatly exceed those generally assumed for practical expectations formation. The "context free/sensitive" designations allude to an isomorphic system for classifying linguistic complexities—the Chomsky ordering.

Modeling Considerations

The four qualitative categories exhaust the dynamic potentialities for reciprocally interactive systems. The characteristic signatures appear in systems with more states (color printing is required), narrower or broader neighborhoods of interaction, higher-order lags, mixtures of rules and neighborhood boundaries, and additional dimensions (Smith, 1971; Albin, 1975; Wolfram, 1986). This particular modeling scheme was chosen for a number of reasons. The three-state plan specification corresponds quite closely to the familiar (worst-case, normal, best-case) scenario format for expectational data and is convenient for black and white printing. The five-firm neighborhood is suggestive of an industry size in which strategic interaction is likely. Finally, the model is small enough so that all strategic rules (of the integer type specified) can be investigated. This is probably the simplest model that is "recognizably economic" in its information cost assumptions, consistent with a general equilibrium growth framework, and capable of generating the full range of dynamics. The model was stripped of obscuring detail, hence the austere assumptions. Note, finally, that this type of system is characterized by "complexity tradeoff," wherein a particular level of dynamic richness can be obtained in narrow-neighborhood models with many states or in broad-neighborhood models with fewer states. Thus, the dynamic behaviors of a fully-elaborated model can be no richer than those exhibited here.

Dynamics and Expectations

Limit-point, and limit-cycle trajectories are, of course, quite familiar in the literature pertaining to monetary dynamics. The strange-attractor (chaos) case is of comparatively recent interest—mostly following work by Day (1982)—but is produced with some awkwardness and considerable obscurity by curvature tricks in nonlinear systems. The extremely rich irregular dynamics of the fourth type are not considered in the literature at all, although a natural consequence of a market economy acting as a mesh of interconnected computers. How important are the rich cases? In models of appropriate scale—2 to 5 expectational states, 3- to 7-firm neighborhoods—the extremely-rich type 4 cases are almost as likely to occur as limit-point equilibria (for approximately 6% - 10% of the rules in a given model). The limit cycle appears somewhat more frequently (generally, between 10% and 20% of the time), while the varieties of chaos are the most likely to occur and increase in frequency as model size grows.

Are there *a priori* grounds founded in economic theory for anticipating one or another type of dynamic behavior to prevail? I think not. A case can be made for just about any one of the rules as a strategy for reacting to specific expectational data. So long as there are advantages (timeliness, reliability, availability) to be gained from drawing on low-cost local data channels and direct observation, these sources will be used. The assumption made in each simulation that all firms in the economy adhere to the same rule is, however, patently implausible. It is employed in the spirit of experimentation. I conjecture that in an actual market economy only a fraction of firms are situated in industries where there is play for reciprocal interactions. Furthermore, such industries may differ as to the prevailing rule, and rules may alter over time either spontaneously or in an evolutionary way. Thus, the actual system might be viewed as a photo mosaic made up of several snapshots with accordingly complex composite dynamics.

Industry Structure

According to the above conjecture, there may be zones of differing intrinsic dynamic behavior within the economy. Furthermore, tendencies for self-organization into expanding or contracting "pseudosectors" have already been seen within several snapshots. What about industry structure *per se*? Included in the policy simulations to come are heterogeneous specifications which assume the strategic leadership of key firms, along with restrictions on channels whereby firms within an industry draw information on conditions outside the industry. Briefly, the four complexity types reappear. However, sectors of like behavior persist longer, and frequently the system is easier to stabilize in the manner to be next described.

Policy Interventions

Active stabilization policy, in general and in the context of our model, involves attempts to achieve one or more of the following objectives:

1) centering the trend of the economy on a target path (taken here to mean the line of zero excess aggregate investment);

2) reducing the amplitude of fluctuations in key aggregates (thus reducing the real burdens of excess-capacity and tight-capacity production;

3) reducing sectoral imbalance within the aggregate (zero excess aggregate investment achieved with a sectoral boom and offset by depression in other sectors is likely to reduce the potential growth rate of the system;

4) reducing within-sector variability (thus reducing excess startup and shutdown burdens at the level of the firm or industry);

One might think of these objectives as priority ordered. In practice, though, loss functions might be such that the system is better off sacrificing a primary objective, e.g., straying somewhat from the target path may yield better results than centering on the path at the cost of wider fluctuations. In brief, the objectives may also be viewed as ends whose attainment can involve tradeoffs because of system interdependencies. In addition, two ancillary outcomes of intervention which might be viewed as policy significant under certain circumstances will be considered. The circumstances are where authorities co-operate and the actions of one authority may facilitate the operations of another. These outcomes are:

5) transforming the qualitative dynamics of the system; and

6) selective simplification of dynamics.

The notion here is that if monetary intervention can turn a chaotic economy into a periodic one or reduce the complication of pre-existing periodicity, the tasks of another policy agency may thereby be made easier—or, perhaps, the economy becomes less sensitive to shocks which otherwise might have to be sterilized.

In modeling policy interventions, an "external entity," e.g., the monetary authority, is specified as the shared neighbor of all firms in the system. This entity transmits a common signal to each neighborhood, in effect, through the agency of the banking system. Firms interpret this signal as an expectational datum. Recall that firms prepare three-contingency investment plans that incorporate assumptions regarding long-term real interest rates and monetary conditions. Thus, capital-allocative effects are already built into the plans. The choice of plan option in the short-run rests on a reading of the local and aggregate business climate. The current monetary signal is viewed as an early warning indicator to be included with observations of the immediate past actions of the firm's economic neighbors.

There is, to be sure, a degree of artificiality in this attempt to isolate the cyclical and expectational from the capital-theoretic—no provision is made for plan revision based on realized experience. The scheme does, however, have the virtue of simplicity and captures salient aspects of the signaling function.

The authority bases its signal (policy) on observation of the immediate past value of excess aggregate investment. It follows either a myopic countercylical rule (tightening credit in response to excess investment) or a procyclical rule. In different experiments, the policies are applied with greater or lesser sensitivity to the margin of excess (coarse or fine tuning).

Simulating Monetary Interventions

The computations are performed as follows:

1. A 100-firm economy is simulated; first, for a homogeneous model and a selection of rules, then for several different heterogenous models and the same rules.

2. The economy is allowed to run without intervention for 20 periods in order to display its basic dynamics and characteristic signature. A control regime is instituted in period 21 and then "inverted" in period 41.

3. The control is based on SUM, the algebraic sum of $(-1, 0, +1)$ actions of all firms. Thus, SUM can range (for a 100-firm economy) from -100, connoting total slump, to $+100$, connoting exuberant boom. SUM $= 0$ can result either from all firms uniformly investing at the normal level or from above-normal outcomes offsetting below-normal outcomes. In the present implementation of the system, the authority does not differentiate between these cases (which surely matter in a real economy) nor are there real output effects from persistent over- or under-investment.

4. SUM is plotted to the right of the characteristic diagram. The dashed line indicates zero net aggregate investment.

5. The monetary control MON can be set at $(-1, 0, +1)$ according to experimental rules. The current value of MON is plotted as a dot, blank, or black square, respectively, just to the left of the rule line at the right of the diagram.

Properties of the System and Experimental Protocols

MON is treated by each firm as the equivalent of a unit of expectational information received from firms in its neighborhood. Thus, if a firm would expand investment if three of its neighbors signaled positively in the preceeding period, it will now expand investment if MON $= 1$ and two firms signaled positively.

In the first group of experiments, an "accommodative" rule is applied in period 21: if SUM > 0, SUM $= 0$, SUM < 0, then MON $= -1$, 0, $+1$, respectively. The rule is inverted in period 41 to become "countercyclical." In a second grouping of experiments, MON $= 0$ only if SUM deviates from 0 by more than 5 in absolute value. In the third and fourth groups of experiments, the countercyclical rule is applied first with different degrees of fineness.[2] In a final group of experiments, interventions are initiated in period 1 for models whose inherent dynamics are of type 1 or 4.

Figure 2. Qualitative Effects of "Monetary" Interventions Working Through Cellular Automata Expectational Models.

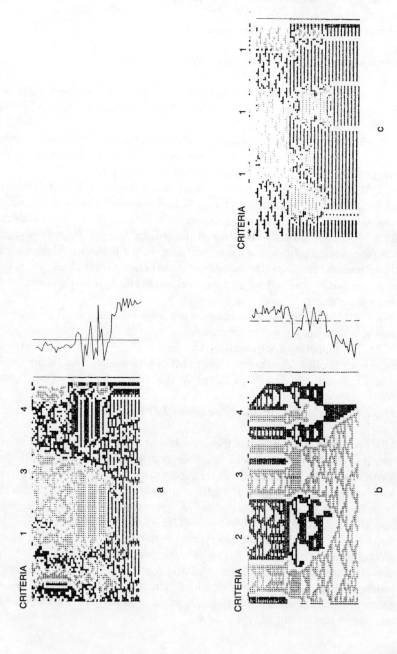

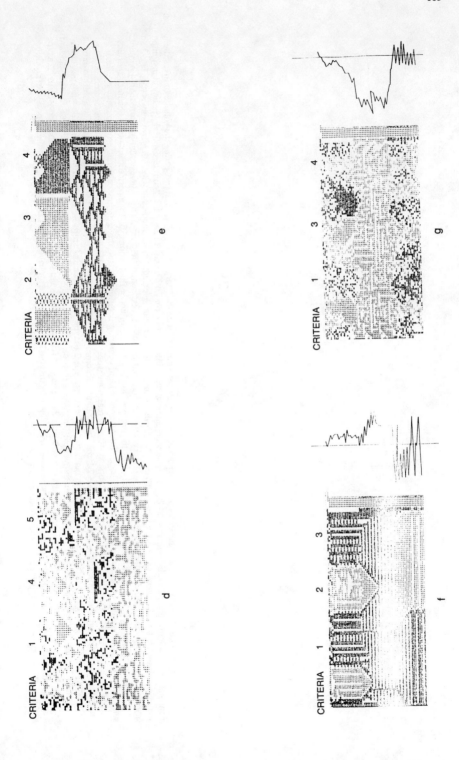

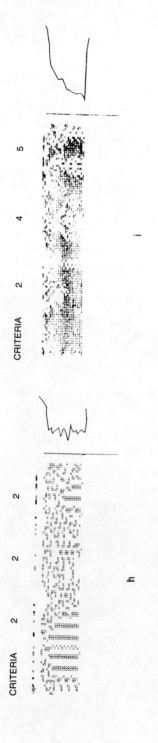

CRITERIA 2 2 2

h

CRITERIA 2 4 5

i

Notes: The plot to the right of each panel gives the time path of "aggregate investment" with the "target" or "0" level representing the volume of investment consonant with a Solow growth path. In panels 2a–2g, the system develops without intervention for 20 periods. In 2a–2d, a "countercyclical" policy is instituted in period 21 and an "accommodative" policy in period 41. In 2e–2g, the sequence of regimes is reversed (but for models in which the firm's own state is not an argument of its expectation function). In both regimes, an intervention is triggered if actual investment differs from target investment by more than 4 percent.

In 2a, an initially chaotic regime is "centered" on target by the intervention but at a cost of wider fluctuations. In 2b, a periodic economy becomes aperiodic with wider fluctuations, but again, improved centering. In 2c, fluctuations widen, centering deteriorates, and the economy becomes pronouncedly cyclical. 2d comes close to being a success for "stabilization": a chaotic system increases measured entropy, corrects a tendency towards depressed output, centers on target but with a relatively high fluctuation range. In each of 2a – 2d, the later shift to "accommodative" policy results in greater homogeneity and often a shift to or back to aperiodicity. Cases 2e–2g also show dramatic shifts in qualitative type, e.g., type 2 to type 3 in case 2e and shifts between different periodic subtypes in 2f.

Panels 2h and 2i show what happens when a "countercyclical" regime is instituted immediately after the initial shock—leaving no time for the standard behavior to develop. In 2h, a rule which ordinarily results in type 1 equilibrium leads to complex persistent forms which mix features of other models. In 2i, a type 4 system displays a number of unusual forms not otherwise observed. It appears that the imposition of a global control can lead to any of the 12 possible transitions between Chomsky-Wolfram types and to many subtypes as well.

Results and Preliminary Interpretations

At this pilot stage of the research, visual classification of model dynamics and verbal descriptions should suffice. We see from inspection of the pattern changes in Figure 2 instances in which the monetary intervention leads to increases in dynamic complexity (e.g., from limit cycles to chaos [2e]) and decreases in complexity (e.g., from chaos to simple limit cycles [2f]). In fact, all possible transitions between the four complexity types have been generated by the imposition of a stabilization rule or its inversion. Careful inspection also suggests that interventions can also lead to higher or lower "complication" within a dynamic complexity classification (e.g., shortening or lengthening of cycle periods, more or less chaotic disorder). This casual observation is supported by calculations of system entropies but further experimentation is needed on this point. One tentative conclusion is offered, however. On the record of several hundred experiments covering a wide variety of firm decision rules and authority stabilization protocols, interventions are highly likely to affect the qualitative dynamic properties of the system. Such effects change the statistical properties of the system, often in ways that would encumber firm or industry forecasters or other policy makers.

Incomplete Stabilization

But what of conventional stabilization? The moment of intervention is easily detected in the time-series graph of SUM to the right of each characteristic diagram. A typical sort of result is that illustrated in 2a and 2b where the economy is better centered but at the tradeoff cost of wider fluctuations in the aggregate. In many other instances, the tradeoff cost of wide fluctuations within the aggregate is encountered. The outcome in 2c, worse centering and dramatically wider oscillation, occurs infrequently but is a thought-provoking illustration of the dangers in fine tuning. A few of these dangers are exemplified in 2h and 2i, which illustrate systems that are stable in isolation but not if "stabilized" from outside. Actually, the result in 2d, escape from a low fluctuation "recession" to a fluctuating centered economy, is as near to a stabilization success as any observed. It is a rarity in economies whose basic dynamics are of type 3. Accommodative policy (Figures 2e, 2f, 2g) tends to drive the system off center, as one might expect; but it also tends to eliminate fluctuations within the aggregate, thus making a later countercylical intervention more effective.

Economic Implications

Results at this point must be judged as preliminary and conjectural; nonetheless, a few themes emerge from the analysis.

  1. A monetary instrument based on a macroeconomic criterion, when mixed

with micro or local "leading indicators," can alter the qualitative dynamics of an expectations-driven economy.

2. The alterations may increase or decrease the complexity and complication of system dynamics. System behavior appears to depend more on the way firms use expectational information than on the procyclical or countercylical intent of the intervention.

3. Preliminary procyclical interventions may be needed to stabilize a system; countercylical interventions may increase aggregate or within-system disorder. Interventions may also work in the manner usually ascribed to them—but do so rarely. What happens depends primarily on firm-level expectational procedures.

4. The coarseness or fineness of filter rules for intervention matters—usually, but not necessarily in the manner expected.

In brief: monetary intervention does alter the dynamics of systems whose dynamics are already rich, but it does not do so in a way that suggests definitive rules for policy. Although the models here abstract from realism to a considerable degree, the results support the view that the expectational effects of monetary interventions are uncertain and potentially perverse.

Notes

1. The underlying mathematical structure of the model is that of a one-dimensional cellular automation. Wolfram (1986) is the primary source of foundation papers and detailed bibliography concerning this form. Also see Albin (1975) for a general discussion of cellular automata models in economics.

2. These rules are quite naive. In future work, I will experiment with higher-order autoregressive schemes and built-in artificial intelligence geared to devising the best adaptive rule.

References

Albin, P. S. 1975. *Analysis of Complex Socio-Economic Systems.* Lexington, Mass.: Lexington Books.

Albin, P. S. 1987."Microeconomic Foundations of Cyclical Irregularities or Chaos." *Mathematical Social Sciences* 13:185–214.

Chomsky, N. 1959. "On Certain Formal Properties of Grammars." *Information and Control* 2.

Chomsky, N. 1963. "Formal Properties of Grammars." *Handbook of Mathematical Psychology* 2. Pp. 323–418. New York: John Wiley and Sons.

Day, R. H. June 1982. "Irregular Growth Cycles." *American Economic Review* 72 (June): 406–14.

Farmer, D., T. Toffoli, and S. Wolfram, eds. 1984. *Cellular Automata.* Amsterdam: North Holland.

Kuenne, R. E. 1979. "Rivalrous Consonance and the Power Structure of OPEC," *Kyklos* 32:695–717.

Li, T., and J. A. Yorke. 1975. "Period Three Implies Chaos," *American Mathematical Monthly* 82 (December): 985–92.

Mandelbrot, B. 1982. *The Fractal Geometry of Nature.* New York: W. H. Freeman and Co.

Martin, O., A. M. Odlyzko, and S. Wolfram. 1984. "Algebraic Properties of Cellular

Automata." *Communications in Mathematical Physics* 93:219–58. Reprinted in Wolfram, 1986.

Smith, A. R. 1971. "Cellular-Automata Complexity Tradeoffs." *Information and Control* 18:466.

Solow, R. M. 1956."A Contribution to the Theory of Economic Growth." *Quarterly Journal of Economics* 70:65–94. Reprinted in Sen, A. ed. 1970. *Growth Economics*, pp. 161–92. Harmondsworth, U.K.: Penguin Books.

Wolfram, S. 1983a. "Statistical Mechanics of Cellular Automata." *Review of Modern Physics* 55. Reprinted in Wolfram 1986.

―――――. 1983b. "Universality and Complexity in Cellular Automata." *Physica D.* Reprinted in Wolfram 1986.

―――――, ed. 1986. *Theory and Applications of Cellular Automata*. Singapore: World Scientific.

Debt Commitments and Aggregate Demand: A Critique of the Neoclassical Synthesis and Policy

Steven Fazzari and
John Caskey

In the *General Theory of Employment, Interest, and Money* (1936), Keynes analyzed the persistent, massive waste of productive potential so evident during the Great Depression. Keynes's theory questioned the viability of *laizzez-faire* capitalism. The "invisible hand" of self-interested market activity, that seemed to coordinate economic behavior effectively at the micro level, did not guarantee the full utilization of productive resources in the system as a whole.

In the postwar period, economic theorists responded to the Keynesian challenge by presenting a view of aggregate economic activity that integrated the seemingly revolutionary results of *The General Theory* into neoclassical general equilibrium analysis. This "neoclassical synthesis," in which Keynesian results are interpreted as a special case of neoclassical orthodoxy, came to dominate mainstream academic thinking, especially in the U.S. In this view, the concept that market economies can be fundamentally flawed was transformed into the notion that "real world" institutions create rigidities in the adjustment mechanisms of market economies. These rigidities may cause the natural, endogenous stabilizers of the system to act slowly when the general equilibrium is disturbed. The economy could have Keynesian characteristics in the short-run, but the system ultimately returns to its full employment general equilibrium state.

The neoclassical synthesis is based on a simple model of the institutional structure of modern capitalism. Financing arrangements are not specifically considered. The feedback from the financial side of the economy to the real side works only through the interest rate that equates the supply and demand for a narrowly-defined money stock. These assumptions keep the model clear and simple. But do they allow enough detail to make the neoclassical synthesis relevant to the analysis of modern capitalism?

This is the question addressed in this chapter. The analysis focuses on whether the stability results of the neoclassical synthesis hold up in a model of the market economy that specifically recognizes the effects of debt contracts on aggregate demand. The conclusions show that in spite of its widespread acceptance, the neoclassical synthesis provides a fragile theoretical basis for the analysis of modern market economies. Its central result, the endogenous stability of the system, is called into question when the institutional details of financial structure are considered in more depth. The ideas presented here also lead to a critique of many current monetary policy views.

The Stabilizers of the Neoclassical Synthesis

The theory behind the neoclassical synthesis predicts that the economy will eventually reach full utilization of productive resources through two disequilibrium adjustment processes. First, a supply-side process assures that when unemployed resources exist, prices will fall. Second, a demand-side process translates deflation into higher aggregate demand that pushes the system back to full capacity. Both of these adjustment processes are essential for the theoretical predictions of the neoclassical synthesis to hold. Each of them are briefly considered.

Suppose a resource, labor for example, is in excess supply. Its nominal factor price, the money wage, falls in a competitive market. When wages fall, marginal cost falls below marginal revenue, output supply expands, and the price level of goods falls. The essential result from the supply side is that under-utilization of resources generates deflationary pressure.

In Keynesian theory, however, a contraction in aggregate demand initially causes unemployment. According to the neoclassical synthesis, the deflation caused by excess supply stimulates aggregate demand through two channels. First, there is the "Keynes effect." Lower prices increase the real value of outside money. The increase in the real supply of liquidity reduces the premium agents are willing to pay to hold money, and the interest rate falls. Lower interest rates stimulate additional expenditure, and aggregate demand rises. The "liquidity trap" causes potential problems here because increases in the real outside money stock may lead to negligible declines in the interest rate. But this can be overcome by the "Pigou effect." With higher real wealth caused by deflation, households directly increase their expenditure. The stability of the system need not depend on interest rate reductions alone.

The adjustment process is summarized graphically in Figure 1. After aggregate demand shifts from D_0 to D_1, excess supply in factor markets pushes factor prices down. This increases aggregate supply for a given price level of output,

Figure 1

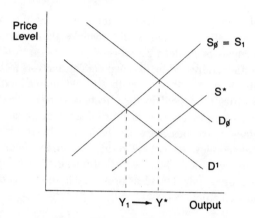

causing the aggregate supply curve to shift outward, and it creates downward pressure on the price level. Due to the Keynes and Pigou effects, falling prices increase aggregate demand, so expenditure rises to reduce the excess supply. The process continues as long as under-utilized resources exist, and the system converges to full capacity, denoted by Y* in Figure 1. Thus, to the extent that prices do not adjust instantaneously, the neoclassical synthesis model allows for short-run output losses due to insufficient effective demand, but endogenous stabilizers operate to restore full employment general equilibrium in the long-run.[1]

The Macroeconomic Effects of Debt Financing: A Critique of the Synthesis

While the neoclassical synthesis represents a widely held view in macroeconomics, there have been criticisms of both the supply and demand sides.[2] In this chapter, we join the critics by questioning the stabilizing effect of deflation on aggregate demand. Our approach explicitly recognizes that debtors have payment commitments with fixed nominal terms. An unanticipated deflation or reduction in the inflation rate will reduce nominal cash flows relative to agents' previous expectations. Thus, the "margin of safety" for debt payments declines. We argue that this can *reduce* agents' expenditures, so when prices fall, aggregate demand may also fall. If this is the case, the dynamic adjustment of an otherwise standard neoclassical synthesis model can be very different from the stable process described in the last section.

Debt contracts set up a stream of payment commitments through time. The parties to contracts make these commitments with certain expectations in mind. Both borrowers and lenders have a plan as to how cash flows will be generated to meet the obligations. For example, if high inflation is expected, borrowers will be more willing to commit to higher future cash payments because they expect the high rate of inflation to increase their future cash flows. These expectations become *embodied* in the debt contracts. They are implicit in the contract's terms, and they cannot be changed until the contract expires or is abrogated.

What happens if events differ from the expectations held at the time payment commitments were determined? Most of the literature has focused on distributional effects. Because actual prices differ from the price expectations embodied in debt contracts, the real value of the payment commitments changes, and the real distribution of wealth between debtors and creditors will differ from what was anticipated in the contract. With a reduction of prices, the debtor loses just what the creditor gains. For this reason, these distributional effects have generally been assumed to cancel in the aggregate.[3]

But more is happening than just a redistribution of wealth between debtors and creditors. When the system receives a deflationary shock, the margin of safety between debtors' cash flows and their cash commitments declines, and the probability of insolvency rises. Because insolvency is costly, debtors have an incentive to avoid it by reducing discretionary expenditure. Even if debtors would choose bankruptcy, their creditors will use all available means to force "austerity measures" on them.[4]

We should not expect that debtors' expenditure reductions in this situation will be offset by increased creditor expenditure. While lenders' real wealth increases by an amount equal to debtors' losses from the deflation, the riskiness of that wealth also increases due to the increased likelihood of bankruptcy. Lenders' liquidity preference will increase in the face of increased risk. This will change the relative price structure of assets. The greater demand for safe liquid assets, government bonds for example, may drive down their yields, *ceteris paribus*, but lower interest rates on these assets will not lead to increased expenditure. On the other hand, as lenders shift away from the risky loans used to finance consumer and business expenditure, interest rates on these loans will rise. This can significantly curtail expenditure.[5]

Unanticipated price declines or reductions in inflation can also depress expenditure due to a breakdown in the financial intermediation process. The literature on credit rationing has shown that adverse selection problems can cause financial intermediation to be curtailed when the riskiness of lending increases. If this happens, as it did during the Great Depression in the U.S., it will also depress demand.[6]

These effects all point in the same direction. A decline in prices or the rate of inflation relative to previously anticipated levels need not stimulate aggregate demand. The net effect on aggregate demand depends on whether our *cash flow effect* dominates the Keynes and Pigou effects emphasized by the neoclassical synthesis. There is no reason to assume *a priori* that the aggregate demand curve is downward sloping.[7]

If the demand depressing effects of falling prices dominate the expansionary tendencies caused by the Keynes and Pigou effects, macroeconomic analysis must be carried on with an upward sloping aggregate demand curve. This wreaks

Figure 2

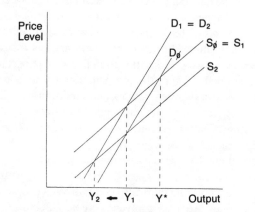

havoc with the neoclassical synthesis stabilizers discussed in the previous section. Suppose we accept the standard microfoundations of the supply-side and assume that unemployment causes factor prices to fall after demand declines. As shown in Figure 2, this outward shift of the aggregate supply curve with an upward sloping aggregate demand curve makes unemployment worse, as price reductions *depress* demand. Also, the greater the deflationary pressure, that is, the faster money wages fall in response to unemployment, the worse will be the result. From an initial situation of depressed demand, falling wages and prices aggravate the situation due to the existence of nominal debt contracts. This directly contradicts the neoclassical synthesis view that the real effects of changes in aggregate demand can be attributed to sticky or inflexible money wages.

When aggregate demand includes the cash flow effect based on nominal debt commitments, the analysis of macroeconomic adjustments with a fixed aggregate demand curve, as in Figure 1, is no longer adequate. For changes in the price level will also change nominal cash payment commitments as agents recontract debts with new expectations. After a negative shock that lowers the price level, new debt contracts will be based on lower price expectations. Thus, debtors and creditors will be able to tolerate a lower price level without reducing expenditure. This shifts the aggregate demand curve outward. Holding the supply curve constant, outward shifts in the demand curve push the system in the direction of full employment.

On net, the direction output moves when there is unemployment depends on the combination of the supply-side and demand-side adjustment processes. When the demand curve slopes upward and prices fall, downward wage adjustments reduce output while downward revisions in the price expectations embodied in debt contracts stimulate output. The net result depends on which of these movements dominates. Figure 3a and Figure 3b present some of the possibilities after a negative demand shock pushes output below its full employment equilibrium level to Y^1. Figure 3a shows a case in which the demand shift dominates the

Figure 3a

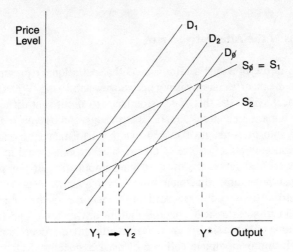

Figure 3b

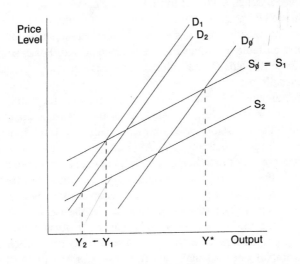

supply shift to push output back toward its full utilization level (Y*) in period 2. In figure 3b, the supply shift dominates and output falls further from Y* in period 2.

In Caskey and Fazzari (1987), the dynamic paths that can result from this kind of model are analyzed. The adjustment paths can be cyclical and they may be asymptotically unstable. If the demand curve is upward sloping, greater downward flexibility of wages leads to less stable macroeconomic dynamics. Again, these results directly contradict the neoclassical conventional wisdom that attributes the real effects of demand movements to "sticky" wages.

Implications of the Alternative View

The analysis in the previous section shows that deflationary pressure resulting from slack in the macroeconomy is not necessarily stabilizing. When compared to the neoclassical synthesis, this conclusion leads to significant differences in the view of how a market economy functions at the aggregate level. It also provides new insights into the linkages between macro performance, economic institutions, and economic policy. Some of these issues are considered in this section.

At the theoretical level, the most striking implication of our results is the possibility that the natural adjustment processes in a market economy may not be sufficiently strong to overcome destabilizing forces, even in the long-run, typically the domain of neoclassical general equilibrium results. The fact that our approach allows the possibility of unstable adjustments does not predict the ultimate explosion or complete collapse of market systems. Rather, it suggests that we must search beyond the price and quantity adjustment processes emphasized in the neoclassical synthesis to find a complete explanation for the general stability exhibited by postwar market economies. It is likely that other aspects of the economy not considered in our approach, or in the mainstream theory, limit the potentially unstable dynamics that we have identified. For example, government interventions, planned or accidental, may have provided barriers that have contained unstable paths.

Of course, another possible explanation for the general stability of market economies over the last several decades is that the empirical parameters of the system are such that the stable case prevails, and the long-run implications of the neoclassical synthesis remain relevant. After all, we do not argue that the aggregate demand curve *necessarily* slopes upward, but only point out that the unstable case cannot be ruled out theoretically. But simply claiming that *ex post* results rule out instability on empirical grounds is not a satisfactory response to the issues raised in this chapter. The relative importance of the cash flow effect is not constant through time but will vary with changes in financial conditions and institutions. Given the secular trend toward increasing private debt burdens in the U.S., for example, one can make a strong case for the proposition that the monetary authorities should design policy and institutional structures to contain endogenous instability even though the recent behavior of the system may appear generally acceptable.[8]

These results emphasize the importance of the link between financial institutions and macroeconomic performance. This crucial relationship is prominent in the work of Keynes (1936) as well as Davidson (1972) and Minsky (1975), for example. Yet, it has not received much attention within the mainstream theories of the neoclassical synthesis. As discussed in the last section, the adjustment path of the system when it is out of long-run equilibrium depends on how quickly cash payment commitments can be brought into line with changing cash flows. This speed of adjustment will depend on the term structure of outstanding debt. The dynamic properties of the adjustment will also depend on the level of indebtedness in the economy as well as the nature of the payment obligations set up in debt contracts. As these institutional features of the economy evolve, the dynamic properties of the aggregate market system may change in significant ways. Macroeconomic theory cannot be separated from the study of changes in financial practices and institutions.[9]

This conclusion is particularly relevant for policy analysis. Much of the literature in macroeconomics proposes universal policy rules, applicable to all market economies at all times. The results of our alternative analysis suggest that this quest is destined to fail. The macroeconomic impact of policy changes will depend on the particular institutional environment in which they occur. In a system with low levels of indebtedness and simple financial relationships, a tight money policy may be effective against inflation and may have low costs in terms of foregone real output. In an economy with extensive and complex debt contracts, however, the same policy can cause persistent changes in output and can lead to instability.

Let us consider this point in more detail. In the previous section, we demonstrated that the net effect of falling prices on aggregate demand is a key determinant of the economy's dynamic behavior. The conventional wisdom of the neoclassical synthesis generally holds when the demand curve is downward sloping, but an upward sloping curve leads to a system in which the deflationary pressures generated by unemployment are destabilizing. Now suppose that firms and households have sufficient financial resources so that a small decline in prices or the inflation rate increases aggregate demand through the conventional channels. If prices fall farther from their previously anticipated levels and financial problems become more severe, however, the destabilizing cash flow effect dominates the stabilizing Keynes and Pigou effects and demand begins to fall as prices fall. A demand curve that has these characteristics will be nonlinear; an example is graphed as D^0 in Figure 4a.

This kind of demand curve can cause the system to exhibit "corridor effects." When small disturbances occur, the endogenous response of the system will be stabilizing, but large disturbances push the economy outside its stable corridor and unstable dynamics result. Consider the effect of a small contraction in demand represented by the backward shift of the demand curve from D_0 to D_1 in Figure 4a. The new equilibrium point lies on the downward sloping portion of the demand curve. Therefore, the deflationary pressure caused by the downward shift of supply pushes output toward its full employment level as Y_2 moves toward Y^*. In Figure 4b, however, the same system receives a larger initial

Figure 4a

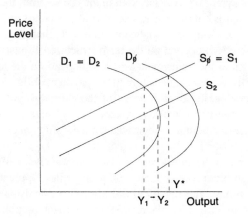

Figure 4b

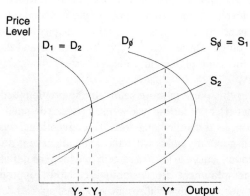

demand shock. The equilibrium after the shock now lies on the upward sloping portion of the demand curve, and deflation will push Y_2 further away from full employment.[10]

This nonlinear analysis provides a basis for "gradualism" in policy implementation. If the monetary authorities tighten money growth to fight inflation, for example, then the policy must be implemented slowly. If the system receives too large a shock, so that the expectations embodied in payment commitments differ significantly from actual circumstances, the stabilizing adjustment mechanisms in the system may break down. This also suggests that policies designed to contain instability in the financial sector, such as lender of last resort policies, may be very important when the system receives large shocks.

This result fundamentally differs from the "new classical" macroeconomics view of monetary policy. In the neoclassical synthesis model, changes in monetary policy only affect nominal variables in the long-run steady-state; real output converges to the full capacity level determined by tastes and technology. When one incorporates rational expectations into this model, agents are assumed to fully understand the long-run consequences of changing monetary policy. Therefore, they instantaneously arbitrage away any differences between current nominal values and the steady-state levels as soon as information about monetary changes becomes available.

In our model, this kind of process cannot occur. Price expectations established prior to a monetary change are more than subjective forecasts that can be costlessly abandoned when new information emerges. The expectations become embodied in objective nominal debt commitments. The legacy of past expectations cannot be erased immediately when a policy change occurs, even if the monetary authorities are fully credible.[11] The *real* expenditure effects caused by squeezing *nominal* cash flow relative to payment commitments implies that the nominal level of economic variables can have an important impact on the adjustment dynamics of the system. Thus, whether expectations are "rational" or not, monetary policy must not interfere with agents' ability to validate debt contracts. Otherwise, our analysis shows that real instability can result.

*   *   *

Ever since the publication of *The General Theory*, mainstream macroeconomics has attempted to overturn Keynes's conclusion that endogenous market mechanisms do not necessarily lead to a stable, full employment equilibrium. The neoclassical synthesis emerged out of this effort. But the synthesis rests on some fragile theoretical propositions. A reasonable and seemingly small change in one of these propositions can cause a large change in the implications of the theory.

In this chapter, we have analyzed the consequences of changing one of the underlying assumptions of the neoclassical synthesis model: the proposition that deflation will stimulate aggregate demand. When payment commitments in nominal terms are extensive, deflation has a negative cash flow effect on aggregate demand because the reduction of nominal cash flows relative to nominal payment obligations increases the likelihood of insolvency. We have indicated how this can reduce the expenditure of both debtors and creditors. If this effect is large enough, deflation causes aggregate demand to fall, and the market response to the system may be unstable. The faster that wages and prices fall, the more severe an economic contraction can be. This overturns a central result of the neoclassical synthesis that attributes the real costs of aggregate demand contractions to the failure of these nominal variables to adjust quickly enough.

It is important to recognize that our results do not lead to the prediction that market economies will be unstable at all times. We claim only that the convergence to general, full employment equilibrium cannot be taken for granted. A market economy can behave in qualitatively different ways based on the institutional settings. The neoclassical synthesis is not sufficiently detailed to provide a

basis for macroeconomic analysis in contemporary, financially complex economies. We need a theoretical framework that explicitly recognizes the links between financial structure and macroeconomic performance. This chapter provides a step in that direction.

Notes

1. Of course, there is considerable latitude within the broad bounds of the neoclassical synthesis for different policy perspectives. Some neo-Keynesians assume that the
endogenous adjustment of wages and prices is sufficiently sluggish that the convergence to
full employment can be quite protracted. Government demand management policies are
required to make the system perform acceptably. Monetarists generally believe that the
lags involved in the adjustment process are so complex and variable that stabilization
policy will most likely fail. Finally, the "new classical" macroeconomists argue that the
endogenous stabilizers work very fast due to "rational" expectations, and that macroeconomic policy has no systematic effect on real variables.
2. The idea that deflation would stimulate aggregate demand contradicts Keynes's
conclusion; see chapter 19 of *The General Theory.* Similar views are also expressed by
Fisher (1933), Davidson (1972), Minsky (1975) and Tobin (1975). A critique of the
supply-side of the neoclassical synthesis can be found in Fazzari (1986).
3. A notable exception can be found in Tobin (1975) where the distributional effects
of a deflation affect aggregate consumption because debtors and creditors are assumed to
have different propensities to consume.
4. Mishkin (1976, 1978) presents empirical evidence that financial conditions affect
consumption behavior. Fazzari and Mott (1986) and Fazzari and Athey (1987) find significant empirical effects of financial variables on firms' investment spending.
5. This analysis becomes more complicated when existing debt contracts carry variable rate financing terms. Then interest rate changes affect outstanding as well as prospective payment commitments. This issue is considered further in Caskey and Fazzari (1986).
6. See Stiglitz and Weiss (1981); Bernanke (1981); Greenwald, Stiglitz, and Weiss
(1984); and Calomiris and Hubbard (1985).
7. This issue is discussed more fully and modeled formally in Caskey and Fazzari
(1987). Similar points are made by DeLong and Summers (1986). In their model, anticipated future deflation reduces aggregate demand by increasing current real interest rates.
8. The chapter by Wolfson in this volume and Wolfson (1986) provide empirical
support for increasing secular debt burdens and declining margins of safety for debt.
Similar evidence from a cyclical perspective is presented in the chapter by Niggle in this
volume. In the framework considered here, these observations increase the likelihood of
instability and make the need for containing policy intervention more critical.
9. These issues are analyzed in greater depth in Caskey and Fazzari (1986).
10. Of course, a full dynamic analysis of this kind of model can lead to many different
kinds of qualitative system behavior, as the chapters in the first part of this volume
demonstrate.
11. In this sense, our nominal debt contracts play a role similar to nominal wage
contracts in models such as Fischer (1977).

References

Bernanke, Ben. 1981. "Bankruptcy, Liquidity and Recession." *American Economic Review* 71(2).
Calomiris, Charles, and R. Glenn Hubbard. 1985. "Price Flexibility, Credit Rationing

and Economic Fluctuations: Evidence from the U.S., 1879–1914," NBER Working Paper No. 1767.

Caskey, John, and Steven Fazzari. 1986. "Macroeconomics and Credit Markets." *Journal of Economic Issues* 20(2).

———. 1987. "Monetary Contractions with Nominal Debt Commitments: Is Wage Flexibility Stabilizing?" *Economic Inquiry,* 25(4): 583–97.

Davidson, Paul. 1972. *Money and the Real World.* New York: John Wiley and Sons.

DeLong, J. Bradford, and Lawrence Summers. 1986. "Is Increased Price Flexibility Stabilizing?" *American Economic Review* 26(5): 1031–44.

Fazzari, Steven. 1986. "Sales Expectations and Output Constrained Firms: A New View of the Microfoundations of Aggregate Supply." Washington University, St. Louis. Mimeo.

Fazzari, Steven, and Michael Athey. 1987. "Asymmetric Information, Financing Constraints, and Investment." *Review of Economics and Statistics,* 69(3): 481–87.

Fazzari, Steven, and Tracy Mott. 1986. "The Investment Theories of Kalecki and Keynes: An Empirical Study of Firm Data 1970–1982." *Journal of Post Keynesian Economics* 9(2): 171–87.

Fisher, Irving. 1933. "The Debt Deflation Theory of Great Depressions." *Econometrica* 1: 337–57.

Fisher, Stanley. 1977. "Long-Term Contracts, Rational Expectations, and the Optimal Money Supply Rule." *Journal of Political Economy* 85(1): 191–205.

Greenwald, Bruce, Joseph Stiglitz, and Andrew Weiss. 1984. "Informational Imperfections in the Capital Market and Macro-Economic Fluctuations." *American Economic Review* 74(2).

Keynes, John M. 1936. *The General Theory of Employment, Interest, and Money.* London: Harcourt, Brace and World.

Minsky, Hyman P. 1975. *John Maynard Keynes.* New York: Columbia University Press.

Mishkin, Fredric. 1976. "Illiquidity, Consumer Durable Expenditure, and Monetary Policy." *American Economic Review* 64(4): 642–53.

———. 1978. "The Household Balance Sheet and the Great Depression." *Journal of Economic History* 38(4): 918–37.

Stiglitz, Joseph, and Andrew Weiss. 1981. "Credit Rationing in Markets with Imperfect Information." *American Economic Review* 71.

Tobin, James. 1975. "Keynesian Models of Recession and Depression." *American Economic Review* 65(2).

Wolfson, Martin. 1986. *Financial Crises: Understanding the Postwar U.S. Experience.* Armonk, New York: M.E. Sharpe, Inc.

III

Empirical Evidence on Debt and Financial Instability

The Cyclical Behavior of Corporate Financial Ratios and Minsky's Financial Instability Hypothesis

Christopher J. Niggle

This chapter presents an empirical evaluation of several aspects of Hyman Minsky's theory of systemic financial instability and fragility. Minsky argues that mature capitalist economies are financially unstable in expansions: certain key financial ratios change systematically as such economies grow.[1] Nonfinancial firms' profit expectations and risk evaluations encourage them to increasingly leverage their capital as expansions proceed and seek external sources of capital to finance positions in real and financial assets. Financial intermediaries and other lenders are willing to supply funds to these borrowers (allowing the nonfinancial firms' leverage ratios to increase beyond levels previously considered prudent) as their own expectations of profit and risk are revised; a collective "euphoria" sets in and debt grows rapidly as a result. Simultaneously, the firms' perceptions of diminished risk, coupled with the usual expansion-induced increase in interest rates, encourage the nonfinancial corporations (NFCs) to reduce their holdings of liquid financial assets ("cash kickers" in Minsky's evocative language). As a consequence, the financial balance sheets of firms in the nonfinancial corporate sector deteriorate in expansions: debt/asset and borrowing/investment (leverage) ratios rise, the short-term composition of their debt increases, and they become increasingly nonliquid.

Minsky argues that in contractions these processes are reversed. Borrowing, investment, and purchases of financial assets decline. Because borrowing declines more rapidly than investment expenditures, leverage ratios also shrink,

Thanks to Martin Wolfson, Willi Semmler, Gary Evans, and Bob Pollin for their comments on earlier versions of this paper; of course, all errors and omissions are my own.

while perceptions of increasing risk lead firms to attempt to increase the liquidity of their asset portfolios. In an economy in which relatively high and stable levels of employment and profits are increasingly seen as normal (because of a long period of relative prosperity, such as during the first three postwar decades) and recessions as temporary aberrations, perceptions of risk decline from cycle to cycle. Consequently, an upward ratchet effect in leverage and nonliquidity takes place from cycle to cycle. This deterioration in the balance sheets of the NFCs has implications for both the stability of the economy and countercyclical policy. The economy may be financially fragile and deflationary macroeconomic policies consequently dangerous. It faces the threat of debt deflation (a collapse of asset values) which may precipitate a severe depression.[2]

In order to determine the extent to which corporations' behavior coincides with that postulated in Minsky's model, the cyclical behavior of the sources and uses of funds for the U.S. nonfinancial corporate sector over six complete business cycles (1953 to 1982) was studied, using the National Bureau of Economic Research's Reference Cycle Program.[3] This program, based upon the business cycle analysis begun by Wesley C. Mitchell and continued by Arthur F. Burns and others at the NBER, is known as the *Standard Business Cycle Analysis of Time Series*. The program translates a time series into reference cycle units which normalize the values of a series with respect to its average value over the cycle (thereby correcting for intracycle trend), defines turning points for the time series, calculates the amplitude of the rise and fall of the series, and computes an "average cycle" on the basis of the cycles analyzed. The business cycle is divided into expansion and contraction phases. They include nine stages: trough; early, mid, and late expansion; peak; early, mid, and late contraction; trough.[4]

Nonfinancial Corporations' Sources and Uses of Funds and Federal Reserve Board Accounting Concepts

In order to clarify some aspects of the analysis of the NFCs' financial behavior presented below, this section will review the sources and uses of funds for nonfinancial firms. It will also discuss the relationship between those abstract concepts and the somewhat different accounting techniques underlying the statistics found in the Federal Reserve Board's Flow of Funds Accounts (FOFA), which furnish the data base for this study.[5] A corporation (and the entire NFC sector) can run a deficit or surplus on capital account (or match capital expenditures with internal funds). The internal funds available for capital expenditures come from two source: retained earnings (profits net of taxes and dividends) and depreciation allowances. Capital expenditures include expenditures on plant and equipment, construction of residential units, and inventory investment. The NFC sector usually runs deficits on capital account, but occasionally runs surpluses during contractions as investment expenditures fall below the level of internal funds (which usually increase throughout contractions due to the strong upward trend in the stock of capital and depreciation allowances).

The deficit (D) or surplus (S) on capital account is defined as the difference between internal funds available for investment (N) and actual investment (I):

(1) $$D(S) = I - N$$

These variables correspond to the Federal Reserve Board FOFA statistics "Finance Gap," "Capital Expenditures," and "Internal Funds." Expenditures on capital account are the sum of fixed investment (F) and inventory investment (V):

(2) $$I = F + V$$

Internal funds (N) are retained profits net of corporate income tax liabilities (P) and depreciation allowances (A):

(3) $$N = P + A$$

Internal funds are reported by the FRB's Flow of Funds Division at both book value and with an inventory valuation adjustment (IVA) which adjusts reported book profits for the effect of price changes. Price inflation raises reported profits as the market value of firms' inventories increase; internal funds with the IVA are lower than the book value of internal funds during inflationary periods. Although this adjusted value of internal funds would be the most appropriate statistic for many purposes, the actual book value of internal funds is most relevant for purposes of considering the ability of the NFCs to internally finance the nominal levels of investment expenditures which they undertake to finance. The deficit concept most appropriate for our purposes is the difference between the nominal value of investment and the book value of internal funds (see Pollin, [1986] for an interesting discussion of the importance and implications of this issue).

The NFCs' uses of funds on capital account as defined by the FOFA are not, however, restricted to purchases of real assets. Corporations also use funds to acquire financial assets (FA); in the FOFA, these financial assets are divided into liquid financial assets (LFA) which includes cash and other short term assets, trade credit (TC), consumer credit (CC), and miscellaneous assets (MA) which consists primarily of U.S. NFCs' direct foreign investment (all of these statistics are net). The identity for net acquisitions of financial assets (NFA) is:

(4) $$NFA = LFA + TC + CC + MA$$

The *total net uses of funds* for capital expenditures (TNU) by the NFCs then includes their deficit on capital account $(I - N)$ plus net acquisitions of financial assets:

(5) $$\text{TNU} = \text{D} + \text{NFA}$$

Total sources of funds (TS) for the NFCs include external funds (X) and internal funds (N):

(6) $$\text{TS} = \text{X} + \text{N}$$

The FOFA divides the NFCs external funds into net funds raised in credit markets (NF) which are sales of debt (B) and equity (E) securities both net of retirements, trade debt (TD), and foreign direct investment in the U.S. corporate sector (FI).

(7) $$\text{NF} = \text{B} + \text{E}$$

(8) $$\text{X} = \text{NF} + \text{TD} + \text{FI} = \text{B} + \text{E} + \text{TD} + \text{FI}$$

Note that both components of net funds, credit market borrowing (B) and equity issues (E), are net of retirements of the NFCs' own issues; borrowing (B) is equivalent to "net issue of debt instruments" in the FOFA tables and consists of all borrowing by corporations which involves the issue of some kind of a debt security for which a secondary market exists (bonds, mortgages, commercial paper, bank loans, acceptances, finance company loans and government loans).

Another potential source of funds for capital expenditures is the liquidation of financial assets in the NFCs' portfolios (especially money and other liquid assets), and including this in a model of the NFC sector's sources and uses of funds has much appeal. (See Earley, Parsons, and Thompson [1976] for a discussion of this approach and its application to an analysis of expenditures by economic units.) This study utilizes an alternative approach in order to be consistent with the Fed's FOFA approach and data. Net acquisitions of financial assets (purchases net of sales) is treated as a use of funds—net of the source of funds (for some firms in the sector) of disinvestment in their financial assets. Total uses of funds on capital account (TU) must equal total sources of funds; this identity may be written:

(9) $$\text{TU} = \text{TS}$$

(10) $$\text{I} + \text{NFA} = \text{X} + \text{N}$$

(11) $$\text{I} + \text{LFA} + \text{TC} + \text{CC} + \text{MA} = \text{B} + \text{E} + \text{TD} + \text{FI} + \text{N}$$

In order to conform to the FOFA approach which defines a deficit on capital account net of internal funds, total net uses of funds (TNU) is defined and is equivalent to Equation (5):

(12) $$TNU = D + NFA$$

TNU must be financed externally. Since total net uses must equal total external funds:

(13) $$TNU = D + NFA = X$$

Although these sources and uses of funds as defined are equal by definition, in the real world, the FRB FOFA estimates of the NFCs' sources and uses of funds result in large statistical discrepancies. "Accounted for sources of funds" almost always exceeds "the accounted for uses of funds." The FRB FOFA statisticians consider the raw data from which they estimate the sources of funds statistics as more reliable than the data underlying the uses estimates. The "sources" data is taken primarily from IRS and SEC reports, while some of the "uses" data is culled from sources such as reports in specialist journals and business publications. These discrepancies can be interpreted plausibly as reflecting unaccounted for uses of funds—outflows from the NFC sector—which may have some interesting analytic significance which will be discussed below. The basic identity for sources and uses of funds which conforms with FOFA techniques but explicitly includes this statistical discrepancy (SD) and interprets TNU as total reported uses then becomes:

(14) $$TNU + SD = D + NFA + SD = X$$

The Cyclical Behavior of the NFCs' Sources and Uses of Funds and Minsky's Financial Instability Hypothesis

Minsky's financial instability hypothesis may be interpreted as a series of propositions regarding the behavior of certain corporate financial variables and ratios; the hypothesis is specified here as the following cyclical behavior:

First, Minsky argues that upward revisions of profit expectations and other factors cause investment expenditures (I) to increase more rapidly than internal funds (N) in expansions: $d(I)/dt > d(N)/dt$.

Second, since perceptions of both borrowers' and lenders' risk are revised downward in expansions, the use of external funds (X) and credit market borrowing (B) both increase in expansions: $d(X)/dt > 0$ and $d(B)/dt > 0$.

Third, since firms borrow to purchase financial assets and existing real assets as well as to finance capital formation, the ratio of borrowing to investment (a "flow" measure of leverage) increases in expansions: $d(B/I)/dt > 0$ where B/I represents the flow measure of leverage. Note: *ceteris paribus* if B/I increases, the traditional measures of leverage (ratios of total debt to total capital or total assets, however represented) would increase.

Fourth, Minsky argues that firms reduce their holdings of liquid financial assets (LFA) in expansions as their perceptions of risk diminish: $d(LFA)/dt < 0$.

Fifth, these processes should all reverse themselves in contractions, except for borrowing which may increase through the early stages of the contraction because of forced borrowing by firms which have contractual cash obligations which they cannot meet out of their (declining) sales receipts. Fazzari and Caskey discuss forced borrowing in this volume: $d(B)/dt > 0$ in early stages of contractions, but $d(B)/dt < 0$ in late stages.

This specification appears consistent with the descriptions of the expected cyclical behavior of these variables as found in many of Minsky's articles treating financial instability, although Minksy does not formally model this aspect of his theory; see Minsky (1974, 1980) for concise expositions. For comparison, see the detailed discussions of Minsky's views on the behavior of financial variables around the peak of the business cycle which are found in Wolfson (1986) and in Taylor and O'Connell (1985, reprinted in this volume). Because of a lack of data in the appropriate format, the cyclical behavior of the maturity composition of corporate data was not studied.

Corporate Financial Variables and Ratios in Expansions

Since it is the increase in debt and the resultant increase in leverage ratios which Minsky identifies as the most important factor in undermining the financial strength of the nonfinancial corporate sector and, ultimately, in determining the degree of financial fragility of the economy, the behavior of those ratios is the focus of this study. And since the stock measures of leverage (debt/capital, debt/assets or debt/equity) move slowly, adjusting to changes in net borrowing and purchases of assets sluggishly, the cyclical behavior of flow measures of leverage are emphasized. Four such measures of leverage for the NFC sector were studied: the ratios of both credit market borrowing (B) and total external funds (X) to gross investment (I) and to fixed investment (F). All four measures of leverage (X/I, X/F, B/I and B/F) behaved consistently with point three of the specification of Minsky's hypothesis: all increased in the expansions, peaking in the late expansion. Figure 1 illustrates the behavior of B/I which peaks in stage 4 of the average cycle. More complete versions of this study and the behavior of other ratios can be found in Niggle (1984, 1986). Stock measures of leverage fall through the early expansion, then rise to peak late in the contraction. See Figure 2 for the behavior of one stock measure of leverage, Credit Market Debt Outstanding/Market Value of Corporate Equity (CMD/MVE).

Consider the individual behavior of investment expenditures, internal funds, and the deficit on capital account. All measures of investment—plant and equipment expenditures, fixed investment and capital expenditures—rise in the expansion more than either measure of internal funds (book value or with the IVA), and

Figure 1. **Leverage: Credit Market Borrowing/Capital Expenditures (B/I).**

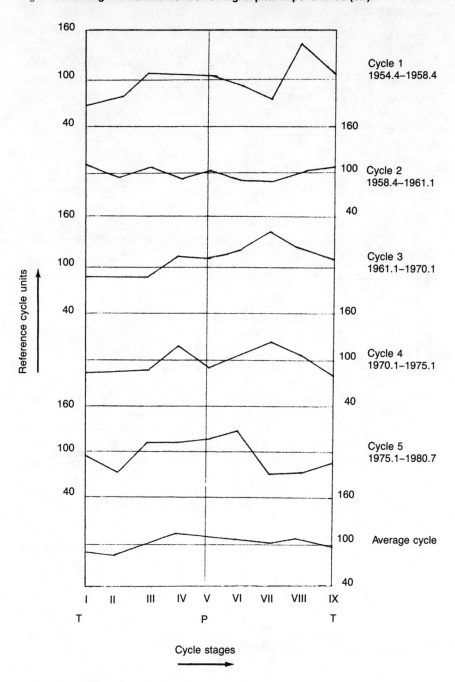

210   CHRISTOPHER J. NIGGLE

Figure 2. **Leverage: Outstanding Credit Market Debt/Market Value of Corporate Equity (CMD/MVE).**

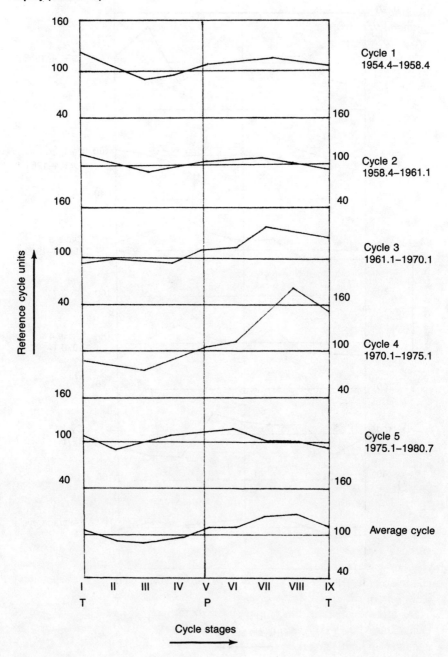

Table 1

"Average Cycle" Values for Trough-Peak and Peak-Trough Changes in Financial Variables and Ratios (U.S. Nonfinancial Corporations, 1953–81)

	B	X	F	I	N	D	NFA	SD	B/I	B/F
	Variable or Ratio									
	Trough-Peak Increase (in Reference Cycle Units)									
(+)	71.3	69.1	44.3	55.6	45.8	246.9	70.9	47.0	20.1	32.8
	Peak-Trough Decrease (in Reference Cycle Units)									
(−)	25.9	18.6	3.4	17.9	4.8	170.6	37.9	+11.8	7.0	19.6

B: Net Credit Market Borrowing
X: External Funds (Credit Market Borrowing Plus Other
          External Sources of Funds, Including Equity Issues)
F: Expenditures on Fixed Investment
I: Capital Expenditures (Fixed Investment Plus Inventory
          Investment)
N: Internal Funds
D: Deficit on Capital Account (I − N)
NFA: Net Acquisitions of Financial Assets
SD: Statistical Discrepancy
B/I: Flow Measure of Leverage
B/F: Flow Measure of Leverage

Source: Federal Reserve Board Flow of Funds Accounts and Niggle (1984).

they also rise more rapidly than do internal funds (see Table 1 for this and other data). The corporate sector begins most expansions with a surplus on capital account which becomes a deficit as the expansions proceed. Capital expenditures rise 55.6 reference cycle units in the average expansion (this means that the variable's increase from cycle trough to peak is equal to 55.6% of its average absolute value over the cycle), while book value of internal funds rises 45.8 points and internal funds with the IVA rises 40.5 points. This behavior is consistent with point one of the specification of Minsky's· hypothesis.

As a consequence of the cyclical behavior of internal funds and investment expenditures, the FOFA deficit on capital account (the gap between investment and internal funds) grows dramatically in expansions, increasing by 246.9 reference points from the initial trough to the cycle peak (Figure 4 and Table 1). This investment gap can be financed in two ways: the corporations can reduce their holdings of financial assets in their portfolios and/or they can resort to external sources of funds. The corporations adopt the latter solution; rather than dissave, the NFCs actually increase their net acquisitions of financial assets by 70.9 reference points in the average expansion (NFA peaks in stage 4—see Figure 3 and Table 1). Consequently, the NFCs must issue securities and raise the necessary funds to finance their growing deficits on capital account externally. Credit market borrowing (B) for the NFC sector rises by 71.3 reference units in the average expansion, peaking in stage 5, the cycle peak; and net funds raised in markets (NF—borrowing plus net new equity issues) rises by 64.1 points, also peaking in stage 5. Total external funds (X) also rises in expansions (Table 1 and Niggle [1986]). This behavior is consistent with point two of the specification of Minsky's analysis.

Thus, some of the increase in external finance which occurs in expansions can be explained as due to differences in the timing or rhythm of the cyclical changes in the flows of internal funds and investment expenditures. Over the course of entire cycles, internal funds are approximately adequate for capital formation (Niggle 1984), but because internal funds increase more slowly than the funds necessary for the desired amount of investment in expansions, firms are forced to seek external sources of funds adequate for their targeted investment expenditures (some of the external funds are necessary to finance the deficit on capital account). And since the flow leverage ratios of external finance and borrowing to capital formation increase in expansions (B/I by 20.1 points and B/F by 32.8 points), borrowing must increase absolutely and more rapidly than either investment expenditures or the finance gap itself. This means that a portion of these external funds must be used for something other than capital formation. Two broad possibilities exist: they may be used to finance increases in working capital (which would appear in the FOFA as acquisitions of liquid financial assets) or for other purposes not tracked by the FOFA, such as speculative purchases of debt and equity securities (including those attendant on mergers and acquisitions).

Consider the identity for total net uses and external sources of funds (Equation 14); dividing this identity by the level of investment (I) gives an expression including one of the leverage concepts (X/I):

(15) $$X/I = (D + NFA + SD)/I$$

This identity shows that the behavior of the flow leverage ratio is determined by the collective behavior of the total net uses of funds (net of internal funds and including the unreported uses reflected in the statistical discrepancy, SD) and investment expenditures; leverage ratios will increase if any of the three variables in the numerator increases. But unless internal funds are declining (increasing D without increasing I), an increase in leverage (X/I) must be the result of an

Figure 3. **Net Acquisitions of Financial Assets (NFA).**

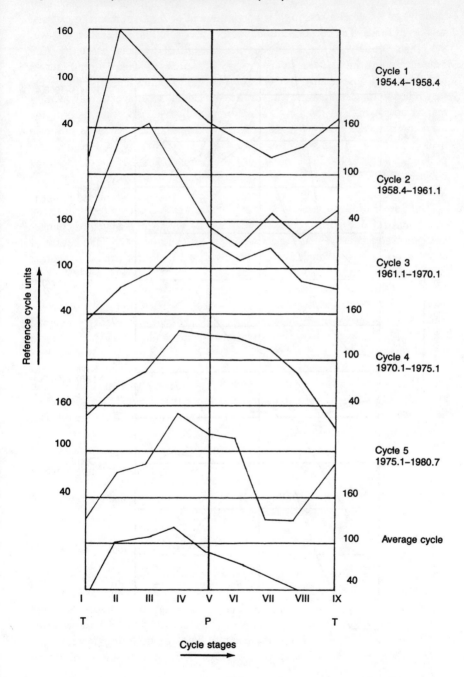

Figure 4. **Deficit on Capital Account (D).**

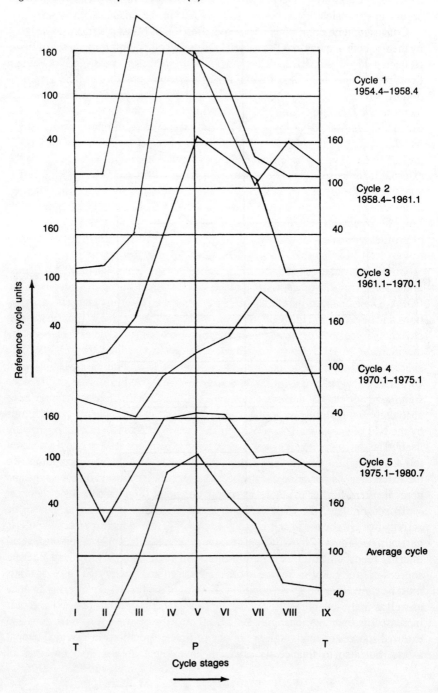

increase in one or both of the other two uses of funds. Since internal funds increase in expansions, the increase in flow leverage ratios such as X/I which occurs in expansions must be due to increases in the other uses of funds.

Consistent with point three of our specification of Minsky's financial instability theory, both acquisitions of financial assets and other, unreported uses of funds (reflected in the statistical discrepancy) do increase in expansions. Although firms reduce their holdings of liquid financial assets—point four of the specification of Minsky's theory—in stages 3, 4, and 5 of the expansion (they initially increase their holdings of liquid assets in stage 2, the first one-third of the expansion), their holdings of other financial assets (trade credit, consumer credit and direct foreign investment) rise rapidly and swamp out the fall in their holdings of liquid assets. These financial uses of funds are large with respect to the external funds raised (the ratio of net acquisitions of financial assets to the deficit was 3/1 in the cycles of the 1970's) and account for much of the growing difference between external funds raised and the deficit on capital account; funds flow out from the NFC sector to finance their customers' purchases and in search of profitable financial investment opportunities. Nonfinancial corporations borrow to lend in expansions, acting like financial intermediaries.

Other financial uses of funds which increase in the expansion may be reflected in the statistical discrepancy between reported sources and uses of funds in the FOFA. Debt-financed purchases of equity securities to effect mergers, acquisitions and buyouts, and the capitalization of interest (borrowing to finance interest payments in periods of financial stringency) are other possible explanations for the increase in leverage ratios which occur in expansions; the original data sources for the FOFA do not track these activities, and casual observation of corporate behavior in recent decades indicates that these activities may absorb significant amounts of borrowed funds.[6] The statistical discrepancy is large both absolutely and with respect to the levels of borrowing and reported expenditures by the NFCs, occasionally approaching the size of total credit market borrowing itself. The statistical discrepancy rises in most expansions (all but one, in which it fell 4.8 points) for an average trough-peak increase of 47.0 reference points. To the extent that its behavior does reflect the speculative financial uses suggested here, it offers further evidence in support of point three of Minsky's theory.

To recapitulate, the increase in external financing of corporate economic activity which occurs in the expansion phase of the typical business cycle is partially explained by the differential rates of increase in capital expenditures and internal funds, in differences in the timing of these uses of funds and internal sources of funds. But increases in other (reported and unreported) uses of funds must be called upon to give a complete account of the increase in external finance as well as in the leverage ratios of the nonfinancial corporations. The NFC sector increases its leverage, changing its capital structure toward a heavier debt and external sources of funds weight not just to finance positions in new real capital assets, but also to finance its sales, its investment abroad, and holdings of financial assets. In addition, the increased leverage might also refinance its outstanding debt, service that debt, and finance restructuring and combinations of firms. As expansions mature, all of these uses of funds outstrip the growth of internal funds, forcing the firms to seek external funds.

This observed behavior in the sources and uses of funds and in leverage ratios is exactly the pattern that Minsky's model of upward financial instability in expansions would predict. Borrowing and leverage both increase in expansions because firms' demand for capital assets (real and financial) outstrip the growth rate of internal funds, and their holdings of liquid financial assets decline, further weakening their financial positions. (Wolfson [1986, and in this volume] also interprets the behavior of financial variables from the perspective of Minsky's theory; although critical of certain aspects of Minsky's model, Wolfson finds that the model gives a plausible account of the behavior of the NFC sector during financial crises, which occur around cycle peaks.)

Corporate Financial Variables
and Ratios in Contractions

In expansions, flow leverage ratios increase because external finance rises more rapidly than expenditures on investment, which in turn rise more rapidly than internal funds. This increase in external finance above that necessary to finance the growing deficit on capital account is necessary to finance other activities of the NFCs such as acquisitions of financial assets, corporate restructurings and combinations of firms. In the contraction phase of the cycle this process is reversed: investment, acquisitions of financial assets, borrowing and leverage ratios all decline, although not back to their levels at the beginning of previous expansions; this behavior is consistent with point five of Minsky's hypothesis.

Flow leverage ratios tend to peak late in the expansion (stage 4 in the average cycle) and then to decline slowly throughout the contraction, often exhibiting a second (lower) peak in the mid-to-late contraction. These contraction peaks in leverage ratios, often higher than the expansion peaks, appear to be a combination of two factors: first, investment declines steadily throughout contractions, reducing the denominator of leverage ratios, and second, borrowing increases in the mid-to-late contraction, increasing the numerator in the ratios. In the cycles in which investment declines a great deal, a relatively small increase in borrowing results in a significant increase in leverage ratios for the sector. The increase in borrowing in the contraction appears to be the result of several factors: one is the increase in the extension of credit by the NFCs to their customers (consumer credit rises in late contractions), and another is direct foreign investment, which also rises in contractions. A third factor, which is consistent with Minsky's financial fragility and instability hypotheses, is forced borrowing by firms to cover operating losses (to pay their fixed costs of administrative overhead, etc.),

Table 2

Average Values of Various Leverage Ratios for U.S. Nonfinancial Corporations During Trough-Peak-Trough and Peak-Trough-Peak Cycles, 1953–81

TPT Cycles (five)	B/F %	B/I %	CMD/MVE %
1 (1954.4–1958.4)	29.0	27.3	36.2
2 (1958.4–1961.1)	29.2	28.1	33.4
3 (1961.1–1970.10)	38.6	34.6	33.4
4 (1970.10–1975.1)	55.2	48.9	50.4
5 (1975.1–1980.7)	45.7	42.0	74.3
PTP Cycles (six)			
1 (1953.7–1957.7)	26.0	23.9	37.9
2 (1957.7–1960.4)	29.7	28.8	39.9
3 (1960.4–1969.10)	36.9	32.9	32.5
4 (1969.10–1973.10)	50.3	46.1	41.5
5 (1973.10–1980.1)	49.6	44.5	73.7
6 (1980.1–1981.7)	43.3	41.5	71.1

B: Net Credit Market Borrowing
F: Fixed Investment
I: Capital Expenditures (Fixed Investment Plus Inventory Investment)
CMD: Credit Market Debt Outstanding
MVE: Market Value of Corporate Equity

Source: Federal Reserve Board *Flow of Funds Accounts and Balance Sheets for the US Economy* 1945–81; Niggle 1984.

to make interest payments, and to refinance outstanding debt. (See Minsky's discussion of forced borrowing in credit crunches and their aftermaths [Minsky, 1982b]; forced borrowing is also discussed by Fazzari and Caskey, and Wolfson, both in this volume.)

The leverage ratios are almost always higher at the end of the trough-peak-trough (T-P-T) cycle (stage 9) than at the beginning (stage 1), producing an upward trend. Table 2 illustrates this upward ratchet effect in the flow measures of leverage which occurred in the first four of the five T-P-T cycles; the stock measures of leverage (such as credit market debt outstanding to the market value of corporate equity) reflect that upward ratchet effect.

The long-run intercycle behavior of these leverage ratios is also consistent with Minsky's model, which is a synthesis of cyclical and secular analysis (Pollin 1982, 1986). The flow measures of leverage peaked in cycle 4 (1970–75); the expansion phase of this cycle succeeded the long expansion of the 1960s (105 months) and the brief recession of 1969–70 (12 months). One could argue from a Minskian perspective that the brief and shallow recession following the 1960s' boom was not severe enough to dissipate expectations of profit and perceptions of risk which, if no longer "euphoric," were still strongly optimistic for the representative firm and its bankers. The greatest relative increases in leverage (in reference cycle units) occurred in cycle 3 (the long 1960s expansion) and cycle 4 (Table 2).

The upward drift in leverage during the period analyzed paused after the fourth cycle (1970–75). Although leverage increased in the expansion of the subsequent cycle (1975–80), it did not rise as rapidly as in the previous cycles, and it fell back farther than in those cycles. This appears to be due to a combination of two factors. First, the sector's deficit on capital account was lower during this cycle than during previous expansions, damping the increase in external funds raised (see Figures 1 and 4); second, the sector's acquisition of financial assets (especially consumer and trade credit) plunged precipitously in the 1980 contraction, lessening the demand for funds by the NFCs (Figure 3).

This reduction in flow leverage over the last cycle may imply a return toward a lower "normal" leverage ratio, the attainment of a new plateau as foreseen by Gurley and Shaw (1956) for financially mature and developed economies, or simply a temporary pause in the secular pattern. Notice (Table 2) that the stock measures of leverage reflect the reduction in flow leverage very slightly: CMD/MVE only fell from 73% to 71% between cycles 5 and 6 (P-T-P cycles), and the decade averages for the stock measures are much higher for the 1970s than for the earlier period. This behavior can also be interpreted as consistent with Minsky's model: the more frequent and severe recessions of the late 1970s and early 1980s, coupled with the deteriorating asset portfolio quality of financial institutions, reduced speculative expectations, effecting a decline in borrowing and leverage. And although the current expansion (which began late in 1982) continues, making cyclical analysis inappropriate, leverage began increasing again in the mid 1980s, so that B/I averaged 50.5% for 1986 (see FRB Statistical Release Z7, June 5, 1987).

*   *   *

This analysis confirms that leverage and borrowing by nonfinancial corporations (taken as a sector) behave cyclically and secularly much as Minsky's theory would have it (at least as that theory has been specified for this paper). Expenditures on capital assets (real and financial, existing and new), borrowing and leverage ratios all increase in expansions. The greatest increase in leverage occurred during the longest expansion (that of cycle 3, 1961–70) and the absolute level of leverage peaked in cycle 4, after the brief 12 month contraction of 1969–70 which followed the long expansion of the 1960s. And although leverage temporarily declined in the late 1970s and early 1980s, that process reversed itself as the economy recovered from the latest contraction of 1981–82; currently leverage ratios are the highest ever recorded for U.S. nonfinancial corporations.

Notes

1. Minsky has discussed financial instability and financial fragility in a series of books and articles. His *John Maynard Keynes* (1975) and *Can "It" Happen Again?* (1983) contain extended discussions of his theory. "A Theory of Systemic Fragility" (1977) contains a concise statement of his views.

2. See Minsky (1977); Minsky (1978), pp. 17–20; Minsky (1980), pp. 508–11; and all of his 1981 paper for discussions of the financial crises and possible ensuing deep depression which the state of financial fragility implies. Minsky (1977) explains the role of liquid reserves in preventing economic collapse. Minsky attributes the argument that debt deflations and ensuing deep depressions occur when economic units are financially fragile to Irving Fisher's pioneering work in the 1930s (Fisher, 1933).

3. Another attempt at comparing Minsky's theory with the empirical record is Martin Wolfson's *Financial Crises: Understanding the Postwar U.S. Experience* (1986); also see his chapter in this volume.

4. Wesley C. Mitchell's *What Happens During Business Cycles* (1951), and W. C. Mitchell and Arthur F. Burns, *Measuring Business Cycles* describe the techniques they developed for business cycle analysis. Gerhard Bry and Charlotte Boschan describe the NBER programs in a thorough but non-technical manner in their *Cyclical Analysis of Time Series*, Technical Paper 20 (1971), NBER. For a detailed discussion of an application of the NBER program to the nonfinancial corporations' sources and uses of funds which discusses the strengths and weaknesses of the NBER approach, see Niggle (1984, chapter 3).

5. The Federal Reserve Board's Flow of Funds Accounts attempt to represent the interaction between financial and nonfinancial economic activity on the macroeconomic and sectoral levels. The FRB began developing the FOFA in 1947; *Introduction to the Flow of Funds* (FRB 1980) describes the accounting concepts utilized, the organization of the accounts, the sources of data, and the various publications which report the time series. Morris Copeland's pioneering work forms the conceptual basis for the accounts (see Copeland 1952). Cohen (1972) offers an assessment of Copeland's contribution to flow of funds accounting techniques and their usefulness for economic analysis.

6. See the statement by Preston Martin, then Vice President of the Board of Governors of the Federal Reserve Board, in the *Federal Reserve Bulletin* 71 (July 1985): 514–17 for the Fed's views on the extent of the nonfinancial corporations' use of funds for corporate combinations and restructurings.

References

Bry, Gerhard, and Charlotte Boschan. 1971. *Cyclical Analysis of Time Series*. Technical Paper No. 20. New York: National Bureau of Economic Research.

Cohen, Jacob. 1972. "Copeland's Moneyflows After Twenty-five Years: A Survey." *Journal of Economic Literature* 10:1–25.

Copeland, Morris. 1952. *A Study of Moneyflows in the United States*. New York: National Bureau of Economic Research.

Earley, James, Robert J. Parsons, and Fred A. Thompson. 1976. "Money, Credit, and Expenditure: A Sources and Uses Approach." *The Bulletin.* Center for the Study of Financial Institutions, Graduate School of Business Administration, New York University, No. 3.

Fazzari, Steven, and John Caskey. 1988. "Debt Commitments and Aggregate Demand: A Critique of the Neoclassical Synthesis." In this volume.

Federal Reserve Board. 1980. *Introduction to the Flow of Funds.* Washington, D.C.: Board of Governors of the Federal Reserve.

Fisher, Irving. 1933. "The Debt Deflation Theory of the Great Depression." *Econometrica* I:337–57.

Gurley, John G., and Edward S. Shaw. 1956. "Financial Intermediaries and the Saving-Investment Process." *Journal of Finance* (May):257–66.

Minsky, Hyman P. 1974. "The Modelling of Financial Instability: An Introduction." *Modelling and Simulation Volume 5: Proceedings of the Fifth Annual Pittsburgh Conference,* Instrument Society of America, pp. 267–73.

————. 1975. *John Maynard Keynes.* New York: Columbia University Press.

————. 1977. "A Theory of Systemic Fragility." *Financial Crises: Institutions and Markets in a Fragile Environment.* E. D. Altman and A. W. Sametz, eds., New York: John Wiley and Sons, pp. 138–52.

————. 1978. "The Financial Instability Hypothesis: A Restatement." *Thames Papers in Political Economy* (Autumn):5–10.

————. 1980. "Finance and Profits: The Changing Nature of American Business Cycles" *The Business Cycle and Public Policy.* Washington, D.C.: U.S. Government Printing Office, pp. 209–44.

————. 1982. *Can "It" Happen Again?.* Armonk, New York: M.E. Sharpe, Inc.

Mitchell, Wesley C., and Arthur F. Burns. 1946. *Measuring Business Cycles.* New York: National Bureau of Economic Research.

Mitchell, Wesley C. 1951. *What Happens During Business Cycles.* New York: National Bureau of Economic Research.

Niggle, Christopher J. 1984. The Cyclical and Secular Behavior of Leverage for the U.S. Nonfinancial Corporate Sector 1953–81: A Sources and Uses Approach. Ph.D. diss., University of California, Riverside.

————. 1985. The Cyclical Behavior of U.S. Nonfinancial Corporations' Financial Ratios and Minsky's Financial Instability Hypothesis. University of Redlands. Mimeo.

Pollin, Robert. 1982. Corporate Financial Structure and the Crisis of U.S. Capitalism. Ph.D. diss., The Graduate Faculty, New School for Social Research, New York.

————. 1986. "Alternate Perspectives on the Rise of Corporate Debt Dependency: The U.S. Postwar Experience." *Review of Radical Political Economics* 18:205–35.

Taylor, Lance, and Stephen A. O'Connell. 1985. "A Minsky Crisis." *Quarterly Journal of Economics* 100:871–85.

Wolfson, Martin. 1988. "Theories of Financial Crises." In this volume.

————. 1986. *Financial Crises: Understanding the Postwar U.S. Experience.* Armonk, New York: M. E. Sharpe, Inc.

Theories of Financial Crises

Martin H. Wolfson

With the increase in financial crises in recent years, there has also been an increase in theoretical analysis concerning the causes of this phenomenon. Several theorists writing on this topic recently have approached the problem from a relatively similar perspective. For want of a better term, this perspective could be termed the "business cycle, credit market" perspective.

Although there is broad agreement on a general approach, there are important differences in the actual analyses of various writers. The purpose of this chapter is to discuss the major theories of financial crises within this general perspective, to indicate how they differ, and to note some ways to compare the theories with the experience of financial crises in the postwar U.S. economy.

A Perspective on Financial Crises

The business cycle perspective sees financial crises as the result of the normal functioning of the economic and financial systems over the course of the business cycle. Endogenous developments near the peak of the cycle create the conditions that make financial crises likely.

According to the credit market perspective, the use of credit is essential to the business cycle expansion. Near the peak of the expansion, the demand for credit becomes increasingly inelastic. However, limitations on the supply of credit imply that all demands for credit cannot be accommodated. The financial crisis is associated with the end of the expansion of credit.

This general perspective is an important framework of analysis, but nonetheless it is only a framework, not a theory of financial crises. Important and significant differences in analysis are contained within the overall perspective. In order to gain a better understanding of these differences, several contemporary

---

The views expressed in this chapter are those of the author and do not necessarily represent those of the Board of Governors or of any other staff member.

theories of financial crises will be briefly highlighted, followed by a discussion of the important points of difference.

Particular Theories of Financial Crises

The view of Albert M. Wojnilower (1980, 1985) is that the demand for credit near the peak of the business cycle expansion is not only interest inelastic; it is essentially unbounded. Corporations seek to expand production and to finance this expansion with as much credit as they can obtain. According to Wojnilower, the banks are willing and able to supply the credit required. The expansion of credit is halted, however, by sudden shocks that make the banks either unwilling or unable to continue lending. The abrupt limitation of credit puts an end to the business cycle expansion and initiates a recession.

The perspective of Allen Sinai (1976, 1977; Eckstein and Sinai, 1986) is quite different. He does not see the economy as out of control near business cycle peaks; rather, his view is that limitations on the supply of credit are slowly and surely bringing the expansion to an end. Tight monetary policy over a prolonged period and reduced deposit inflows make the banks increasingly unable to meet the demands for credit. Production is gradually curtailed, and the economy slowly moves into recession.

The analysis of Hyman P. Minsky (1975, 1982, 1986) is focused on the endogenous development of financial fragility, and the implications of fragility for the development of financial crises. An important aspect of a fragile financial environment is the increasing inability of units to meet payment commitments, especially commitments due to debt. According to Minsky, an important reason for an inelastic demand for credit near the business cycle peak is the need to borrow to pay these debts. Another important reason is the need to finance ongoing investment projects that had been initiated at an earlier time.

Like earlier theorists of financial crises, such as Thorstein Veblen (1904) and Wesley Clair Mitchell (1971), Minsky notes the unwillingness of banks to debt-finance investment because of the decreasing creditworthiness of business borrowers. These earlier theorists emphasized a decline in profits as the key variable in changing the assessments of lenders. Minsky notes the role of profits, but his main emphasis seems to be on rising interest rates. He stresses their negative effect on the ability of borrowers to meet debt commitments, and on the outlook for future profitability. His emphasis is also different from that of Karl Marx (1967, 1968), who stressed the key role of a decline of profits in the inability to meet fixed payment commitments.

Differences Among the Theories

As can be seen from the above discussion, there are important differences among the theorists even though there are similarities in the overall perspective. These differences generally concern (a) the demand for credit, (b) the supply of credit, and (c) the nature of the financial crisis.

An important difference concerns the reason that the demand for credit becomes inelastic near the peak of the expansion phase of the business cycle. One perspective is that business firms are actively seeking to expand production, and higher interest rates are not a sufficient deterrent to these plans. An alternative perspective is that the demand is inelastic because it is necessitous. Firms need money either to finish investment projects that had been started in the past (and whose abandonment would result in unnecessary loss), or to meet payment commitments on outstanding debt.

This difference of opinion is related to another one, concerning the relationship between the financial crisis and the business cycle recession. Those who view the demand for credit as a demand for funds to finance the growth of production consider the interruption of the supply of credit to be responsible for halting this growth and initiating the recession. On the other hand, the view of the demand for credit as a necessitous one, involving funds to meet debt payment requirements and to finish partly completed investment projects, sees the financial crisis as occurring either during the recession or after the conditions for recession have already been established (because plans for new investment have been curtailed).

The distinction is important, not only for pinpointing the causal relationship between the financial crisis and the recession, but also for understanding the potential threat of the crisis itself. If the crisis involves a denial of funds to borrowers who cannot meet debt payments, then a cascading downward spiral of defaults, bankruptcies, and credit liquidations, typical of the debt-deflation process (Fisher 1933), is set to occur. However, if production can be curtailed without requiring debt repudiation, then perhaps the economy can avoid the threat of these severe repercussions.

There is a further difference of opinion among those who emphasize the inability of borrowers to meet debt payment commitments. It is whether this situation is due primarily to an increase in interest rates, or whether a decline in profits is mainly responsible.

A second major issue is the reason for the limitations on the supply of credit. The differences of opinion revolve around the ability and willingness of creditors, especially the banks, to extend credit. One point of view is that the main reason for the limitation is the voluntary restriction of credit by the banks, due to the decreased creditworthiness of business borrowers. The alternative perspective is that the banks try to meet the credit demands of their borrowers but are prevented from doing so either by the slow squeeze on reserves and deposits or by a sudden shock to the system.

A third issue is the nature of the financial crisis. One dimension of difference is whether the crisis occurs slowly or abruptly. Another is whether it is only a squeeze on the supply of credit, or if it also involves a sudden jolt to confidence and a disruption of normal financing patterns. In other words, the controversy is over whether the financial crisis involves a slow winding down of credit extensions or a sudden cutoff of credit and a desperate scramble for money to meet payment commitments.

Theories and the U.S. Experience

It is not easy to reconcile these differences, because they involve attitudes and motivations as well as questions of fact. Although it is not possible to get definitive answers, some light can be shed on the relevant issues by examining the recent experience of financial crises in the United States. Timing relationships and surveys of behavior will be particularly useful.

First of all, it would be useful to briefly identify the timing of the postwar crises. The first crisis following World War II in the United States was called the Credit Crunch of 1966, which took place in August, 1966. It was followed by a crisis surrounding the bankruptcy of the Penn Central Railroad in June of 1970. In May of 1974, the troubles of the Franklin National Bank precipitated another crisis and was followed in March, 1980 by the events surrounding the Hunt brothers' unsuccessful silver speculation. During the summer of 1982 (June through August), a series of events associated with the collapse of Drysdale Government Securities, Inc., the failure of Penn Square Bank, and the threatened default of Mexico on its international obligations created a crisis of confidence in the nation's commercial banks.

If we count the growth recession of 1966–67, then a financial crisis has taken place near the peak of each business cycle expansion since 1966. Each of the above mentioned crises, in fact, has taken place shortly *after* the recession has begun. All of them took place within six months after the peak of the expansion (except for the crisis in 1982, which took place approximately one year afterwards). Thus it appears that this timing evidence is incompatible with the view that sees the recession caused by the liquidation of credit during the financial crisis.

There are also the most recent crises: the effective failure of Continental Illinois National Bank, the runs on deposits of state-insured thrifts in Ohio and Maryland, and the stock market crash. These took place during the business cycle expansion, before the peak had been reached. Their timing is related to long-term structural and institutional changes which will not be discussed further here.[1]

Let us now consider the other issues raised in the previous section. The first issue concerns the reasons for the inelastic demand for credit near the business cycle peak. There is some basis to think that this is a necessitous demand for funds to meet payment commitments.

The financial condition of the nonfinancial corporate sector has shown a strong cyclical deterioration as the peak of the expansion has approached. The traditional measures of balance-sheet strength have worsened: debt/equity and debt/maturity ratios have increased, and liquidity ratios have declined.[2] In addition, the interest coverage ratio has declined near the peak of the expansion. This measure, which is the ratio of gross profits before tax plus interest paid to interest paid, indicates the ability to pay interest costs out of capital income.

The peaks of the interest coverage ratio closely coincide with the peaks in the profit ratio. This closeness in timing suggests that the decline in profits near the expansion peak is responsible for the debt payment difficulties observed. Interest rates, on the other hand, have typically begun to increase from six months to a year before the interest coverage ratio begins to fall. This timing pattern suggests that corporations can use debt to exploit profitable investment opportunities, and these actions can increase interest rates without necessarily creating debt repayment problems. It is only when the means to repay the debt—profits—begin to decline that repayment problems become more severe.[3]

The alternative view concerning the demand for credit is that corporations are seeking credit in order to finance increases in production. However, the empirical record indicates that real investment in plant and equipment has generally peaked before the financial crisis, although it has remained at a relatively high level. In addition, the series on contracts and orders for plant and equipment, which indicates plans for future investment, has consistently peaked approximately one to two quarters before the investment series itself.

The most likely interpretation of these relationships is that a form of "involuntary" investment is responsible for at least part of the demand for credit in the period immediately preceding the financial crisis. During the time in which plans for investment have been curtailed but investment spending is still relatively high, it is likely that corporations are seeking to fund not new investment projects, but those which had been initiated in the past and which require continued funding in the present. This "involuntary" investment takes the form of a payment commitment similar in some respects to debt payment requirements.

The second major issue concerns the reasons for the limitations on the supply of credit. In examining the conditions affecting lenders, we find that monetary policy has consistently tightened near the postwar business cycle peaks. In addition, losses on loans of commercial banks have risen as the peak of the expansion has approached. Thus banks have had an incentive to cut back on their lending and have also had to deal with pressures from the monetary authorities to limit their lending. How they have reacted to this situation, however, has differed for different types of customers.

Generally, banks have restricted credit near the business cycle peaks, but at the same time have tried to meet the necessitous loan demands of their long-standing corporate customers. The pressures on their reserves have led banks to limit the growth of their investments and to slow the growth of nonbusiness loans in favor of business loans. Evidence from the Federal Reserve Board's Survey of Bank Lending Practices indicates that during these times, banks have tightened lending policies much more for new business borrowers than for established customers.

They have been able to meet the needs of their best customers by using liability management and "purchasing" relatively expensive, volatile, and uninsured funds in the money market, e.g., large negotiable certificates of deposit, Eurodollar and commercial paper borrowings, and fed funds.

The final issue concerns the nature of the financial crisis. The difference of opinion centers around the issue of whether the financial crisis is a slow liquidation of credit or a more abrupt reaction. In fact, the pressures on the banks referred to above have led to a slow reduction of credit for many borrowers prior to the business cycle peaks. However, the banks' attempts to meet the needs of their best customers have also led to a lending situation which has been disrupted suddenly by surprise events.

There were two types of surprise events in the postwar experience in the United States. The first was an institutional constraint imposed by government authorities; in 1966 Regulation Q interest rate ceilings were kept in place, and in March, 1980 explicit credit controls were instituted. The second type of surprise event was either a default or failure (or the threat of one) which shocked investor and/or depositor confidence. In 1970, it was the Penn Central bankruptcy, for example, and in 1974, the threatened failure of Franklin National Bank, etc.

The significance of these surprise events is that they have abruptly cut off the supply of credit to important borrowers. In the case of the institutional constraints, banks were suddenly prevented from further lending by government authority. The surprise defaults and bankruptcies typically caused a rapid withdrawal by institutional investors from the commercial paper market and the markets for bank purchased funds. In both cases, lending suddenly stopped.

It was at this point that the Federal Reserve Board quickly intervened in the financial markets as a lender of last resort. By making money available to those who were desperately in need of it and were abruptly cut off from sources of credit, the Federal Reserve prevented the financial crisis from spreading and deepening. This intervention was usually followed by easier monetary and fiscal policies which, for the time being, moved the economy away from crisis.

Thus the essence of the financial crisis is an intense demand for money, brought about by the sudden cessation of credit. Although much of the economy is subject to a gradual credit squeeze as the business cycle expansion is ending, this alone does not capture the full extent of the threat that financial crises pose to the financial stability of the U.S. economy.

Notes

1. For a discussion of these changes and their significance for the business cycle perspective, see Wolfson (1986, 1987).

2. The empirical record is discussed in detail in Eckstein and Sinai (1986) and Wolfson (1986).

3. Neither is it the case that interest costs, which are a deduction from profits, were responsible for the decline in profits; the profit rate with interest costs added back to profits shows the same cyclical pattern.

References

Eckstein, Otto, and Allen Sinai. 1986. "The Mechanisms of the Business Cycle in the Postwar Era." *The American Business Cycle: Continuity and Change*, pp. 39–105. Robert J. Gordon, ed. NBER: University of Chicago Press.

Fisher, Irving. 1933. "The Debt-Deflation Theory of Great Depressions." *Econometrica* 1:337–57.

Marx, Karl. *Capital*. 3 vols. New York: International Publishers. 1967.

————. 1968. *Theories of Surplus Value*. 3 parts. Moscow: Progress Publishers.

Minsky, Hyman P. 1975. *John Maynard Keynes*. New York: Columbia University Press.

————. 1982. *Can "It" Happen Again? Essays on Instability and Finance*. Armonk, New York: M. E. Sharpe, Inc.

————.1986. *Stabilizing an Unstable Economy*. New Haven: Yale University Press.

Mitchell, Wesley Clair. 1971. *Business Cycles and Their Causes*. Berkeley, California: University of California Press.

Sinai, Allen. 1976. "Credit Crunches—An Analysis of the Postwar Experience." *Parameters and Policies in the U.S. Economy*, pp. 244–74. Otto Eckstein, ed. Amsterdam: North Holland.

————. Discussion of Papers on the American Financial Environment. *Financial Crises: Institutions and Markets in a Fragile Environment*, pp. 187–203. Edward I. Altman and Arnold W. Sametz, eds. New York: John Wiley & Sons, 1977.

Veblen, Thorstein. 1904. *The Theory of Business Enterprise*. New York: Charles Scribner's Sons.

Wojnilower, Albert M. 1980. "The Central Role of Credit Crunches in Recent Financial History." *Brookings Papers on Economic Activity*, No. 2, pp. 277–326.

————. 1985. "Private Credit Demand, Supply, and Crunches: How Different are the 1980s?" *American Economic Review* 75:351–56.

Wolfson, Martin H. 1986. *Financial Crises: Understanding the Postwar U.S. Experience*. Armonk, New York: M. E. Sharpe, Inc.

————. 1987. Financial Instability, the Business Cycle, and Macroeconomic Policy. Paper presented at the Meeting of the Eastern Economic Association. (March 6).

The Political Economy of
the External Debt and Growth:
The Case of Peru

Felix Jimenez and Edward J. Nell

The Baker Plan signaled the U.S. Administration's desire to reverse the slow-down in lending to the Third World from 1986 to 1988. Accordingly, first, debtor countries must adopt free-market policies; second, banks should increase new lending to the debt-ridden nations; and third, the IMF and the World Bank should intensify their monitoring of debt-plagued countries and speed up their own lending programs. Underlying the Plan are the unchallenged postulates of American policy makers: the free market is the best engine of economic growth, and foreign capital always contributes to the long-run economic growth of recipients.

American economic policy has affected Third World countries by implementing two measures: one monetarist (or bastard Keynesian) and the other Keynesian. The first is a dollar devaluation, intended to change both the U.S. level of trade and the terms of trade of the U.S. economy.[1] Since Reaganomics has reduced the already damaged purchasing power of the Third World countries, the second measure is to pump fresh money into the biggest debtor countries whenever they adopt free-market policies; this fresh money, in turn, can be expected to help create demand for the manufactured goods of the U.S. and other industrialized economies.[2]

The general object of this paper is to show that the free-market approach is, at best, useless, since it does not deal with the basic problems which prevent Latin American countries from streamlining their economies, and, at worst, dangerous, since it can destroy the fragile industrial base these economies have developed. The point will be illustrated with the case of Peru, which is reasonably representative. Free-market policies are part of the problem, not part of the solution.

Table 1

Total External Debt

Year[1]	Public	Private	Total[2]	Debt-GDP Ratio[3]	Debt-Export Ratio [3]
1966	604.7	1153.1	1757.8	30.3	194.7
1968	762.0	1199.6	1961.6	36.1	201.3
1971	1000.7	1210.5	2211.2	29.0	207.0
1973	1491.0	1201.0	2692.0	26.5	199.8
1975	3066.0	1286.0	4352.0	28.0	261.6
1978	5135.0	1340.0	6475.0	55.0	272.8
1981	6210.0	1507.0	7717.0	30.7	191.0
1984	9775.0	1464.2	11239.2	53.6	312.5

Notes:
[1]Cycle-peaks: 1966, 1971, 1975 and 1981
  Cycle-troughs: 1968, 1973, 1978 and 1984.
[2]Millions of U.S. dollars.
[3]Variables of this ratio were measured by the same currency at current prices.

Sources:
Banco Central de Reserva del Peru; Instituto Nacional de Estadistica; IMF, *International Financial Statistics*; World Bank, Peru: *Long-term Development Issues*, Vol. III, 1979.

First, the external and internal factors underlying the evolution of the Peruvian debt will be identified. The debt crisis arises not only from the inadequacies of the international financial system,[3] e.g., deterioration in the terms of trade and world recession. It is also a result of internal economic factors, since internal policies to counteract international shocks are ultimately limited by the requirements of domestic capital accumulation.

Second, the contribution of foreign finance to economic growth will be quantified and the macroeconomic consequences of both external debt and foreign direct investment will be identified. We want to stress that the need for external finance mostly reflects the structural dependency of the economic system on imports of industrial inputs and capital goods due to the absence of an integrated input-output system.

Sources of Growth of External Debt, 1973-1984

The figures in Table 1 show three important characteristics of the external debt for the Peruvian economy. First, as can be seen by comparing column 2 and column 4, the share of public debt increased rapidly from 34.4 percent in 1966 to 70.5 in 1975, rising to 87 percent in 1984. Second, the ratio of foreign debt to GDP didn't change significantly during the cycle peaks: its mean was equal to 29.5; however, during the cycle troughs this ratio had a spectacular increase: its

Table 2

Current and Capital Accounts of the Balance of Payments (millions of current U.S. dollars)

	1950–62	1963–68	1969–75	1976–80	1981–84
Resource Balance	−297.7	−254.4	−1507.8	1518.0	−825.1
Net factor Service Income	−529.8	−658.4	−1262.9	−3300.0	−4334.6
(Net Interest Payments)	(n.a.)	(−235.0)	(−843.8)	(−2434.3)	(−3774.2)
(Net repatriated profits)	(n.a.)	(−423.4)	(−419.1)	(−865.7)	(−560.4)
Transfers	145.7	151.8	355.0	615.0	698.0
CURRENT ACCOUNT	−681.8	−761.0	−2415.0	−1167.0	−4461.0
Medium and Long term Loans, Net	242.8	542.4	2243.9	2584.0	4342.2
Direct Foreign Investment, Net	330.8	26.1	423.7	348.0	122.0
Short Term Capital(*)	192.2	102.8	−267.4	−604.5	−176.0
CHANGE IN RESERVES, Net	84.0	−89.7	−14.8	1160.5	−172.0

*This item includes Errors and Omissions.
Sources:
Banco Central de Reserva del Peru; World Bank, Peru: *Long-term Development Issues,* Vol III, 1979.

mean was equal to 42.8. A similar pattern is present in the debt/export ratio, which had an average greater than 200 percent for the whole period.[4] Third, the year 1973 constitutes the turning point in the long-run pattern of the external debt; from that year through 1984, the debt increased almost exponentially.

The current and the capital account of the balance of payments clearly show the existence of two radically different periods in the last 35 years (see Table 2). From 1950 to 1968, the current account deficit represented only 18 percent of the respective accumulated deficit in the last 16 years; repatriated profits constituted the predominant item in the balance of factor service income during the same period; and the short term capital flows were persistently positive.

The picture is radically different for the last 16 years, since financial capital took over the economy. The outflow of interest payments from 1969 to 1975 was 3.5 times greater than between 1963 and 1969. Its amount tripled between 1976 and 1980 and became 4.5 times greater from 1981 to 1984, compared to the levels under the Velasco administration. Moreover, repatriated profits were half the level of the net interest payments between 1969 and 1975, a third between 1976 and 1980, and only 15 percent between 1981 and 1984.

Nevertheless, it is worth pointing out that the average debt/GDP ratio during Velasco's government was 12 points less than its mean for the 1976 to 1984 period. The corresponding values were 30 percent for 1968 to 1975, 42.1 for 1976 to 1980, and 41.8 for 1981 to 1984. The cost of borrowing skyrocketed between 1981 and 1984. In order to estimate the cost, the implicit nominal interest rates are used—which may mean underestimating the contractual nominal interest rates. The average real rate, based on price-of-imports inflation, was 2.8 for the first Belaunde administration (1964–68), –0.2 during the first four years of Velasco's government, and –20.5 from 1973 to 1975. During the Morales-Bermudez government, the average real rate became positive but stayed near zero. But during the second Belaunde administration, the cost of credit increased steeply: the real rate averaged 11.7 percent. The cheap credit during Velasco's era and the low debt/GDP ratio (30 percent) contrasts with the high cost and the high debt/GDP ratio (42 percent) during the last Belaunde administration. Are the key factors which determine the differences in the behavior of the foreign debt in these periods chiefly external?

When the debt service is related to exports of goods and services, the resulting ratio for the later period is systematically higher than during the sixties. From 1950 to 1967, the debt service ratio averaged significantly less than 10 percent, only reaching the neighborhood of 10 percent in 1966–67, which is when the GDP rose furthest above its trend values for the entire period from 1950 to 1984 (see Table 3).

What follows is a detailed analysis of the internal and external factors underlying the spectacular growth of foreign debt during the 1973–84 period. This examination will help to evaluate the consequences of different economic policies adopted by the last three governments: the administration of Velasco Alvarado and the governments of Morales-Bermudez and Belaunde Terry. The first of these is well known for its expansionary and interventionist stance, while the last two welcomed subordination to the IMF's monetarist policies.

A methodology based on the balance-of-payments identity is used, which makes it possible to decompose the difference between the actual and the expected increase in debt into internal and external factors.[5] The accounting identity for the net flow of total external debt is:

(1) $NB_t = Pm_tM_t - Px_tX_t + r_tD_t - 1 + FI_t - TR_t - SE_t + RA_t$

where: NB = net flow of total medium- and long-term debt;
   M = imports of goods and non-factor services;
   Pm = import prices;
   X = exports of goods and non-factor services;
   Px = export prices;
   r = nominal interest rate on external debt;
   D = total debt stock in current dollars;

Table 3

External Debt Flows and Debt Service Ratios

Year	Net Flow[1]		Interest Pay-ments[2]	Interest Export Ratio[3]	Debt Service Ratio[4]	Cover-age Ratio[5]
	Total	Public				
1963–88	542.4	474.7	235.0	4.8	9.7	99.2
1969–72	340.4	359.0	297.0	6.6	19.4	16.7
1973	333.5	313.5	101.0	7.5	32.5	71.6
1974	751.0	693.0	176.4	9.6	24.9	152.0
1975	819.0	793.0	269.4	16.2	28.5	167.2
1976	471.0	446.0	331.1	21.0	30.7	92.0
1977	674.0	659.0	384.1	18.1	29.4	105.9
1978	419.0	405.0	562.1	23.7	29.6	57.7
1979	585.0	617.0	540.8	12.6	19.3	74.8
1980	435.0	371.0	616.2	13.4	28.7	28.0
1981	523.0	388.0	767.8	19.0	43.5	22.1
1982	1152.0	995.0	915.9	22.8	39.8	62.2
1983	1346.0	1431.0	971.2	27.9	50.7	80.9
1984[6]	1321.2	1436.0	1119.3	31.1	56.5	70.7

Notes:

[1]Medium- and long-term loans, in millions of U.S. dollars.

[2]Total net interest payments, in millions of U.S. dollars.

[3]Ratio of total net interest payments to exports of goods and non-factor services.

[4]Ratio of amortization plus interest payments on public loans to exports of goods and non-factor services.

[5]Inverse ratio of amortization plus interest payments on public loans to net foreign public debt flows.

[6]Values of debt service ratio and coverage ratio for 1984 are preliminary.

Sources:

Banco Central de Reserva del Peru; Instituto Nacional de Estadistica; World Bank, Peru: Long-term Development Issues, Vol III, 1979.

$$(D_t = NB_t + D_{t-1})$$

FI = net repatriated profits minus the net flow of foreign direct investment;

TR = net transfers;

SE = net flow of short term capital plus errors and omissions;

RA = changes in international reserves;

t = current year t

On the other hand, the expected net flow of total foreign debt can be defined:

(2) $NB^*_t = Pm^*_t M^*_t - Px^*_t X^*_t + r^*_t D^*_{t-1} - TR^*_t$

where: NB^* = expected net flow of total foreign debt;

Pm^* = expected value of import prices;

Px^* = expected value of export prices;[6]

M^* = amount of imports in year t given by applying the propensity to import of year $t-1$ to the volume of domestic demand (apparent consumption) of year t;

X^* = amount of exports in year t given by applying the ratio of exports to world demand in year $t-1$ to the level of world demand of the same year;

r^* = forecasted value of the implicit interest rate estimated by regressing the natural log of the implicit interest rate on time for 1966–72.

D^*_t = is equal to $NB^*_t + D^*_{t-1}$. The expected value of D^*_0 (stock of foreign debt for 1972) was estimated by regressing the natural log of the net interest payments on time for 1966–72. The forecasted value for 1972 was divided by r^* of 1973 to calculate D^*_0.

By subtracting (2) from (1) and assuming:

$$FI^*_t = 0$$
$$TR^*_t = TR_t$$
$$SE^*_t = 0$$
$$RA^*_t = 0$$

the additional external debt can be decomposed as follows:[7]

$NB_t - NB^*_t =$

  (i) $Px_t[x_{t-1}(W^*_t - W_t)]$

  (ii) $(Pm_t - Pm^*_t)M^*_t - (Px_t - Px^*_t)X^*_t$

  (iii) $(r_t - r^*_t)D_{t-1}$

  (iv) $Pm_t[(m_t - m_{t-1})DD_t]$

  (v) $Pm_t[m_{t-1}(DD_t - DD^*_t)]$

  (vi) $Px_t[(x_{t-1} - x_t)W_t]$

  (vii) FI_t

  (viii) $r^*_t(D_{t-1} - D^*_{t-1})$

  (ix) SE_t

  (x) RA_t

where: x is the share of exports in the world demand;
        W is the real world demand proxied by imports of industrialized countries;
        W^* is the expected world demand;[8]
        m is the ratio of imports to domestic demand;
        DD stands for the domestic demand, DD = GDP + M - X;
        DD^* is the expected domestic demand.

The term in row (i), the difference between expected and theoretical values of exports calculated under the assumption that the share of exports in world demand remains constant, accounts for the effect of deviation in world demand from its trend values on the country's real exports. It was named *World Recession Effect* and is measured at current prices. The two terms in row (ii) constitute the *Terms of Trade Effect*. Changes in actual prices are measured against expected prices only in order to capture the unexpected effect of inflation on the terms of trade. The term in row (iii) indicates the effect of changes (with respect to expected values) in the interest rate paid on the external debt. This *Interest Rate Effect* is purely an external shock. All of these three first rows constitute the debt-inducing effects of external disturbances. We named them *External Factors*.

The term in row (iv) accounts for the *Import Penetration Effect*. This effect constitutes the increase in the country's imports explained only by the increase in the propensity to import. Since this effect is also measured at current prices, it incorporates the external shock due to unexpected inflation. The *Austerity Policy Effect* is accounted for in row (v). Assuming a constant propensity to import, it is the estimated increase in imports explained only by deviations of domestic demand from its trend. Again, since this effect is measured at current prices, it incorporates the external shock due to unexpected inflation. The term in row (vi) quantifies the *Export Reorientation Effect*[9] which is measured by the difference between theoretical and expected values of exports under the assumption that the share of exports in world demand remains constant. These last three effects are basically associated with internal factors that further overloaded the debt problem.

The rows (vii) to (x) also constitute the debt-inducing effects of internal policy reactions to internal or external shocks. Row (vii) accounts for the short-run and the long-run impact of continuous foreign direct investment on the balance of payments. It was named *Foreign Investment Policy Effect*. An economic policy which permits profits to be repatriated in excess of net foreign direct investment only exacerbates the financial distress in an economy with structural disequilibrium in its external sector. Row (viii) accounts for the *Debt Stock Effect on Interest Payments*. The effect of policy decisions on speculators is accounted for in row (iv). It was named *Speculation* or *Smuggling Effect*. Since it includes errors and omissions it probably conceals smuggling, which itself is mainly a result of the policies adopted by the government. Finally, row (x) accounts for the *Reserve*

Table 4

**Sources of Growth of External Debt, 1973–1984
(Millions of current U.S. dollars)**

Factor	Velasco 1973–75	Morales-Bermudez 1976–80	Belaunde 1981–84
1. World Recession Effect	326.0	664.3	2747.5
2. Terms of Trade Effect	−216.3	−461.9	4207.4
3. Interest Rate Effect	197.8	1092.3	1740.0
TOTAL EXTERNAL SHOCKS	307.5	1294.7	8694.9
4. Import Penetration Effect	54.6	−85.1	−664.7
5. Austerity Policy Effect	485.6	−2824.8	−1666.7
6. Export Reorientation Effect	687.8	−163.5	641.3
7. Foreign Investment Policy Effect	−372.9	517.7	437.6
8. Debt Stock Effect on Interest Payments	39.9	26.0	996.2
9. Speculative or Smuggling Effect	160.7	604.5	176.0
10. Reserve Accumulation Effect	−281.6	1160.5	−172.0
TOTAL INTERNAL SHOCKS	774.1	−764.7	−252.3
TOTAL ADDITIONAL EXTERNAL DEBT	1081.8	529.8	8442.7

Accumulation Effect, which basically reflects the financial pressure on monetary authorities to maintain the external value of the currency.[10]

The results are summarized in Table 4. As far as the additional external debt (NB-NB*) is concerned—see the last row of Table 4—it amounted to $1,081.8 million in Velasco's period, decreased to $529.8 million in the Morales-Bermudez administration and jumped up to reach the impressive value of $8,442.7 million in the second Belaunde administration.

One striking result concerns the role played by internal factors. These factors explained a significant part of the additional debt only during the Velasco administration: 71.6 percent against −144.3 percent during the Morales-Bermudez's government and −3.0 percent during the second government of Belaunde Terry.

Velasco's administration represents the last political effort to develop a national manufacturing sector based on the internal market, while biasing production toward import-competing industries. The implementation of this strategy required increasing capital goods, technology, and food imports, which meant financing these imports not only from export earnings but also by increasing external debt.[11]

While the average increase in the propensity to import accounted for only 5 percent of the total additional external debt, it is worth noting that the import substitution policy didn't avoid import penetration. The Velasco expansionary policy and the absence of a significant export reorientation accounted for 108.5 percent of the total additional net flow of foreign capital (see Table 4). The foreign investment effect was negative in accord with the nationalist attribute of this administration. By the same token, the smuggling effect was positive. As for external shocks, it can be seen that their contribution to the additional debt only amounted to about 28.4 percent. The favorable terms of trade effect more than made up for the interest rate effect which, in turn, explained not more than 18 percent of the additional external debt. The associated process of import substitution was spurious; it didn't create an integrated national input-output system but only intensified the necessity of importing capital and intermediate goods.[12]

The industrialization process spurred by Velasco's government coincided with the change in the form in which foreign capital has "migrated" to the less developed countries. In the 1960s, foreign direct investment accounted for about 30 percent of all foreign capital inflows into Latin America, with bank loans and bonds accounting for 10 percent. In the 1970s, the multinational share had dropped to 21 percent, while the share of private international financiers had risen to 59 percent;[13] consequently, the interest costs overwhelmed not only the outflow of repatriated profits, but also the inflow of foreign direct investment.[14] According to some analysts, the foreign financial borrowing, by facilitating the trade of capital equipment, know-how, technologies, and the hiring of foreign consultants to help set up the investment projects, has decreased the economic and political risks associated with foreign direct investment.

In the subsequent two administrations, the role of internal factors decreased primarily because of the draconian austerity policies. Without the effect of external factors, the net flow of the total additional external debt would have been negative. The positive additional debt was, therefore, explained basically by the external shocks (see Table 4).

The interest rate effect was the worst external shock during the Morales-Bermudez administration. But, the bulk of this effect was concentrated in the last three years of that administration, just when the cost of the credit started to grow in the international financial system.[15] On the other hand, the world recession effect, discounting the favorable terms of trade effect, only amounted to about 15.6 percent of the total additional debt arising from external shocks.

As far as the internal factors are concerned, the government of that time "succeeded" in driving down the net flow of foreign loans: the import bill was cut by almost $3 billion through its severe austerity measures (see Table 4). Yet, the export promotion policies were not significant in terms of relaxing the need for foreign borrowing.

It is worth noting that without the draconian austerity policy, the accumulated resource balance would have been negative and approximately equal to −$1,307 million (see Tables 2 and 4 for the 1976–80 period). Moreover, it is not surprising that the open-door external policy—a well-known element of the IMF austerity package—prevented a significant decrease in the average propensity to import in the corresponding period. Finally, the most striking internal factor was the reserve accumulation effect. Rather than draw down the reserves to finance the current deficit, the Morales-Bermudez regime borrowed abroad to add to the reserves; the increase in reserves was nearly $1,161 million between 1976 and 1980 (see Table 4).[16]

Trade liberalization started out in 1979 with the elimination of the Registro Nacional de Manufacturas[17] introduced by Velasco's government to control import competition.[18] The consequent significant increase in the propensity to import and its negative impact on the consumer durables-producing sector intensified the vulnerability of the state to pressures of international financial capital. With foreign loans kept down, the state had to divert export earnings to finance import penetration (and also increases in repatriated profits) and could accumulate reserves only in order to manage the dollarization of the economy on the local currency. De-industrialization and the dollar driving the local currency out of the internal market were the two main consequences of control over the state by international financial capital.

Once the IMF and the World Bank paved the way for "restructuring" the manufacturing industry, the international financial institutions increased the flow of loans to the new government of Belaunde Terry. Hence, the additional external debt skyrocketed between 1980 and 1984. The import bill decreased significantly, again due to the austerity policies: − $1,667 million between 1981 and 1984 (see Table 4). President Belaunde weakened the austerity prescriptions at the beginning of his administration, perhaps because of enthusiasm generated by the recent performance of the country's exports and the previously accumulated reserves. This temporary alleviation occurred within a framework of free trade and consequently resulted in a massive inflow of imports: the rise in the propensity to import created a pressure on the balance of payments equivalent to 139 percent of the same effect during the deepest import penetration period—1973 and 1974—of Velasco's administration (See Table 4).

The upward cycle begun in 1979 peaked in 1981 simultaneously with the current account deficit, which reached its highest value in the last 35 years. The crisis of the external sector forced a reversal of the cycle and the story was repeated—with an identical scenario imposed by the IMF. The government decreased the import bill by austerity measures; it fell − $1,766 million—which might have been expected during 1983–84. The draconian austerity package was imposed on an economy deeply dependent on imports, which also put a downward pressure on the ratio of imports to domestic demand. As a result of this and other restrictive external policies, the influence of changes in the propensity to import on the additional external debt was severely negative in 1983 and 1984.

The policy of trade liberalization, begun in 1979, was halted in 1982. The government decreed a general temporary tariff increase of 15 percent. But this occurred at a point when the process of de-industrialization had already increased the income elasticity of demand for imports to more than twice its value for 1968–75 (see Table 8).[19]

On the other hand, the attempt to reduce the financial squeeze by export-promoting policies was fruitless. The depressed international environment during Belaunde's administration only showed, in a dramatic way, the unfeasibility of the so-called export-led growth model, popularized by the apparent successes in Asia. To try to penetrate international markets for nontraditional exports in an unfavorable environment is likely to be a waste of effort.

Although the export reorientation effect during Morales-Bermudez's administration had an opposite sign, the policies were basically the same as those of the second administration of Belaunde Terry. The first was luckier than the second, but both shared the free-market-conservative ideology. As a matter of fact during both administrations, the sum of repatriated profits, discounting the net flow of foreign direct investment, amounted to over $955 million. That was almost 34 percent of the outflow of international reserves due to the increase in the interest rate in the international financial system (see Table 4). By the same token, the outflow of short-term capital, which usually depends on confidence in internal policy making, was approximately equal to $780 million. In absence of these two effects, the net flow of foreign borrowing would have been $1,070 million less than its expected value, calculated on the basis of the internal austerity and trade policies adopted during 1981–84. Finally, the contrasting behavior of the reserve accumulation effect during Belaunde's government doesn't mean a recovery of monetary sovereignty, but shows a state unable to resist the pressure to devalue. The highest rates of depreciation occurred between 1981 and 1984, and the government was forced to change the monetary unit by creating the so-called INTI.

In order to appreciate the foregoing analysis properly, it is important to remember that the total effect of internal factors on the additional debt was negative for both administrations. Therefore, the positive inflow of foreign borrowing was basically connected to external shocks. As mentioned, during Belaunde's administration the external shocks worsened. The world recession effect was quadrupled; the deterioration in the terms of trade was of such a magnitude that it created an additional need for international reserves approximately equal to $4,207 million; and the interest rate effect was around 60 percent more than the value reached during the previous government (see Table 4).

To show the nature of the debt crisis during the last two governments, we need to also consider the effects of the IMF policies on the internal economy as whole. The average rate of growth during Morales-Bermudez's administration was only about 1.9 percent, and it fell to –0.5 percent in 1981–84, to mention only one of the more important economic indicators. Hence, the striking moral—for the monetarists—that can be derived from the analysis so far is that free-market policies cannot solve the persistent crisis of the balance-of-payments. The continuous dismantling of the machinery of state economic intervention only exacerbated the financial squeeze on the economy. This was reflected in the spectacular rates of growth of external debt reached during the last two administrations. Trade liberalization increased the vulnerability of the economy to import penetration; this brought about de-industrialization, which further increased the income elasticity of demand for imports. The lack of control over the outflow of repatriated profits and over the inflow of foreign direct investment did not bring any relief for the financial distress of the economy. Furthermore, the austerity measures alleviated this distress in an irrational way—by deadening the economy and, hence, worsening the financial misery of the country.

So far, it is clear that the Peruvian debt picture was overwhelmingly complicated by external conditions in the last ten years. With world demand, terms of trade, and interest rates growing at their trend rates, the net flow of foreign capital would have been equal to $-\$4,100$ million between 1981 and 1984. If this hypothetical situation had occurred, could we argue that the free-market policies would have resolved the current account crisis in a medium- or long-run perspective as Baker's plan assumes? In other words, could the economy reach a sustained and stable rate of growth without incurring an increasing external debt, by introducing free-market policies and assuming a favorable international scenario? This question is answered in the following sections.

The Contribution of External Borrowing
to the Rate of Economic Growth

The discussion so far shows that for the Peruvian economy, the major constraint on the rate of growth of output is the current account of its balance of payments. The persistent tendency to deficit on current account sets the limit to the growth of domestic demand,[20] a limit which certainly need not be compatible with the needs of the economy. But this tendency is just a consequence of a mode of accumulation which reproduces the non-integrated industrial structure. Hence, there is a bias toward a diversified production of consumer-durables with its concomitant income distribution. The absent, or scarcely developed, domestic sector of capital goods and industrial inputs makes the process of accumulation highly dependent on imports.

By the same token, the demand effect of public and private investment is exported and consequently, the full internal operation of Verdoorn's and Kaldor's law—growth of productivity and capital accumulation endogenous to the economic system and dependent on final demand[21]—is weakened. The multiplier effect of investment is lost at the same time that it generates an increase in imports of capital goods and their corresponding inputs. Therefore, the tendency to external disequilibrium is associated with the increasing import bill generated by the basic process of accumulation in the domestic economy. So a rise in growth has to be associated with an increase in pressure on the external balance. Without public expenditure (not directed to generate capacity), the effect of investment on profit will be nil although it enlarges production capacity. Therefore, the accumulation process also creates a tendency to excess capacity, eventually creating downward pressure on the rate of profit.[22]

At the beginning of the import-substitution-led industrialization of the fifties, the failure of investment to create additional effective demand for domestic products was offset by the creation of new industries directed to produce goods which were previously imported. This transformational growth ended as private capital developed a bias toward the production of consumer durables between 1960 and 1966. Consequently, industrial development failed to integrate the productive structure and to eliminate dependence on foreign technology and equipment. Since the mid-sixties, the increasing public deficit offset the rising tendency to export effective demand, but at the cost of permitting a growing deficit on current account and thereby creating an increasing flow of foreign borrowing. The root of the financial distress is, therefore, structural: the presence of a nonintegrated input-output system with a new dynamic sector—manufacturing industry—which is increasingly dependent on imported inputs and capital goods.[23]

Under these circumstances, expansionary policies are both self-defeating and increasingly difficult as this spurious process of industrialization unfolds. The relative contribution of foreign financial capital to economic growth will decrease partly because of austerity policies to overcome potential crises in the balance of payments and partly because free-market trade policies will increase the income elasticity of demand for imports. Open international competition will force the economy to return to pre-industrial structures—as in Chile—but now with higher elasticities due both to higher levels of consumption and to the more diversified composition of consumption originated by the industrialization process.

To test these propositions quantitatively, we divide the actual rate of growth as follows: one part attributable to the rate of growth of exports, and the other attributable to the financial flows of foreign capital. The relative price movements (for example, the terms of trade effect) are dealt with as a residual factor which also affects the rate of economic growth. A methodology based on a balance of payments identity[24] is followed to analyze the contribution of foreign capital to economic growth during the last three administrations. With an initial current account deficit, the balance of payments can be expressed as:

(3) $$Px_t(X_t) + C_t = Pm_t(M_t)$$

where: X_t is the level of exports at constant prices in the year t
   Px_t is the domestic price of exports
   M_t is the level of import at constant prices
   Pm_t is the price of imports expressed in domestic currency
   C_t is the value of capital flows measured in domestic currency

Taking rates of change of the variables in the previous equation we obtain:

(4) $(E/R)(px_t + x_t) + (C/R)(c_t) = pm_t + m_t$

where the lower case letters represent rates of growth of the variables, and E/R and C/R represent the share of exports and the capital flows in the total inflow of international reserves or the total import bill financed by export earnings and foreign borrowing.

Assuming a multiplicative import function and taking rates of change of its variables,

(5) $m_t = w[pm_t - px_t] + n[y_t]$

where: m_t is the rate of growth of imports
        w is the price elasticity of demand for imports (w < 0)
        pm_t is the rate of growth of import prices
        px_t is the rate of growth of export prices
        n is the income elasticity of demand for imports (n > 0)
        y_t is the rate of growth of domestic income

Substituting equation (5) into (4), we get the balance of payments constrained growth rate:

(6) $$yb_t{}^* = [w(px_t - pm_t) + (px_t - pm_t) \\ + (E/R)x_t + (C/R)(c_t - px_t)]/n$$

where: $[w(px_t - pm_t)]/n$ measures the import volume effect of relative price changes on income growth
        $[px_t - pm_t]/n$ gives the terms of trade effect
        $[(E/R)x_t]/n$ stands for the export growth effect
        $[(C/R)(c_t - px_t)]/n$ gives the effect of the rate of growth of foreign capital flows.

Assuming a residual price effect, the balance of payments constrained rate of growth can be written as follows:

(7) $yb_t = [(E/R)x_t + (C/R)(c_t - px_t)]/n$

Hence, the difference between the actual rate of growth of output and that estimated by (7) becomes a measure of the terms of trade effect and any import volume response from relative price changes.

In order to obtain yb_t, first, the corresponding import functions were estimated—the results are shown in Table 8. Second, in the export variable, not only

Table 5

Relative Contribution to the Rate of Economic Growth

Regime	Actual Growth Rate	Estimated Growth Rate	Exports	Foreign Financial Capital
Velasco				
1969–75	4.6	2.2	−2.3	4.5
(1973–75)	(5.4)	(3.7)	(−5.5)	(9.2)
Morales-Bermudez				
1976–80	1.9	−1.6	1.1	−2.7
Belaunde				
1981–84	−0.5	0.5	−0.2	0.7

Note: The income elasticities of demand for imports of goods and non-factor services were 1.90 for 1969−75 and 5.98 for 1976–84.

exports of goods are included but also exports of non-factor services. Finally, the variable C, which represents the foreign capital flows, includes the net inflow of medium- and long-term loans plus the net foreign direct investment, minus the net interest payments and repatriated profits adjusted for transfers.

Table 5 gives data on the actual growth rate and the growth rate predicted by the model (7). The latter was decomposed into two parts: one associated with the growth of export volume and the other connected with the growth of real foreign capital.

Three important conclusions can be derived from the results of the estimated model. First, the potential growth of GDP attributable to the growth of exports of goods and non-factor services increased during the last two administrations, but its significance was reduced by the spectacular increase in the income elasticity of demand for imports. It is worth pointing out that the economy reached the highest rate of growth during Velasco's government in spite of the sharpest drop in the rate of growth of its exports. The Baker plan encourages export-led growth at the expense of social programs, although adopting export promotion policies within a free-trade framework implies an immense social cost, particularly when the tiny contribution of exports to economic growth during the last two liberal administrations is considered. Even in the best international scenario, from 1977 to 1980, the contribution of exports to growth was significantly less than the rate of growth of the labor force. It is not possible to consider the various measures of social cost here; the point simply is that neither export promotion nor free-market policies, let alone their combination (for they work at cross purposes), provide a path to sustained growth.

The second important conclusion refers to the contribution of foreign capital.

Table 6

The Current-account-equilibrium Rate of Growth and Balance-of-payments Constrained Rate of Growth

Regime	Actual Rate of Growth of Output	Actual Rate of Growth of Export	Estimated Growth Rate by Harrod Trade Multiplier	Estimated Growth Rate Including Foreign Capital Flows
Velasco				
1969–75	4.6	−4.6	−2.4	2.2
(1973–75)	(5.4)	(−10.6)	−5.6	3.7
Morales-Bermudez				
1976–80	1.9	6.9	1.2	−1.6
Belaunde				
1981–84	−0.5	−1.3	−0.2	0.5

Note: The estimated rate of growth of output by Harrod Trade Multiplier is the ratio of exports growth to the corresponding income elasticity of demand for imports.

External saving enabled the economy to grow rapidly during the expansionary period of 1969 to 1975. However, during the free-market administrations, its contribution decreased tremendously: from 1981 to 1984 when the largest increase in the debt took place, the contribution of foreign capital was only 16 percent of its 1969–75 contribution. In Morales-Bermudez's period, the positive rate of growth of output was exclusively linked to export growth.

The third conclusion concerns the impact of the terms of trade effect on the rate of economic growth. The difference between the actual and the predicted rate of growth was not significantly explained by the positive rate of growth of the terms of trade during Velasco's administration. But when the open-door policy was introduced, the difference between the two rates was almost perfectly correlated to the changes in the terms of trade.

As may be noticed, the balance-of-payments constrained growth rates do not provide a good prediction of the actual growth rates. As previously mentioned, the difference between them is basically a measure of the extent to which the "constrained" growth rates have been affected by relative price movements in international trade. However, two qualifications are necessary. On the one hand, only during Velasco's period did the balance-of-payments constrained growth rates give a good prediction of the actual growth rates. The foreign capital inflow allowed growth to be faster than otherwise would have been the case. The contribution of exports was significantly negative (see Table 6). On the other, the relatively unimportant role played by foreign capital loans during the last two "liberal" administrations is correlated with the emphasis that they put on equili-

Table 7

Components of the Difference between the Actual Growth Rate and the Estimated Growth Rate by Harrod Trade Multiplier

Regime	y_t-yh_t	yb_t-yh_t	Relative Price Effect Total	Terms of Trade
Velasco				
1969–75	7.0	4.6	2.4	1.0
(1973–75)	(11.0)	9.3	1.7	1.7
Morales-Bermudez				
1976–80	0.7	−2.8	3.5	2.0
Belaunde				
1981–84	−0.3	0.7	−1.0	−1.0

Notes: y_t is the actual rate of growth of output, yh_t is the rate of growth estimated by Harrod Trade Multiplier, and yb_t is the balance of payments constrained rate of growth which includes foreign capital flows. The total price effect and the terms of trade effect are adjusted by the income elasticity of demand for imports.

brating the current account of the balance-of-payments, one of the basic targets of the IMF policy prescriptions. Only during these two governments did the rate of growth estimated by Harrod trade multiplier give a good prediction of the actual growth rate, as shown in Table 6. To better understand this, note that when the current account equilibrium is a policy objective, then:

$$(8) \qquad \frac{\Delta Yt}{\Delta Xt} = \frac{1}{m}$$

where Y is the level of output, X is the level of exports, and m is the marginal propensity to import. The inverse of this propensity is the so-called Harrod Trade Multiplier. When this equation is made "dynamic" and it is assumed that exports

(X) are equal to imports (M), we obtain:

$$(9) \qquad yh_t = x_t/n$$

where yh_t is the estimated rate of growth by the Harrod Trade Multiplier, x_t is the rate of growth of exports, and n is the income elasticity of demand for imports.[25]

The previous two qualifications can be assessed by looking at Table 7. As pointed out before, real capital inflows growing faster than exports (4.6 percent)

Table 8

Import Demand Functions
[log M_t = log a + w log(Pm_t/Px_t) + n log GDP_t]

Period	Con-stant	Elasticities Price(w)	Income(n)	R	F	SSR
1968–82	−64.2	−0.302	5.770	0.83	15.8	0.102
	(−3.31)	(−1.955)	(3.918)			
1968–75	−13.5	−0.225	1.901	0.91	10.6	0.014
	(−1.20)	(−1.260)	(2.184)			
1976–82	−67.1	−0.433	5.981	0.87	6.50	0.046
	(−1.56)	(−1.043)	(1.833)			

Notes: The import variable incorporates goods and non-factor services. Bracketed terms under the coefficients are t ratios. All the regressions were corrected for autocorrelation. SSR is the sum of squared residuals which gives us a Chow's statistic equal to 1.87. The end-year of each period is a peak-cycle; this allows us to not understimate the import functions.
Source: Instituto Nacional de Estadistica.

only confirms that the balance of payments equilibrium was not a policy target during the Velasco government. By the same token, the terms of trade effect, though positive, played an insignificant role in the economic performance of that period. Furthermore, reflecting the industrialist strategy based on foreign technology and capital goods, the import volume effect due to the price elasticity of demand for imports was "perverse."

This pattern is drastically modified during the latter two administrations. Between 1976 and 1980, the rate of growth of output was linked almost exclusively to the positive and significant rate of growth of exports and the favorable terms of trade. The real capital inflows grew more slowly than exports (−2.8 percent as seen in Table 7).

During the Belaunde Administration, the rate of growth of output was again associated with export growth and the terms of trade effect. In the first free-trade administration, the export promotion program (intended to ease the financial distress of the economy) succeeded, but only because of the existence of favorable external markets. The gloomy international scenario of later years proved the unfeasibility of that model conceived, as in the Baker plan, within a free-market policy framework.

At this point it is appropriate to assess the Baker free-trade policy proposals. Free trade has conclusively failed in the case of the Peruvian economy. As shown in Table 8, the external structural disequilibrium brought on by the spurious process of import substitution,[26] was exacerbated first by the strategy of export promotion but also by the significant increase in the income elasticity of demand for imports due to the open-door policy imposed by the IMF. With the increased dependence of the economy on imports, the external disequilibrium worsened between 1976 and 1984, contrary to what the official economists had expected.

An economy with a structural external disequilibrium requires a permanent growth of real foreign capital flows to maintain a given positive rate of growth of output. If the rate of growth of capital inflows becomes zero, the rate of growth of output will be less than yb_t. To maintain a rate of growth equal to what would be possible by considering only the Harrod Trade Multiplier, the real capital flows would have to increase at the same rate as exports. In general, to maintain a given rate of growth of output, say yb_t, $(c_t - px_t)$ would have to be equal to x_t. If x_t becomes zero or less than zero, $(c_t - px_t)$ would have to increase correspondingly to compensate for the drop in exports.[27] If the implicit assumption of constant terms of trade is dropped, an adverse international scenario to export and of export prices would imply a greater increase in the rate of growth of real foreign capital to maintain an initial positive rate of growth of output. For example, to grow at the average 1969–75 rate of growth (i.e., 4.6 percent) during Belaunde's period, the rate of growth of real capital inflow would have had to be equal to 34.7 percent, given an income elasticity of imports equal to 5.98, a negative rate of growth of exports equal to –1.3, and an average terms of trade deterioration equal to –6.0 percent. However, as mentioned before, the weighted average rate of growth of real capital inflows was only equal to 4.3 percent.

Therefore, it is not difficult to figure out that continuous borrowing within an adverse international scenario has to cause an explosive increase in the debt/GDP ratio and, by the same token, in the debt/service ratio. This will be so even with a constant real rate of interest, provided it is greater than the rate of growth of exports. The situation will be worse, of course, when the adverse international scenario is accompanied by growing real rates of interest.[28] Moreover, in Peru, the structural lack of financial capacity of the manufacturing sector created a constant inflow of foreign financial capital. This, in turn, kept real national income permanently below its potential level due to the constant outflow of capital for interest payments and repatriated profits.[29]

*   *   *

The facts analyzed and evaluated in this chapter show an economy entrapped by international financial capital and without enough autonomy to pursue fiscal and monetary policies. The IMF backed the commercial banks' demands for full repayment by imposing free-market policies as a condition to get short-term financial relief in the balance of payments. Its adjustment programs have indeed contributed to the world recession by cutting the debtor countries' current account deficit. Baker's proposal to deregulate and free up the Third World economies is linked to this effect.

The difference between the IMF programs and the Baker plan does not center on the nature of the policy prescriptions. The issue now is the direction of the new loans. While the IMF made balance of payments loans on the condition that countries accept the austerity package, Baker's plan contemplates the World Bank making loans with the exclusive purpose of raising efficiency in trade and industry. Efficiency in the free-market ideology means trade liberalization, a reduced role of government, elimination of state-owned companies, and so on. So, the new loans will be to assist these objectives. As with IMF conditionality, the commercial banks would provide new financing after the countries had reached lending agreements with the World Bank. But the borrowing terms will be harder: only countries that commit themselves to free-market-oriented economic reforms would get the help.

The Baker plan for a free-market economy doesn't contemplate, of course, an economic restructuring based on the development of the internal market together with the construction of a domestic capital goods sector.[30] A structural change of this kind would mean developing an integrated national input-output system by selectively controlling the external sector and reinforcing the economic role of the state. Baker calls for just the opposite: divestment of public enterprises, lower taxes and elimination of industrial subsidies, de-regulation, and trade liberalization.

The Baker plan resolves the conflict between the Latin American states and international capital in favor of the latter. It doesn't introduce structural changes into the present organization of international financial capital. Belying its free market ideology, the plan doesn't even allow the market to resolve the crisis. From the market point of view, international commercial banks share responsibility for debt crises, since they seem to have made mistakes about the risks they were taking when they financed the increasing expenditures of public sectors. Thus, creditors should simply sell their claims in the free market and take the losses. Why should the United States' government help them out? Free market advocates have no business calling on the government to bail them out of their mistakes.[31]

Our analysis also suggests the existence of domestic conflicts associated with the crises in the model of capital accumulation. As observed, continuous financial capital inflow is a direct result of a manufacturing sector highly dependent on imports. In this context, the external factors (sluggish demand for exports or increases in real interest rates) only accelerate financial distress. The current crisis has spurred internal conflicts between the export-led growth advocates and the interests tied to the current import substitution regime, between the supporters of a national re-industrialization and capital linked to the manufacturing "white line" production, between the pro-agricultural strategy to re-industrialize the economy and the native imitators of industrialization in the central countries, between interventionists and free-market supporters, between the followers of the statism and the participationists, etc. And finally, all the national economic interests are confronted with international financial capital.

The development of the Peruvian external debt has revealed, over the last fifteen years, some of the historical dynamics of these conflicts. The external debt rocketed during the expansionary period of Velasco's government. The "liberal" (conservative) policies applied from 1976 to 1980 to deal with the consequent financial crisis worsened the structural problem. The priority given to servicing the debt decreased the rate of growth of the net capital inflow (medium- and long-term debt) and hence put a brake on economic growth. The positive—but insignificant—average rate of growth reached in this period was closely associated with the export sectors which had the benefit of a favorable international environment. But the vulnerability of the economy to international competition and the financial pressures on monetary authorities increased.

As occurred in 1976–80, the net inflow of the total debt due to internal factors during the Belaunde administration did not increase significantly. But total debt soared again, this time because of growing real interest rates and a depressed international scenario which drastically undercut export earnings. All export-promoting policies of this period proved fruitless, and the vulnerability of the economy increased.

Notes

1. The Keynesian aproach to devaluation—the elasticity approach—can be transformed easily into the monetarist. The monetarist approach incorporates the role of real balance effect with money treated as a capital asset. See Dornbusch (1976).

2. An economist of *Financial World* comments, "Baker's approach reflects a more sophisticated sense of macroeconomics than the administration's prior statements on the debt crisis did. Having recently moved to devalue the dollar in concert with the West's biggest central banks . . . the Treasury Secretary seems to be trying to ensure that nations like Brazil the world's eighth largest economic entity, will be capable of importing some of the United States' prosperity less expensive exports. . . . And an increase in American exports might help forestall the drive for the sort of protectionist tariffs that also contributed to the Great Depression." See Peter Hall (1985).

3. For example, the average maturity of new medium- and long-term loans decreased from 10 years in 1973 to five years in 1975. See I. Mehdi Zaidi (1985).

4. In 1981, this ratio was equal to 271.5 for Latin-American countries and 77.0 for East Asian countries. The higher ratio of debt to exports is, according to Jeffrey Sachs (1985), the critical factor in making Latin America so vulnerable to the external shocks of the early 1980s.

5. The methodology used in this and in the following section as well as the results were taken from Jimenez (1987). See also Jimenez and Schatan (1983).

6. The expected values of import and export prices are derived from their trend rates of growth estimated by regressing their natural logs on time for 1960–72, 1960–75, and 1960–80. The rate of growth associated with the first regression was applied to obtain the expected import and export prices for Velasco's administration; the second one to obtain similar expected values for Morales-Bermudez's period; and the third one for the administration of Belaunde Terry.

7. The assumption of expected values equal to zero is not an accurate reflection of correct policy in relation to the corresponding economic variables. However, by assuming $FI^* = 0$, we are only hoping that we can avoid an outflow of capital greater than the net inflow of foreign direct investment. On the other hand, by assuming SE^* and RA^* equal to

zero, we are presupposing the absence of speculative capital outflow and that the monetary authorities are not vulnerable to international financial pressures.

8. The expected values of W and DD were estimated by their corresponding trend rates of growth observed during 1960–72, 1960–75, and 1960–80. The trend rates were obtained by regressing the natural log of W and DD on time for the same periods. The set of expected values associated with the regressions for the first period was used to analyze the Velasco administration; the set corresponding to the regressions for the second period was used to examine Morales-Bermudez's government; and the third set of expected values was used to analyze Belaunde's administration.

9. Kate and Wallace (1980) introduced this suggestive name, but they estimate it in a different way.

10. When private short-term capital movements become part of the balance of payments deficit or surplus, the related concept of equilibrium, as Thirlwall (1980) points out, gives a measure of the financial pressure on the monetary authorities to maintain the external value of the domestic currency.

11. See Angell and Thorp (1980), pp. 865–86.

12. The argument against industrialization based on the internal market doesn't take into account the fact that the capacity of this market to drive and sustain economic growth depends upon the social and institutional forces which are embodied in the specific industrial strategy. For example, a growing purchasing power of the peasant economy can indeed be important as a motive of industrialization. Gerschenkron (1966, 114) assessed the importance of the internal market referring to the substitutes for the demand of the peasantry. He says, "The internal market as represented by the peasantry can become unimportant for industrialization . . . if someone else, say the state, is willing and able to engender industrial production and at the same time constitute the market for the goods produced. This is one of the substitution patterns that occur in the industrialization of backward countries. Besides, the demand of the state is not the only possible substitution of this kind. . . . Such substitutions often are very likely to take place, but there is no assurance that they actually will. If they do not, the rate of industrial growth is likely to suffer, but the rate that is maintained will surely depend on the existence of the demand emanating from the internal market."

13. See Interamerican Develoment Bank (1979, 1980, 1982).

14. "Throughout the 1970s, direct foreign investment flows to developing countries were on the order of $10 billion annually; net external borrowing was six to eight times as large. At current rates, interest obligations are more than $50 billion per year. It is conceivable that direct investment could rise enough to meet these interest costs." See Eaton and Taylor (1985).

15. The typical interest rate on developing country loans—LIBOR (London interbank offered rate) plus a spread of 1 percent—increased from 7.0 percent in 1977 to 9.7 percent in 1978, 13.0 percent in 1979, 15.4 percent in 1980, and it has fluctuated around this level since then. "Borrowers became accustomed to low real interest rates in the 1970s. For 1961–70, LIBOR on U.S. dollar deposits minus the U.S. wholesale price increase produced an average real interest rate of 4.1 percent. But for 1971–80, this average was –0.8 percent; real interest rates were negative, on average, for the decade. By 1979 and 1980, nominal interest rates were high (LIBOR averaged 13.2 percent) and although U.S.inflation was virtually equal to LIBOR, high nominal rates caused a cash flow squeeze for borrowers. . . . By 1981–82, declining inflation without a corresponding decline in interest rates meant high real interest rates (7.5 percent in 1981 and 11.0 percent in 1982), making matters worse." See Cline (1983), pp. 18–23.

16. This type of policy reaction to financial pressures seems to have been common in the majority of developing countries just when the external debt was increasing exponentially. In this regard, Dornbusch (1980) comments: ". . . the striking fact is that rather than

draw down their reserves to finance their deficits, the developing countries have borrowed abroad to add to their reserves at a rate of nearly $12 billion over 1976–78," pp. 18–19.

17. See Banco Central de Reserva del Peru (1983).

18. The World Bank emphasizes the fact that trade liberalization, the exchange rate and the interest rate policies were in consonance with its position expressed in its report of April, 1981. See World Bank (1981), p. 26.

19. To see the negative impact of liberalization on the manufacturing sector, consider some figures: in 1981, $52.6 million was spent on imported TVs, $370.6 million on automobiles and automotive vehicles, $3.4 million on footwear products, and $5.5 million on clothing. Of course, in all these industries the domestic product decreased due to international competition. A dramatic example of de-industrialization is the case of the public steel enterprise SIDERPERU, whose capacity utilization fell from 75 percent in 1980 to 50 percent in 1982, while the economy imported 240 tons of competitive products in 1981. See Iguiniz (1984).

20. See Jimenez (1984).

21. See Jimenez (1982).

22. See Casar and Ros (1983).

23. See Jimenez (1985). For an interesting analysis of Latin American industrialization see Fajnzylber (1983).

24. We follow the methodology suggested by Thirlwall and Hussain (1983).

25. See Harrod (1933) and Thirlwall and Hussain (1983).

26. See Jimenez (1984).

27. See A. P. Thirlwall and M. N. Hussain (1983), pp. 503–4.

28. In general, when income and export growth depend on the growth rate of world demand, ". . . the slower is the growth of world demand, the greater the debt and the higher the debt/GDP ratio; further worse terms of trade cause a higher import propensity which raises the debt/GDP ratio." See Spaventa (1983), pp. 330–1.

29. For an explanation of the behavior of the real national income and import capacity, see Jimenez (1987).

30. Thirty five years ago, the ECLA started out its theoretical work to show that the de-regulated or free-market economy would only reproduce the structural problems and limit the growth capacity of Latin American countries. Thirty years later, in 1979, Raul Prebish (former conductor of ECLA), would say it is surprising to still find in our continent advocates of the free-market ideology. They think, he said, that by opening up the economy, the central countries, impressed by their devotion to the neo-classical principles, will receive generously all of that they export or want to export. They have lost, he added, the most elemental political realism. See Prebish (1980).

31. This solution was suggested by Wiesner (1985).

References

Angell, A., and R. Thorp. 1980. "Inflation, Stabilization and Attempted Redemocratization in Peru 1975–1979." *World Development* 8.

Banco Central de Reserva del Peru. 1983. *El Proceso de Liberalization de Importaciones: Peru 1979–1982*. Lima.

Casar, J. I., and J. Ros. 1983. "Trade and Capital Accumulation in a Process of Import Substitution." *Cambridge Journal of Economics* 7:257–67.

Cline, W. R. 1983. *International Debt and the Stability of the World Economy*. Washington: Institute for International Economics.

Dornbusch, R. 1980. *Open Economy Macroeconomics*. New York: Basic Books.

————. 1976. "Devaluation, Money and Non-traded Goods." J.A. Frenkel and H.G. Johnson, eds. *The Monetary Approach to the Balance of Payments*. London:

George Allen and Unwin Publishers, Ltd.

Eaton, J., and L. Taylor. 1985. Developing Country Finance and Debt. Mimeo.

Fajnzylber, F. 1983. *La Industrializacion Trunca de America Latina*. Mexico: Nueva Imagen.

Gerschenkron, A. 1966. *Economic Backwardness in Historical Perspective*. Cambridge: Harvard University Press.

Hall, P. 1985. "How Safe Are the Banks." *Financial World*, November.

Harrod, R. 1933. *International Economics*. New York: Cambridge University Press.

Iguiniz, J. 1984. La Crisis Peruana Actual: esquema para una Interpretation. Mimeo.

Interamerican Development Bank. 1979. *Economic and Social Progress in Latin America*. Washington, D.C.

—————. 1980 and 1982. *Economic and Social Progress in Latin America, the External Sector*. Washington, D.C.

Jimenez, F. 1982. "Peru: la expansion del sector manufacturero como generadora de crecimiento economico y el papel del sector externo." *Socialismo y Participacion*, No. 18.

—————. 1984. "La balanza de pagos como factor limitativo del crecimiento y el desequilibrio estructural externo de la economia Peruana." *Socialismo y Participacion*, No. 25.

—————. 1985. Peru: inflacion, deficit publico, desequilibrio externo y crecimiento economico. Una critica al enfoque monetarista. Mimeo.

—————. 1987. Capital Accumulation, the State and Effective Demand: A Non-Neoclassical Structuralist Approach to Peruvian Development 1950-1984. Ph.D. diss.

Jimenez, F., and C. Schatan. 1983."Mexico: la nueva politica comercial y el incremento de las importaciones de bienes manufacturados en el periodo 1977-1980." *Aspectos Metodologicos para el Analisis del Sector Externo*, 2.

Kate, A. T., and R. B. Wallace. 1980. *Protection and Economic Development in Mexico*. New York: St. Martin's Press.

Prebish, R. 1980. "Prologo." Octavio Rodriguez, *La Teoría del Subdesarrollo de la CEPAL, Siglo XXI*.

Sachs, J. 1985. "External Debt and Macroeconomic Performance in Latin America and East Asia." *Brookings Papers on Economic Activity* 2:523-73.

Spaventa, L. 1983. "Risks to the Stability of the International Financial System: Gloom without Drama." *International Lending in a Fragile World Economy*. D.F. Fair and R. Bertrand, eds., Hague: Martinus Nijhoff Publishers.

Thirlwall, A. P. 1980. *Balance of Payments Theory and the United Kingdom Experience*. London: The Macmillan Press Ltd.

Thirlwall, A. P., and M. N. Hussain. 1983. "The Balance of Payments Constraint, Capital Flows and Growth Rate Differences between Developing Countries." *Oxford Economic Papers* 34 (3).

Wiesner, E. 1985. "Latin America Debt: Lessons and Pending Issues." *The American Economic Review*. Papers and Proceedings (May).

World Bank. 1981. *Peru: Principales Cuestiones y Recomendaciones en Materia de Desarrollo*. Washington, D.C.

Zaidi, I. M. 1985. "Saving, Investment, Fiscal Deficits, and the External Indebtedness of Developing Countries." *World Development*(13)5: 573-88.

DATE DUE

APR 2 9 2010		
REC'D APR 0 2 2010		